How France Votes

How France Votes

Edited by
Michael S. Lewis-Beck
University of Iowa

CHATHAM HOUSE PUBLISHERS
SEVEN BRIDGES PRESS, LLC
NEW YORK • LONDON

HOW FRANCE VOTES

Seven Bridges Press, LLC
135 Fifth Avenue
New York, NY 10010-7101

Publisher: Robert J. Gormley
Managing editor: Katharine Miller
Production supervisor: Melissa A. Martin
Cover design: Andrea Barash & Associates
Composition: Bruce Bicknell for TIPS Technical Publishing
Printing and binding: Versa Press, Inc.

Library of Congress Cataloging-in-Publication Data
How France votes / edited by Michael S. Lewis-Beck.
p. cm.
Includes bibliographical references and index.
ISBN 1-56643-069-0
1. France—Politics and government—1981-1995. 2. Presidents—France—Election—1995. 3. France—Politics and government—1995- 4. France. Parlement (1946-). Assemblee nationale—Elections, 1997. I. Lewis-Beck, Michael S.
JN2594.2 .H69 1999
324.944—dc21

98-58099
CIP

Manufactured in the United States of America
10 9 8 7 6 5 4 3 2 1

To Ed and our cassoulet

Contents

Acknowledgments

How France Votes is unique. It offers expert analysis of contemporary French elections from sixteen leading scholars, on both sides of the Atlantic. The student of French politics now has, in English, a comprehensive yet profound discussion of electoral happenings within this most provocative of democracies. The project also represents a serious, and rather rare, cooperation of social scientists who may speak different languages, not only verbally but methodologically. In the end the collection is, we hope, a fine blend, like the best wine of Bordeaux.

Many deserve thanks, beyond the scholars themselves, and their home institutions. Chapters by the French contributors had to be translated, and this was done by two professors of French, Scott Sheridan of Illinois Wesleyan University and Anne Perriguey of University of Nebraska-Lincoln. Tiffani Grimes, an undergraduate Honors student in Political Science and French at the University of Iowa, also helped track down citations and translations. With regard to the physical composition of the book, editorial support at Chatham House was splendid. I wish to acknowledge in particular Melissa Martin and Katharine Miller, who were always professional, tireless, and cheerful.

Finally, I must mention that the book is the brain-child of Ed Artinian, Chatham House founder and publisher, who recently passed away. For years Ed, applying his friendly persuasion to me, had talked up the value of such a book. I am sorry that he is not here to share in its publication.

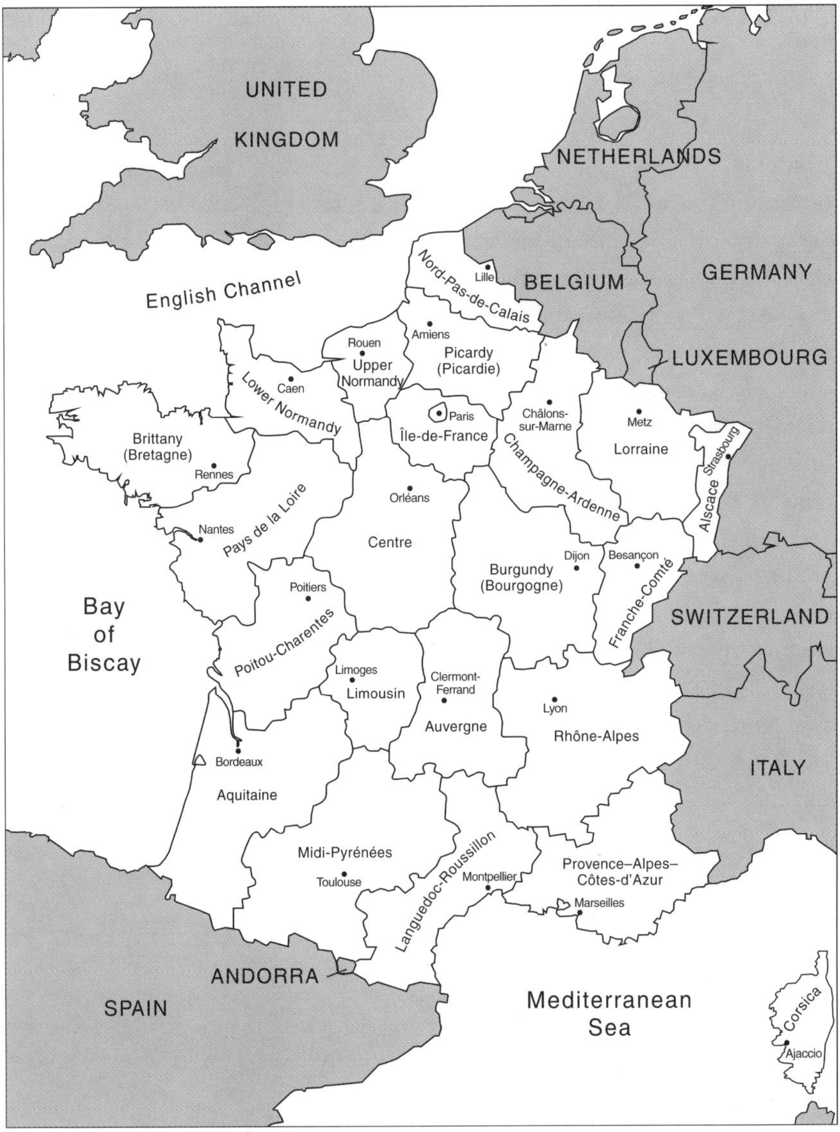

THE REGIONS OF FRANCE

SOURCE: Map redrawn from Michael G. Roskin, *Countries and Concepts*, 6th ed. (Upper Saddle River, N.J.: Prentice Hall, 1998), 83; accompanying table (facing page) assembled from Wayne Northcutt, *The Regions of France* (Westport, Conn.: Greenwood Press, 1996), passim.

THE DEPARTMENTS OF METROPOLITAN FRANCE

Region	*Departments*	*Regional Seat*
Alsace	Bas-Rhin (Lower Rhine), Haut-Rhin (Upper Rhine)	Strasbourg
Aquitaine	Dordogne, Gironde, Landes, Lot-et-Garonne, Pyrénées-Atlantiques	Bordeaux
Auvergne	Allier, Cantal, Haute-Loire, Puy-de-Dôme	Clermont-Ferrand
Brittany (Bretagne)	Ille-et-Vilaine, Côtes-d'Armor, Finistère, Moribihan	Rennes
Burgundy (Bourgogne)	Côtes-d'Or, Nièvre, Saône-et-Loire, Yonne	Dijon
Centre	Cher, Eure-et-Loir, Indre, Indre-et-Loire, Loir-et-Cher, Loiret	Orléans
Champagne-Ardenne	Ardennes, Marne, Aube, Haute-Marne	Châlons-sur-Marne
Corsica (Corse)	Haute-Corse, Corse-du-Sud	Ajaccio
Franche-Comté	Territoire de Belfor, Haute-Saône, Doubs, Jura	Besançon
Île-de-France	Paris, Seine-et-Marne, Yvelines, Essone, Hauts-de-Seine, Seine-Saint-Denis, Val-de-Marne, Val-d'Oise	Paris
Languedoc-Roussillon	Hérault, Aude, Pyrénées-Orientales, Gard, Lozère	Montpellier
Limousin	Haute-Vienne, Creuse, Corréze	Limoges
Lorraine	Meuse, Meurthe-et-Moselle, Moselle, Vosges	Metz
Midi-Pyrénées	Ariège, Aveyron, Haute-Garonne, Gers, Lot, Haute-Pyrénées, Tarn, Tarn-et-Garonne	Toulouse
Nord–Pas-de-Calais	Nord, Pas-de-Calais	Lille
Lower Normandy (Basse-Normandie)	Calvados, Manche, Orne	Caen
Upper Normandy (Haute-Normandie)	Eure, Seine-Maritime	Rouen
Pays de la Loire	Loire-Atlantique, Maine-et-Loire, Mayenne, Sarthe, Vendée	Nantes
Picardy (Picardie)	Somme, Oise, Aisne	Amiens
Poitou-Charentes	Deux-Sèvres, Vienne, Charente-Maritime, Charente	Poitiers
Provence (Provence–Alpes–Côtes-d'Azur)	Alpes-de-Haute-Provence, Haute-Alpes, Alpes-Maritimes, Bouches-du-Rhône, Var, Baucluse	Marseilles
Rhône-Alpes	Ain, Ardèche, Drôme, Isère, Loire, Rhône, Savoie (Savoy), Haute-Savoie (Upper Savoy)	Lyon

Introduction:

The Enduring French Voter

Michael S. Lewis-Beck

French politics, like French food, can be rich, refined, elegant, and sometimes hard to digest, at least for Americans. This collection of readings aims to make French elections a palatable, even pleasurable, subject matter for U.S. students. Written by a team of distinguished scholars from France and the United States, it takes as context the presidential election of 1995, which saw the triumph of Gaullist Jacques Chirac, and the legislative elections of 1997, which saw Chirac's political defeat. To the surprise of most observers, the right lost control of the National Assembly, and Socialist Lionel Jospin emerged as prime minister in June 1997. How this happened, and why, is a common theme of these papers. In addition to questions about the campaign issues and party strategies, concerns about the enduring sociology of the French electorate are raised, and as well, the consequences of Fifth Republic constitutional rules and institutions are considered. By examining the 1997 election from multiple analytic perspectives, the essays give the reader a supple understanding of that event. Indeed, readers finding themselves in a Paris cafe might expect to hold their own in a political debate over not only the 1997 contest, but also the next one to come.

In this introduction, I offer a framework for thinking generally about French voters and elections, one which might be applied to past as well as future elections. I emphasize how French voters differ from American voters because a novice American observer is likely to miss those differences. I begin by examining the French system of electoral institutions and parties and exploring how these bear on political participation. Then I consider long-term traditional cleavages, which commonly influence vote choice, and go on to discuss issues and overall election outcomes. I conclude by assessing the French voter's degree of changeability and the consequences for stability and predictability in the electoral system.

Institutions, Parties, and Participation

Probably no modern democracy changes its basic political rules as often as France does. Since the Revolution, the French have been governed under sixteen constitutions. As one commentator remarked, French political institutions have "been treated as a weapon in the struggle between different political camps and between different political forces for the control of State and society" (Campbell 1965, 17). The current political system, a product of the Fifth Republic Constitution of 1958, is a presidential-parliamentary hybrid, personified in a dual executive, the president and the prime minister. The new constitution, which nominally assigned considerable power to the president, was meant to overcome the party factionalism and weak leadership common during the Third and Fourth Republics. In 1962, the constitution was amended to provide for popular election of the president by majority vote in a two-round ballot. The president serves as head of state for a seven-year term, has no term limit, and may invoke emergency powers. The president oversees Parliament, naming the prime minister, formulating general policy, and validating parliamentary acts. He or she may dissolve the National Assembly and force new elections. Under Charles de Gaulle, presidential executive power was great and unchallenged by the prime minister. As Roy Macridis (1975, 28) expressed it, the prime minister was just "the President's man." (Since that time there has been one female prime minister, Edith Cresson, appointed by President Mitterrand in 1991). Table I.1 gives second-ballot results for the presidential elections of the Fifth Republic.

Until the 1981 election of Socialist François Mitterrand, the presidency was captured by candidates from the traditional right. Despite some early concerns, presidential powers easily survived this *alternance* to the left. The first serious assault on the supremacy of presidential authority came in the aftermath of the 1986 legislative elections. Throughout the Fifth Republic, National Assembly deputies had been directly elected from single-member districts in two rounds of balloting. After defeating incumbent Valery Giscard d'Estaing in 1981, President Mitterrand dissolved the National Assembly and called for new elections under the established selection rules. The 1981 parliamentary elections returned an unprecedented absolute majority of seats to the Socialists, and allowed President Mitterrand to launch his left-wing legislative program. However, by 1986, the five-year terms of the deputies had expired, and another election was necessary. Its

TABLE I.1. PRESIDENTIAL ELECTION RESULTS, FIFTH REPUBLIC SECOND BALLOT, 1965 (IN PERCENTAGES)

	Incumbent		*Opponent*	
	Candidate[a]	*Vote*	*Candidate*	*Vote*
1965	de Gaulle	54.5	Mitterrand	45.5
1969	Pompidou	57.6	Poher	42.5
1974	Giscard d'Estaing	50.7	Mitterrand	49.4
1981	Giscard d'Estaing	48.2	Mitterrand	51.8
1988	Mitterrand	54.0	Chirac	46.0
1995	Jospin	47.4	Chirac	52.6

SOURCES: *Le Monde, Dossiers et documents,* various issues.

a. The candidate of the incumbent party (or party coalition).

political timing was bad for the left, for it appeared that the Socialists and their allies would lose heavily to the Gaullist Rally for the Republic (RPR) and the Giscardian Union for French Democracy (UDF). Hence, the Socialist leadership in the Assembly changed the election rules for the 1986 contest, instituting a proportional representation system applied to voting on department-level party lists. Despite that change, the Socialists lost control of the Assembly to the RPR and the UDF, who restored the old election rules. Nevertheless, the 1986 legislative result had two irrevocable consequences: It gave the extreme-right National Front, for the first time, a strong parliamentary presence, with thirty-two seats in the Assembly. And, it ushered in *cohabitation*, which has gravely shifted the center of executive authority in French government.

"Cohabitation" means that a president and a prime minister from opposing party coalitions serve together. After the 1986 National Assembly election, the RPR-UDF coalition on the right commanded a majority of votes. By constitutional authority, President Mitterrand was to name the new prime minister. However, to get the required majority approval from the Assembly, he was forced to pick a leader from the right opposition, headed by the RPR (with 158 seats compared to 132 seats for the UDF). He decided on Jacques Chirac, then mayor of Paris and chief of the RPR. This cohabitation, involving a Socialist president and a Gaullist prime minister, lasted until the elections of 1988. In that year, Mitterrand was reelected president and called for new parliamentary elections, where the RPR-UDF coalition met defeat. President Mitterrand, who now directed a "working" left majority in the Assembly, appointed fellow Socialist Michel Rocard prime minister.

Under this first cohabitation (1986-88), President Mitterrand quickly learned that he could not command the domestic policy agenda of the Assembly, and thereafter he confined himself to international issues. The second cohabitation (1993-95) again found Socialist President Mitterrand pitted against an RPR prime minister, Edouard Balladur. The third cohabitation, begun in 1997, reversed these political tendencies, with RPR President Chirac and Socialist Prime Minister Jospin. Through different cohabitations, the limits of presidential power have become increasingly clear. In practice, the president can do little in any policy arena, foreign or domestic, unless he or she controls a voting majority in the National Assembly. If the prime minister, in opposition to the president, can reliably rally a majority of Assembly seats, then he or she is the effective executive of the French nation. Prime Minister Jospin understands this, as, to his great dismay, does President Chirac, who, under the third cohabitation, has been confined largely to symbolic politics and ceremonial activities as head of state.

There is considerable continuity among candidates competing to lead France. De Gaulle remained president from 1958 until his resignation in 1969. Mitterrand was the second-ballot opponent to de Gaulle in 1965, and to Giscard in 1974 and 1981, when he finally won. Chirac was made prime minister to Giscard in 1974 and to Mitterrand in 1986, and he fought the second ballot for president unsuccessfully against Mitterrand in 1988. Chirac prevailed in 1995 against Jospin, whom he had to appoint prime minister in 1997. Thus entry into this elite group, the *crème de la crème* of French politicians, appears quite restricted. But while key national political leaders have an ongoing presence, they represent deep partisan divisions in French society. For example, the RPR, founded in 1976 to carry on the tenants of Gaullism, and headed by Jacques Chirac, has been the standard-bearer of the traditional right, while the Socialists have assumed that role on the left. These two parties, the RPR and the Socialists, have been the top vote getters in early National Assembly elections since 1978. (See figure I.1 for first-ballot National Assembly results across the Fifth Republic, by party.)

There are many French political parties, and many do not resemble what Americans think of as political parties. In the 1997 contest for the National Assembly, to take an example, at least forty-eight differently labeled partisan groups were running candidates (*Le Monde, Dossiers et documents: Élections législatives 25 mai–1er juin 1997*, 69). Some of these groups represented single issues, for example, the Natural Law Party (PLN); the Revolutionary Communist League (LCR), an extremist splinter; the Liberty Party of Claude Reichman (PPL), an individual following; or a generic category, *extrême gauche* (extreme left). Other labels represented party coalitions, for example, the UDF, a grouping of center-right parties headed by Giscard. In figure I.1, only the leading six or seven parties or party coalitions in each election are listed, but these account for about 90 to 95 percent of voters.

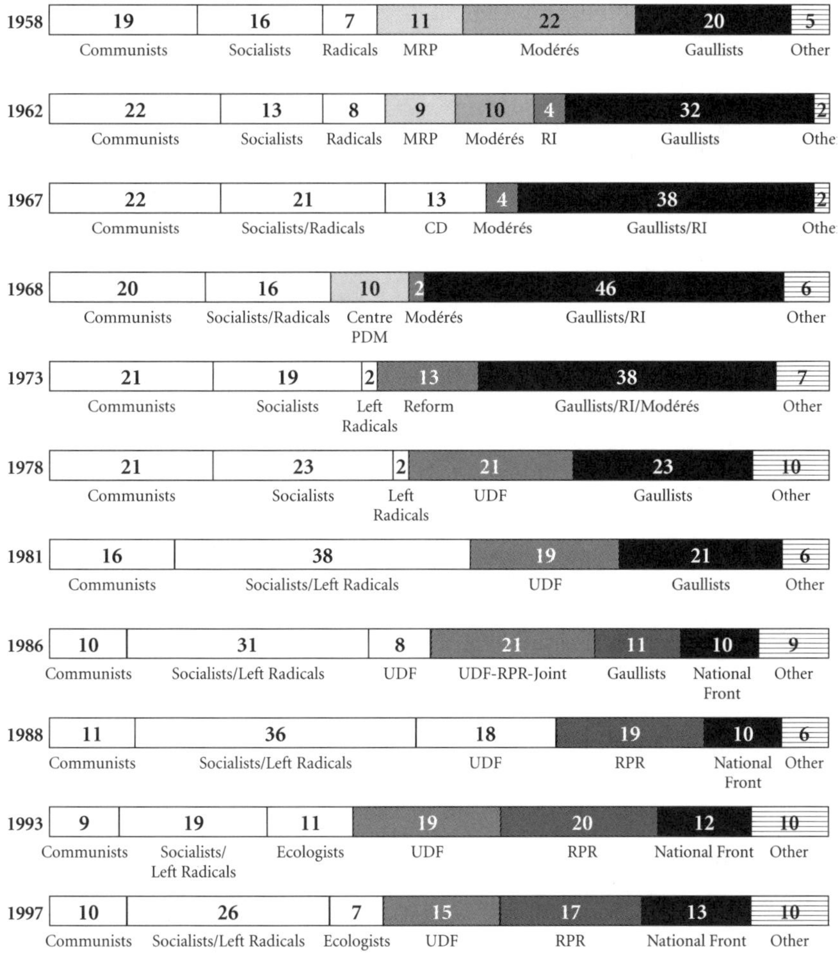

FIGURE I.1. NATIONAL ASSEMBLY ELECTIONS, FIFTH REPUBLIC, FIRST BALLOT RESULTS FOR MAJOR PARTIES, 1958-97 (PERCENTAGE OF TOTAL VOTE)

SOURCES: Data for 1958-88 are from Lewis-Beck and Rice 1992, 118. Data for 1993 are from *Le Monde, Dossiers et documents: Élections législatives 21 mars–28 mars 1993, La Droit sans partage*, 63. Data for 1997 are from *Le Monde, Dossiers et documents: Élections législatives 25 mai–1er juin 1997, Le Président désavoué*, 43.

French parties are arrayed along an ideological spectrum, from left to right. Even among the major parties, the contemporary French voter has to make serious ideological choices, from the Communist Party on the far left to the National Front on the far right. This wide range of choice may be responsible for the high level of participation in French national elections. Voters do not stay home, because all are able to cast their ballots for candidates who closely represent their policy preferences. Turnout is highest in presidential contests. Consider the 1995 race. On the first ballot, each of the following eight candidates for president received at least 3 percent of the vote: Jospin (Socialist), 23 percent; Chirac (RPR), 21 percent; Balladur (RPR), 19 percent; Le Pen (National Front), 15 percent; Hue (Communist), 9 percent; Laguiller (LO, the Worker's Struggle), 5 percent; De Villiers (MPF, *Mouvement pour la France*), 5 percent; Voynet (Greens), 3 percent. Clearly, voters had considerable choice, and they exercised it; 78.4 percent of registered voters actually voted. Overall, in the six popular presidential elections of the Fifth Republic, first-ballot turnout has averaged 81.2 percent. (*Le Monde, Dossiers et documents: Le Élection presidentielle 23 avril–7 mai 1995*, 36-39).

There is slightly more abstention in National Assembly contests. In the seven National Assembly elections since 1973, average turnout was 74.8 percent of registered voters. In 1997, 68 percent of registered voters turned out, which was not as low as the record abstention year of 1988, when just 66.2 percent voted. Across time, however, abstention has increased somewhat in legislative elections. Abstention exceeded 30 percent for the first time in 1988, for instance, and did so again in 1993 and in 1997. (See *Le Monde, Dossiers et documents: Élections législatives 25 mai–1er juin 1997*, 43). While failure to vote is of growing concern among observers of French democracy, the problem remains small compared to that in the United States. French voters appear to be much more politically engaged than are their American counterparts.

Traditional Cleavages and the Individual Voter: Class, Religion, Ideology

Although France is a modern industrial democracy, certain political divisions have remained in force since the nineteenth century. The traditional cleavages of class and religion, what French analysts sometimes call the "heavy variables" (*les variables lourdes*), continue to separate the electorate. As Marx foresaw, citizens' relationship to the means of production, that is, how they make their living, has an impact on the political parties they choose. Blue-collar workers are more likely to vote for parties on the left, particularly the Communists, than are the middle classes, who vote for parties on the right, especially the Gaullists. The association between these two variables, class and vote, is not overwhelming, and many other circumstances also influence choice. This association has persisted at a steady level throughout the national elections of the Fifth Republic, however (Lewis-Beck 1984; 1998).

Such class differences are evident even among young voters. Table I.2 shows occupation data on first-time voters, taken from the second round of a 1995 presidential voting survey. At one extreme, small business owners voted overwhelmingly for the Gaullist Chirac, giving him 77 percent of their votes. At the other extreme, blue-collar workers in this group gave Chirac only 43 percent. The French class structure has evolved, and a strict division between workers and the *bourgeoisie* is in some ways too simple. Class has not diminished in its relevance for the individual voter, however, although class composition may have changed.

TABLE I.2. RELATIONSHIP OF CLASS AND RELIGION TO 1995 PRESIDENTIAL VOTE, SECOND ROUND, FOR FIRST-TIME VOTERS (IN PERCENTAGES)

	Chirac	*Jospin*
A. *Occupation*		
Small business[a]	77	23
Upper middle[b]	59	41
Middle middle[c]	45	55
Lower middle[d]	49	51
Worker[e]	43	57
B. *Religion*		
Practicing Catholic[f]	74	26
Nonpracticing Catholic[g]	59	41
Another denomination or religion[h]	44	56
Not religious	31	69

SOURCES: From a BVA survey of 4,798 voters exiting 150 voting bureaus on 7 May 1995. *Le Monde, Dossiers et documents, l'élection presidentielle 23 avril–7 mai 1995, Jacques Chirac le défi du changement*, 72.

a. Includes shopkeepers, employees of small commercial operations, artisans, farmers.

b. Includes members of the liberal professions and top executives.

c. Includes teachers, bureau chiefs, technicians, social workers, middle-level managers.

d. Includes sales clerks, office employees.

e. Includes blue-collar factory workers, service workers.

f. Attends mass regularly.

g. Attends mass irregularly or not at all.

h. Includes Protestants, Jews, Muslims.

In the early Republics, religion exercised a tremendous influence in French politics. Given the new harmony in church-state affairs, the disappearance of Catholic political parties, the legal status of divorce and abortion, and the diminished attendance at mass, however, it might seem that religion's political force was spent. But such is not the case. Socialist efforts in the early 1980s to bring Catholic schools more fully under the control of the national education administration put a million protesters in the streets of Paris at one point. The public school versus private school issue flared up again in the early 1990s, when the Gaullists pressed for more government support for run-down Catholic primary schools. Religion, and the symbolic and substantive issues surrounding its practice, continue to galvanize French politics. Good Catholic voters still are expected to favor the right. For example, table I.2 on page 7 shows that 74 percent of practicing Catholics said they voted for Gaullist Chirac in 1995, whereas only 31 percent of those with no religion supported him. As I have noted elsewhere, this "is not an external, essentially spurious, link between two behaviors. Rather, it symbolizes a network of beliefs, images, and feelings that define a Catholic's political role" (Lewis-Beck 1984, 438).

Social structure shapes political perspective. A French worker may see things from the left, a faithful churchgoer may see them from the right. What does it mean to see things from the left or right? These ideological terms convey much in France, where they first arose in a 1789 Assembly with revolutionaries grouping on the left side and royal partisans on the right side. This left-right division continued, culminating in the National Convention of 1793, when the groups separated over the execution of the king (Lewis-Beck, Hildreth, and Spitzer 1988). Since that time, French citizens have used a left-to-right ideological spectrum to order their universe of political choices. In contemporary public opinion surveys, French voters are routinely asked to place themselves politically on a left-right scale; almost all can do so, and only about one quarter place themselves in the neutral center of the scale (Michalet 1993). Furthermore, a voter's ideological self-placement is highly predictive of an actual vote. For example, in the 1995 presidential race (second ballot), among voters who said they were "very left" (*très à gauche*), 97 percent selected Jospin, whereas among those who said they were "very right" (*très à droite*), 92 percent selected Chirac. Of those who said they were "in the middle" (*ni à gauche ni à droite*), only 57 percent went for Chirac (*Le Monde, Dossiers et documents: L'Élection presidentielle 23 avril–7 mai 1995, Jacques Chirac le défi du changement*, 72). To discover a French person's ideological leaning is to discover a great deal about his or her politics. For French voters, ideological identification acts as a "standing decision" rule, very much as party identification does for the American voter (Fleury and Lewis-Beck 1993). It tells them which parties and candidates they favor and which they do not.

Campaign Issues and Election Outcomes

While class, religion, and ideology operate strongly on the French electorate, votes are not simply reflexive responses to these traditional forces. French voters weigh issues before arriving at a final decision. The felicitous title of a recent book by French political scientists, *L'Électeur a ses raisons* (The Voter Has Reasons), makes the point well (Boy and Mayer 1997b). In the 1995 presidential campaign, for example, voters saw many issues as important, including unemployment, AIDS, social security, corruption, crime, immigration, the environment, and the European Union. Further, they viewed some candidates as better than others for dealing with particular issues. For instance, the voters surveyed thought Chirac could better handle unemployment, Jospin social security, and Voynet the environment (Chiche and Mayer 1997, 219-27). Certain candidates, such as Dominique Voynet of the Greens or Jean-Marie Le Pen of the National Front, were strongly identified with specific issues. For voters who worry about the presence of the mostly North African immigrant community, Le Pen has long held a particular attraction. Table I.3 shows survey data gathered before the 1986 National Assembly election, when the National Front first established itself as a country-wide political power. National Front supporters were overwhelmingly anti-immigrant, unlike members of other parties.

TABLE I.3. PARTY SUPPORTERS AGREEING "COMPLETELY" THAT THERE WERE "TOO MANY IMMIGRANT WORKERS" (IN PERCENTAGES)

Vote intention[a]	*Agree completely*
Communist	32
Socialist	24
UDF	37
RPR	45
National Front	88

SOURCES: Euro-Barometers nos. 21–24 (April 1984–November 1985, total sample size = 2,778), in Lewis-Beck and Mitchell 1993, 122.

a. Vote intention = "the party you would vote for if a legislative election were held tomorrow."

Le Pen placed fourth in the first round of the 1995 presidential balloting, winning 15 percent of the vote. The two top vote getters, Jospin and Chirac, went on to battle it out in the second round. Voters had to incorporate many issues into that last choice, of course. Some issues come and go, but certain ones remain near the top of the political agenda. Economic concerns have held the highest priority since the end of the Algerian war, according to public opinion surveys (Lewis-Beck 1988, 95-102). If anything, the relevance of economic issues may be increasing. The polling firm SOFRES regularly asks, "Among the following things, which should the government give priority to at present?" In 1981 the mean response was 56 percent for "the fight against unemployment," and that value rose to 83 percent by 1995 (SOFRES 1989; 1996). One could even argue that voter opinion on the state of the economy, and how Chirac might affect it, was critical to his victory (Lewis-Beck 1997, 239-62). Table I.4 shows data from the 1995 French National Election Survey, wherein voters' evaluations of the national economy are related to their second-ballot preferences. Among those who foresaw economic progress, 72 percent favored Chirac; in contrast, among voters who perceived a worsening economy, only 18 percent favored him. It seems plausible that the economic issue brought many voters into the Chirac camp.

TABLE I.4. NATIONAL ECONOMIC EVALUATION AND 1995 PRESIDENTIAL VOTE, SECOND ROUND (IN PERCENTAGES)

Q: Over the next twelve months, do you think that the economic situation of the country will improve, worsen, or stay the same?

	Economic evaluation		
Vote	*Improve*	*Stay the same*	*Worsen*
Chirac	72	36	18
Jospin	28	64	82

SOURCE: Data are from the 1995 French National Election Study, available from the Interuniversity Consortium for Political and Social Research. Sample size = 2,884.

The data in table I.4 support the broad idea that voters weigh issues before deciding. But which issues? There are noneconomic as well as economic ones, and these vary from election to election. Is there some way to summarize the impact of issues, and systematically take into account their impact on French election outcomes? One approach is to aggregate voters and elections, and sort issues into overall categories, thus allowing much of the "noise" from any single choice, contest, or issue to be overcome. Here is one hypothesis to explain voting in National Assembly elections across the Fifth Republic: If voters, on balance, are satisfied with government handling of major economic and noneconomic problems, they vote for a party in the ruling coalition; otherwise, they vote for an opposition party (Lewis-Beck 1985). This could be expressed as an equation:

Assembly Vote = performance on economic and noneconomic issues

Suppose we define Assembly Vote to mean the percentage of first-round votes going to opposition parties. For Economic Performance, measure the growth rate of the Gross Domestic Product (GDP) before the election. When that number is good, government parties should gain votes. To account for Noneconomic Performance, take the president's popularity rating, which encapsulates public opinion on a host of social and cultural issues. When the president is doing a good job on these issues, as registered by his popularity, this should win votes for his party coalition. Using these definitions, the equation can be calculated in a regression analysis on data from the National Assembly elections of the Fifth Republic (Lewis-Beck 1995):

$$\text{Vote} = 68.28 - .13G - .38P$$

where Vote = the first-round vote percentage for government opposition parties, in the ten National Assembly elections from 1958 to 1993; G = the growth rate of the Gross Domestic Product, six months before the election; P = the percentage "satisfied" with the president in the *Institute français d'opinion publique* (IFOP) poll six months before the election.

The coefficients of G and P, respectively, demonstrate that poor economic growth aids the opposition, as does an unpopular president. To illustrate, consider the 1986 National Assembly election. Before that contest, the economic growth rate was only .3, and only 34 percent of the public surveyed said they were "satisfied" with President Mitterrand. On the basis of these numbers, the equation predicts a first-round win for the right opposition of about 55 percent. In fact, the right parties won 56 percent of the first-round vote and went on to obtain a seat majority, which approved Jacques Chirac as prime minister. In general, the equation has predicted the first-round vote rather well and has always tracked the shift in the final government majority from left to right, as in 1986, or from right to left, as in 1981. Table I.5 on page 12 summarizes the prediction accuracy of the equation, for each election from 1958 to 1993.

The equation predicts the political composition of the National Assembly majority, left or right, without error. This suggests that it could be used for fore-

TABLE I.5. PREDICTIONS OF FIRST-ROUND NATIONAL ASSEMBLY RESULTS, 1958–93 (IN PERCENTAGES)

	Opposition vote			*Is majority*
	Actual	*Predicted*	*Prediction error*	*correctly predicted?*
1958	43.4	42.8	0.6	Yes
1962	44.2	44.9	-0.7	Yes
1967	45.0	43.9	1.1	Yes
1968	41.0	48.0	-7.0	Yes
1973	46.4	47.7	-1.3	Yes
1978	49.5	49.6	-0.1	Yes
1981	55.7	54.3	1.4	Yes
1986	56.0	55.4	0.6	Yes
1988	50.3	45.4	4.9	Yes
1993	57.0	56.4	0.6	Yes

SOURCE: Fauvelle-Aymar and Lewis-Beck 1997, 15.

casting election outcomes, a possibility that was tested before the 1997 contest. In April, President Chirac dissolved the Assembly and called for elections almost a year ahead of schedule. Politicians saw this as a wise strategic move, for virtually all observers, including the pollsters, put Chirac's UDF-RPR ruling coalition in the lead. In fact, the polls were seriously biased, and such lead as the traditional right had enjoyed had dwindled away by election day (Jérôme, Jérôme, and Lewis-Beck 1999). The prediction equation appeared in the press a few days before the election and, to widespread skepticism, forecast the defeat of the ruling right party coalition (Fauvelle-Aymar and Lewis-Beck 1997, 15). The relevant numbers on economic growth and presidential popularity, respectively, were G = .2 and P = 30. That is, going into the election, the economy was doing poorly and the president was unpopular. In many ways, it was a repeat of the 1986 scenario, but from the right rather than the left. For either contest, the defeat of the parties of government should not have come as a surprise. The big issues, economic and noneconomic, were working for the opposition.

To an inexperienced American observer, French democracy may seem exotic. The constitution is only forty years old, there appear to be two chief executives, voting takes place in rounds, the voting rules themselves may change, the Senate is not really important, everyone participates, the array of parties is dizzying, and party discourse is highly ideological. But this gaudy democratic fabric is backed by plain cloth: individual French voters whose voting behavior largely can be understood. Long-term forces—class, religion, left/right ideology—continue to mold them, making their choices predictable, especially in the context of current issues. The preferences of French voters endure. Other things being equal, the French will make the same partisan choice election after election. Of course, things are not always equal, and certain issues, such as immigration or economics, will drive some away from their "first" party, perhaps permanently. On balance, though, even such shifts become predictable in the aggregate, as the National Assembly equation demonstrated. In an earlier commentary, I concluded that "French voters are caught in a structure of commitment and choice that reproduces itself, with little variation, from one election to the next" (Lewis-Beck 1993, 11). On the basis of the 1995 and 1997 election results, I continue to affirm that the French electorate is blocked in this way, or "stalled." After reading this volume, however, the reader may disagree—which is what makes the study of French politics an endless source of intellectual adventure.

Chapter 1

The Socialists, Jospin, and the Mitterrand Legacy

William Safran

The parliamentary elections of 1997 must be considered an event of multiple significance for the Socialist Party (PS). It was a dramatic reversal of the party's 1993 defeat, when it was reduced to barely 20 percent of the seats in the National Assembly. The capture of parliamentary control by the PS and the appointment of Lionel Jospin as prime minister attested to the organizational stability of one of the major parties in France and to the continued relevance of the right/left dichotomy in French political life.[1]

The Heritage

The PS victory can be attributed not only to the policy failures of the RPR-UDF governing team and the shortcomings of Prime Minister Alain Juppé, but also to the PS's overall legacy, specifically its achievements in the 1980s. These included socioeconomic reforms, such as an increase in the minimum wage; the institution of a minimum monthly family income (RMI); a fifth week of paid vacations; improvements in civil liberties (Safran 1988); the promotion and subsidization of ethnoregional cultural programs; and the partial privatization and pluralization of the media. The achievements also encompassed institutional reforms that became permanent features of the French political landscape: the reduction of the *cumul des mandats* (the accumulation of simultaneously held elective offices); the upgrading of the role of Parliament; the abolition of the State Security Court; and, above all, administrative decentralization. Finally, the Socialist legacy included the transformation of PS attitudes toward European integration, a less hostile attitude toward Americans and NATO, the dissipation of illusions about the Soviet

Union, and the conversion of the PS to an acceptance of capitalism. Paradoxically, these changes occurred together with the building of a leftist alliance. A major feature of the alliance was the tactical embrace of the Communist Party (PCF), which contributed to that party's domestication, return to respectability, and gradual enfeeblement.

These Socialist achievements are largely those of François Mitterrand, having occurred during his fourteen-year tenure as president of the republic. It is a matter of debate to what extent this legacy was counterbalanced by the negative aspects of the image Mitterrand left behind. These relate to his reputation as a modern "Florentine" prince who practiced nepotism[2] and wielded power for its own sake, and in so doing manipulated his political associates, sometimes betrayed them, and discarded them when they ceased to be useful. His personal antagonisms sometimes worked to the detriment of his own party: the PS, which he had been instrumental in rebuilding from its low point in the 1960s into a major "catchall" party in the late 1970s, was greatly undermined in the early 1990s by disagreements with other left-wing politicians and by Mitterrand's vendetta against Michel Rocard, which culminated in Rocard's elimination in the early 1990s as a viable contender for the presidency.[3] By the time Mitterrand left office, the coherence of the PS had been so weakened by internecine fights that, as one wit (Guy Bedos) remarked, "Mitterrand [intended] to give back the Socialist party in the same condition in which he had received it" (quoted in Friend 1993, 1).

Toward the end of his presidency, Mitterrand's image was further tarnished by renewed revelations about his past, including a dalliance with the extreme right during the 1930s (Péan 1994) and connections with the Vichy regime (Faux, Legrand, and Perez 1994); his continued friendship during the Fifth Republic with René Bousquet, who, as a high police official in the Vichy regime, had been implicated in the deportation of Jews; his involvement in wiretapping; and his personal escapades.[4] Finally, Mitterrand's reputation was damaged by his refusal to reveal information about his long and incurable illness, a refusal that was explained by some as being in the national interest (*raison d'État*), but labeled by others a "state lie" (*mensonge d'État*) (Pégard 1996; Coignard and Guichard 1996).

Jospin and Mitterrand: An Ambiguous Relationship

Jospin's decision about the degree to which he should identify with Mitterrand's record was not easy, given the general public's complex and changeable views of the Socialist president. Mitterrand's approval rating had ranged from a high of 59 percent in 1989 to a low of 37 percent in 1993. This change was not clearly related to his concrete achievements; although the French judged him severely for his failure to solve the unemployment problem, his rating went up in 1995 despite a worsening employment situation.[5] He consistently received higher ratings for his foreign policy performance than for his domestic policy achievements, despite his failures in the international arena.[6] Mitterrand's ratings improved toward the end of his career for reasons that are not entirely clear. Two years before the end of his second term of office, he became a lame-duck president and therefore was no longer held responsible for policy shortcomings; moreover, his terminal illness evoked considerable public sympathy. In a poll conducted shortly after his death in January 1996, more than 80 percent of respondents judged his fourteen years as president to have been one of the great periods of French history (SOFRES 1996, 318).

Jospin's ambivalent position with respect to Mitterrand is explained both by Mitterrand's legacy and by the ambiguous relationship between the two men that had existed during Mitterrand's rise to power and presidency. In the 1960s Jospin was invited by Mitterrand to join the *Convention des institutions républicaines* (CIR), one of his political creations, but Jospin declined because he considered the CIR too centrist for his taste. However, he did join the PS shortly after Mitterrand became the secretary-general of that party in 1971, two years after it was established as successor to the *Section française de l'internationale ouvrière* (SFIO). During the 1970s Mitterrand had relied on Jospin to serve as a link to the more radical members of the ex-SFIO and to improve relations with the PCF, and he had even considered Jospin as a possible heir (Giesbert 1996, 289). However, Mitterrand eventually regarded him as too leftist because of his reputed earlier connections with Trotskyists (and possibly his advocacy of Algerian independence, which Mitterrand had once opposed), and he came to prefer Laurent Fabius (Leclerc and Muracciole 1997, 40-43). During the 1970s, Jospin was one of Mitterrand's most reliable adjutants. He understated his own political ambitions in the service of party unity and, above all, in the interest of Mitterrand's presidential aspirations, only to be sidelined by Mitterrand in favor of Fabius.

In 1981, when Mitterrand was elected to the presidency, Jospin succeeded him as secretary-general of the PS. This promotion was, to some extent, compensation for Fabius's having been chosen over Jospin to manage Mitterrand's election campaign. Throughout his two presidential terms, Mitterrand could count on Jospin's honesty and loyalty, which contrasted markedly with Mitterrand's own deviousness and unsteady commitment to his political associates.[7] As secretary-general of the PS, Jospin demonstrated so much loyalty to the president that many party politicians regarded him as little more than Mitterrand's errand boy

(Dupin 1991, 244). This loyalty was to stand Jospin in good stead, for Mitterrand was not tempted to destroy him politically.

Nevertheless, during the 1995 presidential campaign, Mitterrand did little to help Jospin's candidacy, providing him only a lukewarm endorsement. Given the tense relationship between the two men, perhaps Mitterrand was as little inclined to help Jospin as a professor would be to help someone who was neither his disciple nor an admirer. Jospin reacted in a nuanced manner: although he associated himself with the positive aspects of Mitterrand's presidency, he distanced himself from the negative. He stressed that he was his own man, with his own personality and his own distinct approaches to the party and to politics. Jospin had taken that position even before his nomination as a presidential candidate. At a Socialist Party congress toward the end of 1994, he had expressed reservations about Mitterrand's legacy by publicly denouncing the ethics of his presidency.

The Ascendance of Jospin: Contextual Elements

At the same time, Jospin followed in Mitterrand's footsteps both programmatically and tactically. Mitterrand had asserted his leadership of the PS after forcing Valéry Giscard d'Estaing into a runoff in the presidential elections of 1974; in the same way, Jospin was recognized as the PS party leader after forcing Jacques Chirac into a runoff in 1995. However, unlike Mitterrand, who had been selected by the party's executive committee as first secretary and thereafter as presidential candidate, Jospin was *elected* by the party's activists as presidential candidate and subsequently (in October 1995) as secretary-general. The election procedure endowed Jospin's leadership with some grassroots legitimation. Jospin's stature as party leader also was enhanced by his political origins. Traditionally, all the leaders of the PS, from its founding until 1979 (the party congress in Metz), had emerged not from the party itself but from different movements antedating the party that came to form its factions: Mitterrand (CIR), Rocard (PSU), Pierre Mauroy, and Gaston Defferre (SFIO). Jospin, in contrast, had emerged from within the party apparatus. Although that apparatus had come to be dominated by Mitterrand, he bequeathed no distinct ideology or orientation, so his influence did not outlast him. As Jospin put it, in 1988 Mitterrand cultivated the illusion of having been elected "for himself and by himself," and "he transformed the theme of a rallying of the French around himself into a permanent theory, with which the left could no longer identify" ("Entretien avec Lionel Jospin," *Temps modernes*, June-July 1997, 6). Thus, when Jospin assumed the leadership, the factions led by the Mitterrand generation of political leaders had no clear set of principles by which to maintain their distinct identities (Portelli 1997, 74-77).

As soon as he was chosen as the standard-bearer of the PS, Jospin set about rebuilding the leftist alliance, notably by reestablishing links with the PCF and by embracing clearly leftist policy goals, a course he continued to pursue in the 1997 parliamentary election campaign. Jospin was able to accomplish this task because his relationship with his left-wing partners was easier than Mitterrand's had been. Like Mitterrand himself, the three Socialists who had been in the forefront as possible presidential candidates—Rocard, Fabius, and Jacques Delors—although ideologically diverse, belonged to the right wing of the PS (Portelli 1992, 134).

Mitterrand's relationship with the Communists had been marked by an awareness that they competed seriously with the Socialists for hegemony of the left, and for that reason he asked the PCF for guarantees that it would respect the results of elections (which meant that the party would relinquish office peacefully if voted out of office) and that it would be independent of foreign control (Morray 1997, 62). Jospin had no need to pose such conditions; nor did he have to convince the PCF of his basically leftist orientation. Whereas Mitterrand's socialism was belated, tactical, and of short duration—he was said to have been a Socialist for only two out of the fourteen years of his presidency (Duhamel 1997a, 124)—Jospin had been "viscerally attached to the union of the Left" (Mercier and Jérôme 1997, 43). In short, Jospin, once having emerged from Mitterrand's shadow, retained a leftist credibility sufficient to reconstruct a relationship with the PCF.

Jospin was helped in his efforts, to be sure, by a favorable context. The PCF was in a much more cooperative mode in the mid-1990s than it had been in the early 1980s: the Soviet Union had collapsed, and Georges Marchais, a consistent Stalinist, had been replaced as secretary-general of the PCF by Robert Hue, a voluble and telegenic moderate with whom Jospin quickly formed a friendly personal relationship.[8] He established an equally friendly relationship with Jean-Pierre Chevènement, a former member of the PS and now the leader of his own party, the leftist Citizens' Movement (*Mouvement des citoyens*). Such a relationship was possible because Chevènement's disagreement with Mitterrand over French participation in the Gulf War had become irrelevant,[9] and because Chevènement (once fiercely opposed to NATO and to a supranational Europe) had overcome his earlier hostility to the Maastricht Treaty and now regarded the European Union more favorably. The ecologist Green Party (*Verts*) had evolved in a decidedly leftist direction by the time Dominique Voynet succeeded Antoine Waechter as its leader; this development facilitated a "pink-red-green" coalition.

Jospin gained ascendance in his own party when Rocard was eliminated as a serious presidential candidate, which left only Fabius as Jospin's rival for party leadership. At the party congress in Rennes (1990), Mauroy (a former prime minister) and Louis Mermaz (a former Speaker of the Assembly) formed an alliance with Jospin, not because they shared his ideology or necessarily wanted to advance his career, but because they both were hostile to Fabius and ready to support Jacques Delors (the outgoing president of the European Commission) as the presidential candidate (Portelli 1997, 141-42). Fortunately for Jospin, however, Delors declined to be nominated in 1995. In the subsequent competition with Fabius, Jospin was in a better position than his major rival, who continued to be identified with Mitterrand (Philippe and Hubscher 1991, 119). This illustrates two important points: (1) internal fights are less about ideology and program and more about personal rivalries; and (2) the evolution of a party's direction and the situation of its leadership are often matters of context and unanticipated events.

Jospin also was helped in his efforts by the mediocre quality of Juppé's cabinet ministers, their failure to solve the unemployment problem, and the corruption scandals that beset Gaullist (RPR) and Giscardist (UDF) politicians, which caused many voters to disregard the money-laundering scandals that had earlier dogged Socialist politicians. The decisive contextual factor was, of course, President Jacques Chirac's ill-advised and unnecessary dissolution of the Assembly, which precipitated the 1997 parliamentary elections.

During the 1995 campaign, Jospin had harbored considerable doubt about his voter appeal. The PS had not recovered from its electoral defeat of 1993 and continued to be deeply divided, and Jospin's selection as the standard-bearer of his party was not unchallenged. During the 1997 campaign, however, Jospin felt a degree of "psychological liberation" (Mercier and Jérôme 1997, 17) and believed the election to be winnable for a number of reasons: Juppé's evident unpopularity, the absence of Mitterrand as a constraining force, and his own success in asserting his leadership of the PS. Like Mitterrand, who in 1988 had portrayed himself as a focus of confidence and comfort with his slogan "*la force tranquille*" (Carton 1995, 52), Jospin avoided exaggerated claims and projected an aura of reliability and modesty, although he could not match Mitterrand's avuncular image. He leaned to some extent on Mitterrand's electoral strategy by forming alliances with other leftist parties; but unlike the pattern of his earlier election campaigns, he went beyond a commitment to second-round withdrawals (*désistements*) by giving up more than thirty constituencies in the first round—even *before* Chirac decided on early Assembly elections—and by permitting PS candidates to put rival leftist party candidates on the ballot as alternates (*suppléants*), and vice versa.[10]

The Conflicting Bases of Electoral Choice

To explain the PS victory in the parliamentary election is a complex task. It is simple to argue that the elevation of Jospin to the prime ministership was the people's choice, because during the presidential campaign, Jospin had become the unchallenged leader of the camp of the left to whom all leftist parties rallied in the second round of elections. It is less easy, however, to determine the motivations for that choice. The electoral result can be analyzed in terms of any one of the three dominant explanatory paradigms of political behavior: those based on institutions, political culture, or rational choice. It seems obvious that the left was the logical beneficiary when the government of the right, which was punished for its inability to solve urgent domestic problems, was ousted. The victory of the left confounded many who had argued that the French were victims of ideological disenchantment, reflected in a "breakup of the culture of the Left," especially among intellectuals, largely because of socialism's ideological contradictions (Bergougnioux and Grunberg 1992, 398ff, 413-14). Some observers went even further, arguing that the French electorate had become "neoliberal" (that is, converted to a market-oriented ideology), a thesis that had gained ground with the overwhelming victory of the RPR and UDF in the legislative elections of 1993. The French were so attached to their customary wage, job protection, family income supplement, and health service entitlements, however, that they forgave the PS its previous policy failures.

The acceptance of the Maastricht Treaty and of privatization (however qualified) suggested that the PS had itself evolved in a neoliberal direction, but that evolution must not be overstressed. Unlike Fabius and Rocard, who were said to have embraced a "perverted Mitterrandism" by attempting to transcend socialism, Jospin wanted to preserve as much of the socialist tradition as possible (Philippe and Hubscher 1991, 121-22). He retained the major tenets of the socialist faith. These included, in order of importance, the defense of the "social achievements" of the French people, the protection of workers' rights in the workplace, the reform of education and apprenticeship training, a reduction of the workweek, and the improvement of conditions for the underprivileged sectors of society (SOFRES poll 26–28 March 1996, cited in Allègre 1996, 45). Jospin was perceived as embodying these themes better than all other leaders of the left (both in the PS and in other parties)—not because he was more "leftist" than they, but because he had greater prestige than his rivals, and because the PS realistically was the center around which these themes could be organized. The concrete policies spelled out in the PS platform illustrated Jospin's adherence to tradition. Moreover, any temptation on his part to abandon these tenets could be checked by the gains of other leftist parties, whose support he needed. Several months before the 1997 elections, the PS had reconciled with the PCF and made accommodations with smaller leftist parties (including the Greens), as it prepared a *contrat d'orientation* (guiding agreement) with them. Prior agreements among the parties on a number of issues facilitated such accommodation. Thus, the Greens agreed with the Socialists on reducing the presidential mandate to five years, limiting the *cumul des mandats*, and approaching parity between women and men. Both the PCF and the Greens shared the Socialists' desire to upgrade the role of Parliament, and the PS was receptive to the smaller leftist parties' desire for a return to proportional representation (*Le Monde, Dossiers et documents* 1995, 32-33).

The issue-based, or "instrumental," explanation for Jospin's success is, however, insufficient. Public opinion surveys suggest that the voters, while punishing the right for its policy failures, also remembered the similar failures of the earlier Socialist government and had no optimistic expectations for a succeeding Socialist government. According to a poll conducted before the conclusion of the 1997 elections, a third of the respondents expected nothing from the Socialists, and even 24 percent of those who intended to vote for the PS thought it would make no difference in terms of policy if the PS and its allies were victorious (SOFRES poll of 25-26 April 1997 [*Le Monde, Dossiers et documents* 1997, 20]). Before the elections, Socialists and other leftists of various stripes, abetted by a number of trade unions, organized mass demonstrations to demand the abrogation of the restrictive Pasqua-Debré laws on immigration and naturalization,[11] although the demonstrators derived no personal economic advantage from their actions (and subsequently protested against what they considered Jospin's failure to introduce legislation to improve the situation of legal and illegal immigrants). The chorus clamoring for a generous policy was not unanimous: a number of intellectuals identified with the democratic left wrote a broadside in *Libération* (8 October 1997) opposing a blanket regularization of the status of illegal immigrants. Nevertheless, it can be argued that the electorate made its choice as much for emotional or "expressive" reasons as for reasons of rational economic (i.e., cost-benefit) considerations, and that ideology is not dead but functionally autonomous.[12]

Here the positive evaluation of Jospin's personality must be set against a widespread animus toward Juppé's behavior. Juppé was considered to be patronizing and arrogant; as a prime minister enjoying overwhelming support in the

Assembly, he had presented his program for streamlining the precarious condition of the social security system to the Assembly as a fait accompli, without sufficient prior consultation with "social partners," especially the trade unions. Furthermore, he had been personally involved in corruption: the fact that he lived in a municipally owned luxury apartment at artificially low rent was widely publicized. Jospin, in contrast, was regarded as a person who strove for political consensus by carefully consulting with politicians and labor and business spokespersons. In 1995 he had run as a "citizen-president" willing to listen to all sectors of the population; in 1997 he projected much the same aura, portraying himself as the anti-Juppé candidate who fought against the elitism of the *Énarques*, the graduates of the National School of Administration (ENA), and who dominated the higher administrative corps. Such an approach had its risks, for Jospin, like Juppé and Chirac, was also an *Énarque*. Nevertheless, he was personally untouched by scandal, his behavior was that of a schoolmaster, and he took a moralizing approach to politics. During the 1970s and 1980s Jospin gained a reputation for a dry and reticent personality; because of his reticence, he had been underestimated by most of his colleagues, some of whom had regarded him as a "loser" as recently as early 1995. He acquired a certain charisma after an impressive performance in the 1995 presidential elections, however, when he came out on top in the first round and garnered nearly half the popular vote in the second round. This performance added to Jospin's political authority, which enabled him to transform his leadership into the "bully pulpit" normally associated with the presidency.

Jospin's position as national opposition leader was manifested in discussions about a televised debate between the right and the left before the first round of the 1997 elections. The Gaullists and their allies had suggested that such a debate (normally organized for presidential rather than parliamentary contests) include both Juppé and François Léotard, the leader of the UDF, on one side, and Jospin and Hue, the Communist leader, on the other. Jospin, however, insisted that the debate be a one-to-one affair between himself and Juppé, a demand that the Gaullists found unacceptable. Consequently, the debate never took place. But after Juppé had announced that he would resign as prime minister, the campaign for the second round turned into a personalized confrontation between Jospin and Chirac, that is, almost a reenactment of the presidential elections of two years earlier.

Jospin's inaugural speech to the Assembly on 19 June 1997, wherein he presented his government and program, was one illustration of his quasi-presidential behavior. In length and magisterial tone, that speech befitted a president. It stressed the sanctity of a politician's word (*la parole donnée*), the importance of social solidarity, and the ideas of good citizenship and civic education. It referred to the impartiality of the law, the permanence of the nation-state in the context of a united Europe, and the continuing reality of France as a republican and secular society that welcomes immigrants. It was a "republican pact" that made reference to a number of legislative priorities, which were to be embodied in government bills in due course ("Discours de Lionel Jospin," *Le Monde*, 21 June 1997, 8-9).

In the presidential and parliamentary election campaigns, Jospin had promised to address himself to a number of the electorate's crucial concerns: unemployment, urban violence, immigration, civil rights, the behavior of the police, the maintenance of welfare-state entitlements, a reduction of the workweek, and the fight against the neglect of economically underprivileged sectors. Yet the parliamentary elections had come about so unexpectedly that the PS did not have enough time to work out all the details; moreover, the programmatic promises of the Gaullists and their allies were not much different and could therefore not serve as reliable bases of comparison. According to *Libération*, "both the Right and the Left avoid[ed] posing serious questions, contenting themselves with incantations or 'gadget' solutions," such as vague promises to create 700,000 jobs and to address themselves to socioeconomic inequalities. Meanwhile, the voters continued to defend their privileges and to rely on their lobbies to help protect them (Wyplosz 1997).

It has been argued that "partisan attachments weaken when new parties emerge that appeal to preexistent group loyalties" (Schickler and Green 1997, 453). However, the new parties that have come into existence in France have tended to be limited-issue ones and ephemeral, either because they have been unable to fulfill their promises or because their causes have been taken up by established parties. In view of this fact, "right" and "left" have continued to be important markers of identification in French politics. It may therefore be argued that the voters' choice was made in terms not consistently connected with specific policies, but rather in terms of the ideological identifications that constitute a basic characteristic of French political culture, such as the clash between the generalized collectivist-statist orientation of the left and the individualist and market-oriented outlook of the right. For institutional reasons, specifically, the prevailing system of national elections, there has been neither a credible centrist ideological alternative, nor a lasting or reliable alternative to the PS for left-oriented voters.

The persistence of the right-left dichotomy is illustrated by the results of the national elections from 1988 to 1997, which show that electoral shifts tend to occur "within the family"; that is, the loss of popular votes for the PS usually redounds to the benefit of other leftist parties, save for exceptional years such as 1993. In runoff rounds, the leftist parties "reassemble" around the most favorably placed leftist vote-getter, who is, more often than not, a Socialist (Grunberg and Chiche 1995, 192).

Jospin, the Left, and the "Pluralist" Government

None of the foregoing detracts from Jospin's personal contribution. As a *rassembleur* (unifier), he took a leaf from Mitterrand's book, but he went about his task more systematically, by building alliances early and carefully. Jospin's *Propositions pour la France* (Jospin 1995) and his "Program of the Left" were reminders of Mitterrand's *110 Propositions pour la France* (text in Manceron and Pingaud 1981, 170-89) and of the Common Program of the Left of 1972 in that they contained a number of traditional leftist demands, such as the thirty-five-hour workweek, a raise in wages, and a change in the tax system to make it more progressive. These items were a part of the forty-five key points of the government's "social and moral pact" adopted by Jospin (Colombani 1997). As in the Common Program of two decades earlier, some of these points were included on the insistence of the PCF as a condition of its participation in the government. But that insistence was not categorical, because the Communists were willing to go to great lengths to emerge from their isolation, and this circumstance permitted Jospin a certain interpretive leeway (Bougereau 1997, 32). Thus Jospin, although stressing employment in the public sector, was inclined to reduce the number of positions in that sector in favor of jobs in local government and private associations; although he favored retaining the nationalized sector, he proposed measures to partially privatize industries while allowing the government to retain significant shares (a policy reminiscent of Rocard's position nine years earlier, namely, neither significant privatization nor additional nationalization). Such measures are far from "pure" socialism; instead, they are attempts to navigate between the exigencies of the marketplace and excessive statism, without adopting the U.S. model of a "ruthless capitalism" verging on social Darwinism, and without abandoning the social solidarity that is part of French political culture. In this regard, the Socialists are not diametrically opposed by the mainstream (or "republican") right-wing parties, for they, too, wish to adhere to the principle of a "social republic" (as provided for in the constitution [Article 2]) and attempt to steer a middle course between *dirigisme* (state economic planning) and liberalism. Indeed, in arguing for a "social" Europe and for a reduction of socioeconomic inequalities within France, Jospin represented a position that had also been articulated by presidential candidate Chirac in 1995 and reaffirmed by him in 1997.

The elections of 1997 were remarkable for the attention the PS paid to the role of women in politics. Altogether, 167 (exactly 30 percent) of the 555 PS candidates for election to the Assembly were women; more than 40 of the 246 Socialist deputies elected were women (out of a total of 63 women deputies, compared to 32 in the previous Assembly); and 8 women ministers were appointed to the Jospin government, 5 of them to full cabinet posts. This may not look very original. Juppé's first government, set up immediately after his appointment as prime minister, had included more women, but most of them had been given minor ministerial posts; after a government reshuffle, the number of women had been reduced to four. Shortly before the dissolution of the Assembly, Juppé had proposed amending the constitution to secure adequate representation of women in politics; but this move was largely symbolic, for the number of Gaullist women candidates for the forthcoming legislative elections, and that of women subsequently elected under the Gaullist label, remained small.

The feminization of the Jospin cabinet contributed to the image of a government that was generally representative of society, while downgrading the weight of the "old elephants"—politicians who had been prominent in the SFIO and/or had been heavyweight members of Mitterrand's entourage—conveyed the impression of rejuvenation. Furthermore, in creating the first cohabitation government that did not include any high-ranking "ministers of state," Jospin served notice that there would be no complicated hierarchical differentiation between him and the rest of the cabinet (Dolez 1997). By this move, as well as by appointing two powerful personalities (Martine Aubry and Dominique Strauss-Kahn) to take charge of ministries with expanded responsibilities, he created a programmatic as well as tactical balance, which enabled him to be the final arbiter in socioeconomic policy.

Jospin's program has been a variant of Keynesianism, that is, a mixture of state intervention and reliance on the private sector to create employment and stimulate consumption. This mixture appears to correspond to the preferences of the electorate as a whole, including the Socialist electorate. That electorate ranges across the social-class spectrum: in the recent parliamentary elections, 32 percent of the PS vote came from executives and senior managers (*cadres supérieurs*) and the liberal professions, 29 percent from employers, and only 25 percent from workers (IPSOS exit poll, *Le Point*, 2 June 1997). The "catchall" nature of the PS—now more or less comparable to that of the British Labour Party, whose evolution was instrumental in bringing Tony Blair to power in Britain—is in turn reflected in the government, which includes a large number of young people. In one respect there has been no change from the Mitterrand era: the PS is still a party led by professional *cadres* and intellectuals.

Rejuvenation had its limits, however, and not all the "old elephants" were ignored. A number of Rocard and Mitterrand supporters were given legislative committee chairmanships, and even Fabius, Jospin's old rival, regained his old job as Speaker of the Assembly. Indeed, it was Jospin who expressly urged the PS deputies to choose Fabius for the post (Schneider and Carton 1997, 33). Fabius had been Jospin's main rival in the war of succession, which had begun in the mid-1980s and heated up in 1990 (Dupin 1991, 175, 211ff). In addition, the selection of the chiefs of staff of Aubry and Strauss-Kahn—Dominique Marcel, who had served in the *cabinet ministériel* of Prime Minister Edith Cresson and later on the Elysée staff, and François Villeroy de Galhau, who had been on the staff of Prime Minister Pierre Bérégovoy—signaled an element of Mitterrandist continuity. These individuals were known as fiscal conservatives, as were a number of members of other ministers' staffs, and they provided a counterweight to the decidedly leftist pluralist cabinet (Mauduit 1997a).

Although Jospin has tried to avoid composing a team specifically based on party factions, he has included individuals identified with the various *courants* of both the PS and other leftist formations. Although most of the old PS leaders and seasoned collaborators of Mitterrand have been excluded from the government, their presence, and therefore the echo of the factions they represent, is still felt: the cabinet includes a number of younger Mitterrandists, Rocardians, and even Fabiusians (Julliard 1997, 36). The person who almost ideally embodies a combination of rejuvenation, gender balance, and Mitterrandism is Martine Aubry: a woman, the daughter of Jacques Delors (who was identified both with the Catholic and the "Europeanist" wings of the PS), a former cabinet member, and (as deputy mayor of Lille) closely associated with Pierre Mauroy. Another old politician, now the leader of the PS parliamentary group in the Senate, is Claude Estier, and Jospin consults with him regularly.

So far, Jospin has managed to combine the redistributive orientation of the left with the productivist imperatives imposed by economic realities, including the supranational policy norms of the European Union. He has insisted that adherence to a common European monetary unit (the euro), a crucial element of the Maastricht Treaty, be combined with the retention of the existing features of the French welfare state. This balancing act implies, inter alia, keeping under control the rivalries between Aubry, whose outlook is informed by a Socialist-Christian ethic of solidarity and who favors job-sharing, and Strauss-Kahn, whose socialism increasingly is marked by a productivist ethic and who sees France's adaptation to global competitive pressures as a solution to its economic problems. The success of this combination will, of course, be influenced by future relationships among leftist politicians. Although relations among Jospin and other leftist parties are good, these parties retain their blocking potential in the Assembly, which could emerge should the government's policies depart too much from agreed-upon positions. The same possibility exists with respect to the factions within the PS. At this writing, these seem to be under control. For the first time since the founding of the PS, the party's national council has adopted nearly unanimously a common text synthesizing the views of nearly all its factions; this text was presented at the party congress in Brest in November 1997 (Macé-Scaron 1997b, 13). The existing consensus is a "soft" consensus, however, which could be destroyed if Jospin proves unable to control political egos, especially of those slighted in the apportionment of official roles in the government or Parliament, or if conflicting ideological positions (between the dogmatists and the pragmatists) become manifest (Duhamel 1997b).

Jospin's Policies

Whether the policies of Jospin's government are sufficiently "socialist" is a matter of controversy. Certainly, their overall tenor must be considered redistributive, embracing reduction of the workweek to thirty-five hours (whether or not accompanied by a corresponding reduction in wages); progressive tax reforms, including an increase in wealth and corporate taxes; the proposal to apply a means test to recipients of family income supplements (with families earning more than 25,000 francs a month no longer being entitled to that benefit, and needier families having their supplements increased); and defense budget reduction. All of these could be regarded as standard socialist fare. This applies equally to the continued reliance on the public sector for the creation of new jobs. Much of the increase in public service employment was designated for primary and secondary education, including 100,000 new positions (spread over three years) for teachers, teachers' aides, and school counselors. The state's contribution to culture was to be fixed at 1 percent of the national budget (a contribution that had been reduced by previous Gaullist governments). The educational and cultural measures were introduced in order to propitiate the teachers and intellectuals who continue to be a major part of the PS electoral base. In addition, Jospin, who had been a minister of education, took a particular interest in these measures, and Claude Allègre, the new minister of education, was a personal friend of Jospin's.

A traditionally leftist orientation was also evident in the Jospin government's reserved approach to the privatization of industries (stopping or freezing some privatization projects). Although falling considerably short of the nationalization measures of the Popular Front (1936), the punitive nationalizations of the tripartite (Socialist-Communist-Christian Democratic) government (1944-45) led by de Gaulle, or the massive nationalizations of the Mauroy government (1981-82), Jospin's hesitant privatization measures—as, for example, in the case of France Télécom—actually guaranteed that state control over the affected industries would be maintained. Moreover, a number of privatization initiatives undertaken earlier (e.g., CSF-Thomson and Air France) were frozen due to pressures from the PCF and the more radical unions, as well as opposition by Jean-Claude Gayssot, the minister of transport and the most important Communist in the government.

Other policies are difficult to classify as either conservative or leftist, for example, the proposal to reduce the tax deductions for households employing domestic workers or child-care personnel, as well as the abolition of special income tax reductions for members of more than seventy liberal professions, including journalists (who have fiercely opposed that measure). The same applies to the government's policies on immigration and naturalization. The Chevènement and Guigou bills (so named after the interior and justice ministers, respectively) could be considered either moderate or leftist, depending upon one's perspective. Described by the government as "humane but firm," these bills proposed returning to France's traditional policy of political asylum, regularizing the status of selected illegal immigrants for family reasons, and restoring the virtually automatic acquisition of citizenship on the basis of *jus soli* (birth in France); contrary to preelection promises, they did not fully replace the relatively harsh Pasqua-Debré laws on immigrants. In the opinion of many leftist politicians, such measures do not go far enough because they retain cumbersome documentation requirements; for many Gaullist and Giscardist politicians, however, they go too far, and are not only misguided but also inspired by a tactical consideration: the provocation of anti-immigrant voters, who would desert the RPR and UDF and turn increasingly to the National Front (as happened in 1986 during the Mitterrand presidency). Conversely, there are those who argue that the Chevènement reforms, in their departure from the Socialists' alleged softness toward illegal immigrants, their stress on "law and order," and their interest in limiting the number of immigrants, have stolen the thunder of the right-wing parties.

Another area commonly identified with the Mitterrand presidency has been that of ethnocultural pluralism. The gradual acceptance of the idea of French society as a "multicultural" mosaic (an idea originally propounded by the PSU, when it was led by Rocard) was embodied in an array of government subsidies for cultural programs using the Breton, Alsatian, Basque, Catalan, and Provençal languages and for the teaching of those languages at various levels. During Mitterrand's second term, multiculturalist ardor cooled, owing to both fiscal constraints and increasing pressure for the integration and assimilation of minorities. Ethnocultural concerns did not figure among the campaign themes of 1995 and 1997 both because there were other more important concerns, and because of the hostility of Chevènement and the PCF and the indifference of the Greens. Consequently, ethnocultural pluralism has not figured as a clearly identifiable element of Jospin's government policy.

In any case, the programmatic outlook of individual Socialist ministers is heavily influenced by the portfolios they hold. Before the installation of the Jospin government, Strauss-Kahn, one of Jospin's closest associates, was considered to be ideologically committed to a redistributive policy, whereas Aubry had a reputation for fiscal responsibility and pragmatic socialism. Both experienced role reversals as cabinet members, however. Both ministers have endorsed reducing the workweek to thirty-five hours, in the hope that such a measure would contribute to job sharing and help reduce unemployment; yet whereas Aubry, in her capacity as minister of employment and solidarity, endorsed, with a surprisingly dogmatic rigidity, a quick implementation of this measure, Strauss-Kahn, as minister of economy, finance, and industry, attempted to gain the business community's support for such a policy by promising a more realistic—that is, selective and gradual—approach, and she has argued that neither the business community nor the political right were uniformly opposed to reducing the workweek (Bezat 1997).

At a one-day marathon conference in October 1997 devoted to employment and wages and involving the government and the two major "social partners," the labor unions and the employers' federation, Jospin attempted (unsuccessfully) to merge the two conflicting approaches (although he had argued originally that a reduction of the workweek without a reduction in wages was "uneconomical"). While holding fast to the principle of a thirty-five-hour week (except, initially, for small firms) and insisting that a law would be introduced setting a target for such a workweek by the year 2000 (preferred by Aubry), he called upon employers and unions to achieve that aim by collective bargaining (preferred by Strauss-Kahn), aided by government subsidies and reductions in taxes and social-security contributions. So far, neither approach has been satisfactory: organized business claimed to have been sidelined, and Jean Gandois, the president of the Employers' Association (CNPF), resigned his position in protest. Yet organized labor, especially its two most vocal unions, the pro-Communist General Confederation of Labor (CGT) and the equally radical Workers' Force (FO), seemed far from pacified. The CGT, representing most of the national railroad and Paris subway system workers, argued that the workweek reduction should begin in the public sector, where the government could set an example with its 5 million employees, but the catch was that since public transport workers already had the thirty-five-hour week, they deserved a further reduction to a thirty-two-hour week. At this writing, the transport workers appear to be supported in these demands by Gayssot, the Communist minister of transport.

Gayssot also supported the truck drivers who struck in November 1997 for higher pay and better working conditions. In this instance, Jospin himself did not temporize; he identified clearly with the truck drivers' demands in their confrontation with employers, who were accused of nonfulfillment of commitments they had made during a strike a year earlier. Gayssot affirmed the government's intention to introduce a bill to reorganize the profession and unblock roads for the use of foreign truckers (something Juppé had failed to do), hoping that the problem would be settled as much as possible by collective negotiations (*accords paritaires*). To some extent, the Jospin measures corresponded to those that the Gaullist minister of transport, Anne-Marie Idrac, had prepared earlier but not introduced in the Assembly because of an intervening dissolution. Jospin's support of the truckers was another example of his silencing of Gaullist critics by appropriating their policies. Jospin and Gayssot were firmly supported by Robert Hue and most of the Communist deputies (except Maxime Gremetz, a dogmatic leftist), and their actions elicited a favorable reaction from *L'Humanité*, which commented in an editorial (6 November 1997) that France finally had a prime minister who would fearlessly remind employers of their responsibilities.

The Socialist government's progressive approach will likely have perverse consequences, for, by promoting European integration, Jospin and the PS also accept the growth of transnational competition in the trucking industry, which reduces Jospin's ability to promote a clear goal of the Socialist government, namely, to secure higher wages for French truck drivers. This dilemma explains why Jospin intervened actively in the negotiations, not only to insist that the trucking companies live up to agreements made a year earlier, but also to pressure the unions to accept a 6-percent wage increase.[13]

Problems of Cohabitation

In 1995 Jospin replicated Mitterrand's electoral strategy, and he did so again in 1997. As Mitterrand had done in 1974 and 1981, Jospin had a common PS-PCF platform ready in 1997 and thereafter neutralized the Communist Party by giving it cabinet positions. It is an open question whether a PCF withdrawal of its ministers from the Fabius government, such as occurred in 1984, will be repeated under Jospin. There are reasons for arguing against it, the most important of which is the Communists' fear of political isolation. The development of amicable personal relationships between Jospin and Hue, made possible by the domestication of the PCF, has been reflected in the positive spin Hue has attempted to give to the government's basic intentions. The resulting atmosphere suggests that most of the PCF leadership intends to remain part of the government. A withdrawal of Communist ministers would be accompanied by the withdrawal of support from Communist deputies, which would undermine the Assembly majority upon which the Jospin government relies and bring with it the risk of what the PCF views as a worse alternative: the return of a Gaullist-dominated government. There is an additional incentive for the PCF and the other left-wing coalition partners of the Socialists to cooperate: the construction of joint electoral lists in the forthcoming regional elections.

These considerations explain Jospin's insistence that his government has only *one* policy, and that the PCF and the other coalition partners will not be permitted to hold the government hostage. Jospin's behavior is reminiscent of that of Mitterrand, who resisted including the more extreme demands of the PCF in the Common Program and refused to put the PCF on a level of equality with the PS (Giesbert 1996, 258ff; Philippe and Hubscher 1991, 89). At the same time, however, Jospin has avoided unnecessary moves that would ruffle the PCF's feathers. Thus, when George Marchais, Hue's predecessor as the first secretary of the PCF, died in November 1997, Jospin contributed an acceptable eulogy and asserted that he was proud to have Communists in his government. Hue returned the compliment.[14]

Nevertheless, there is continued dissatisfaction within the more radical rank and file of the party, echoed in part in the discomfort of several Communist ministers. Among the grounds for this discomfort are slights relating to patronage. For example, the Communists received the chairmanship of only one of the six standing Assembly committees, and the other leftist parties got none, which caused the PCF and its allies to complain of the Socialists' "imperialism." Dissatisfactions about policy have been even more important: for example, the Communists (supported by the Greens) had demanded a 10-percent raise in the minimum wage, but got only 4 percent; the Communists and several union leaders had demanded that the government avert the layoff of several hundred workers in a Belgian Renault plant, but the government proved unable (or unwilling) to do so, thereby setting a dangerous precedent for French workers threatened with dismissal; and there was continuing uncertainty about the Air France privatization efforts and the reduction of the transport workers' workweek. Before the 1995 election, in deference to the PCF position, Jospin had backed down from his support of the euro, and his position remained lukewarm in 1997; since then, however, he seems to have come around to supporting a common currency, despite the persistent misgivings of his coalition partners.

These problems have not, so far, resulted in a collapse of Jospin's government coalition. The reason for that is complex. The PCF, having abandoned democratic centralism, is no longer monolithic; it consists of several *courants,* and has become, in the words of a critic, "a sort of UDF of the Left" (Macé-Scaron 1997a, 69). It has lost considerable control over its own parliamentary group; Robert Hue has attempted to keep this group from rebelling because he seems committed to his active role in the Jospin government. In order to retain sufficient credibility in the eyes of labor unions, Communist deputies, and radical party members, however, Hue must be seen to articulate the more leftist demands of all of these segments (Pégard 1997, 10).

Under Jospin's leadership, relations between the government and the unions have improved considerably, not only compared to those during the preceding Gaullist government—here again, Jospin has reaped the benefits of the unions' hostility to Juppé—but also compared to those during Socialist governments, especially since 1984. However, the benefits derived by Jospin from the unions' hostility to preceding governments are not unalloyed. Much of that hostility has been articulated by one union, the FO, which resented Juppé's withdrawal of its monopoly in administering the public medical insurance funds, and whose leadership became radicalized as a result. This hostility, in turn, has led to a continuing bidding war between the FO and the CGT, which has given rise to periodic strikes to warn the government against any significant departure from its leftist agenda, and has threatened the stability of the Jospin government.

At the onset of his term as prime minister, the leaders of several trade unions, notably Louis Viannet of the CGT and Marc Blondel of the FO, demonstrated a benevolent attitude toward Jospin's policy initiatives, but this period of grace was short-lived, and they threatened that unless there were significant wage increases, a commitment to stop privatizations, and a willingness to renegotiate the reform of social security initiated by Juppé, the unions would take to the street.

One scholar (Sawicki 1997, 20-21) has argued that the PS has little power over organized labor, due to the absence of "organic" relations between the party and the unions, a phenomenon that has been one of the cultural and historical peculiarities of the PS. That absence would seem to be less important today than it was earlier, owing to the "postindustrialization" of the French economy and the dramatic decline of union membership (*désyndicalisation*), which now represents barely 10 percent of wage earners. However, the unions cannot be lightly dismissed, for the following reasons: (1) their continued strength in the public and private transport sectors makes their strikes effective; (2) despite the inconveniences massive strikes cause, the general public tends to support the strikers for as long as possible because of the tradition of social solidarity in France; and (3) the "postindustrialization" of the French economy has not been reflected in a postindustrial economic ideology, which makes little room for trade unionism. In earlier years, Socialist governments allied with the PCF might depend on that party to control union excesses, or at least to control the behavior of the CGT, which often acted as the party's "transmission belt." Today, however, the PCF is too divided and too weak to maintain an effective hold over the CGT, which is now freer to act as if it had nothing to lose.

The foregoing discussion has pointed to the problems of Jospin's cohabitation government. Although Jospin has acted on his own and rightfully distanced himself from Mitterrand, his success in maintaining his government must depend to a large extent on the institutional groundwork Mitterrand prepared. Not only did Mitterrand make Europe acceptable to the democratic left; his presidency provided a training ground for young Socialist politicians who, after many years in opposition, gained considerable practical experience in governing and in facing increasingly constricted policy options. Most important, Mitterrand laid out patterns of "system-maintaining" behavior during cohabitation, which functioned as guidelines for both Jospin and Chirac.

These guidelines were not perfect. During his first cohabitation, Mitterrand had attempted to retain as many presidential prerogatives as possible and made life difficult for Chirac. During the second cohabitation, Mitterrand, confronted with a massive Assembly majority hostile to him, retreated to largely symbolic functions (such as arranging international meetings and initiating grandiose building projects [*grands travaux*]), and his political involvements came to resemble those of the British monarch, defined by Walter Bagehot (in *The English Constitution*) as "the right to be consulted, the right to encourage, and the right to warn." Much of the power that Mitterrand retained during the first cohabitation was based on the fact that the Chirac government with which he had to share power was itself a cohabitation of two camps whose relationship was often tense. When the third cohabitation began, the roles were reversed. The quip in *Le Canard Enchaîné* (3 June 1997) that the 1997 parliamentary election result created "*un gouvernement pluriel et un président plus rien*" (a pluralist government in which the president's authority had been reduced to nothing), is probably overdrawn. Nevertheless, whatever political power President Chirac retains is now based on the internal divisions of the Jospin government. Given Chirac's loss of authority over his own party, the RPR, and the divisions within that party and between it and the UDF, however, he is not in the best position to exploit the pluralism of Jospin's government.

Continuities and Innovations

One of the "pattern" innovations of the Jospin government relates to the division of labor between the president and the prime minister. All presidents from de Gaulle to Mitterrand interpreted the ambiguities of the written constitution such that foreign and defense policies were defined as presidential domains; consequently, presidents, rather than prime ministers, have represented France in international summits and negotiations. As prime minister during the first cohabitation episode (1986-88), Chirac endeavored to invade that domain, but Mitterrand was able to resist that attempt, largely because the Chirac *government* was weakened by its internal divisions. Jospin appears to be more successful in his forays into foreign policy because of Chirac's weakness as *president.* Thus Chirac was obliged to take Jospin along to a European summit in Amsterdam and, subsequently, to permit the prime minister to make official trips to Russia and sub-Saharan Africa. Fortunately, this has presented no serious foreign policy problems so far; although Jospin insists that there is no "fusion" between his attitudes and those of the president, he has taken pains to assert that in matters of foreign policy France speaks with one voice.

Indeed, one can observe considerable continuity in the country's international posture. There have been no essential differences between the foreign policies of Jospin, Mitterrand, and Chirac. Jospin appointed Hubert Védrine, formerly chief of Mitterrand's presidential staff, as foreign minister, and this appointment was perfectly acceptable to Chirac. Védrine, much like Claude Cheysson and Roland Dumas, his Socialist predecessors, is more Gaullist than Socialist, which explains why Jospin has had little difficulty in aligning his own views on foreign policy with those of Chirac, which, in turn, have not differed greatly from those of Mitterrand. This has been especially true with regard to the European

Union and the euro; the officially close (and quasi-obligatory) special relationship with Germany; and the Middle East, including an openly pro-Arab position (perhaps articulated with the least self-righteousness and cynicism by Jospin). Foreign policy continuity also has applied to the heavy diplomatic and military French involvement in Africa, especially where France has important economic interests, and to asserting France's continuing importance in European, if not global, affairs, accompanied by periodic attacks on the United States for its alleged economic and cultural imperialism.

Before Jospin became prime minister, his position represented a synthesis of the PS's two conflicting foreign policy positions: the "progressive" position (embraced by Pierre Mauroy, Pierre Joxe, and other leftists of the old SFIO), which called for ending diplomatic relations with nondemocratic regimes, and the "realist" position (embraced by Mitterrand and, with certain qualifications, by Chevènement), which favored dealing with such regimes in the national (that is, commercial) interest (Jospin 1976). As prime minister, Jospin (who once worked as an official in the Foreign Ministry) seems to have embraced the "realist" position (adopted by both Gaullist and Socialist foreign ministers), which includes lip service to fighting terrorism, accompanied by continuation of the "critical dialogue"—that is, business as usual—with authoritarian states that have sponsored terrorism. Jospin's enthusiastic endorsement of a highly profitable contract for oil exploration with Iran and similar deals with Iraq are recent examples of continuity in foreign policy. Fortunately, foreign policy has not been of much concern to the electorate; and Jospin can at least argue that aiding or selling arms to nondemocratic countries contributes to employment, and thus to the success of the Socialists' domestic agenda.[15]

There have been two Chiraquist departures from Mitterrand's foreign and defense policy: the resumption of nuclear testing and the abolition of the draft. Nuclear testing was clearly not acceptable to the left, but it was little more than a symbolic exercise by Chirac in demonstrating his Gaullist credentials and was stopped after massive domestic opposition and foreign criticism. Jospin has endorsed the creation of a professional army, perhaps because it also may contribute to savings in the military budget. A professional military runs counter to the Jacobin (and general leftist) preference for a citizen army, however, which may explain why Jospin's leftist coalition partners abstained in an Assembly vote on the bill.

Like most governments in industrialized democracies, the current government's policy options are constrained by internal electoral pressures, external influences, and resource limitations. Yet Jospin appears to be striking out in new directions, particularly in the area of institutional policies, among which the following deserve mention:

Cabinet meetings. Regular meetings are being held every other week in Hôtel Matignon, the prime minister's residence, without the presence of Chirac. In addition, Jospin has decided to assemble *all* government ministers once a month.

Reduction of the presidential term. The government has committed itself to shortening the presidential term to five years, in order to make it harmonize with that of the National Assembly. Such a measure had been advocated by Mitterrand before he became president, but he dropped it after his election. It is now supported by the Greens and not opposed by the Communists, whose preference is for the weakening of presidential power and a return to a more "classical" parliamentary system.

Cumul des mandats. The tradition of holding an unspecified number of elective offices simultaneously was modified by a law passed in 1985 that limited the number to two. Upon becoming prime minister, Jospin contributed to a further undermining of *cumul* when he required all his ministers to relinquish their positions as mayors. That measure was to make it possible for his ministers to devote their full energies to their dossiers without being distracted by local obligations. This innovation figured in Jospin's government program, and legislation is being prepared to make holding a cabinet position incompatible with being mayor of a large city. If this incompatibility is extended to the members of Parliament (as the legislation is likely to provide), it should improve attention spans, reduce deputies' chronic absenteeism (including that of Socialist deputies, even during crucial debates), and contribute to further upgrading the role of Parliament, a process that was significantly advanced by former speaker Philippe Séguin and that no doubt will be continued by his successor, Fabius. The passage of such legislation is far from certain, for it is opposed by numerous left-wing deputies, many of whom (including several older PS politicians) are mayors of towns.

The Constitutional Council. Jospin, like Mitterrand before him, favors a constitutional amendment that would (following the example of the German Federal Republic) give ordinary citizens the right to appeal to the Constitutional Council violations of basic rights.

The judiciary. Among Jospin's projected measures are those intended to reform the system of justice. These measures are largely based on the work of a blue-ribbon commission (the *Commission Truche*), appointed by Chirac at the beginning of 1997. Its report, issued after Jospin's appointment as prime minister, included a proposal that henceforth ministers of justice would cease interfering in the state's attorney's prosecutorial activities, as they had done on occasion in politically charged cases (such as those involving corrupt politicians and Middle Eastern terrorists) both under conservative presidents and Mitterrand. During the 1995 campaign, Jospin refrained from taking a clear position on such matters, owing to the Socialist Party's own problems with the financial misdeeds of its politicians. However, in view of the prosecutorial zeal of the Gaullist minister of justice (Jacques Toubon) in selected instances and the conviction of a prominent Socialist politician (Henri Emmanuelli) for the misuse of party funds, such a reform easily became part of Jospin's government program. Nevertheless, the judicial reform proposal was soon subjected to a somewhat flexible interpretation by Elisabeth Guigou, the new minister of justice.[16]

"Affirmative action" for women. Among the items on the Socialist legislative agenda is a feminine "quota" to insure equality of access for women. Such a measure would be of questionable constitutionality, however, and would open the door to an American-style "affirmative action" that would violate the Jacobin principle of the equality of individuals as such.

The postelection dynamism of the new Jospin government regarding both institutional matters and public policy recalls the dynamism of the first Socialist government under Mitterrand's presidency. The spate of reform proposals introduced and promised by Jospin was almost as ambitious as the legislative agenda in the wake of the Socialist victory in 1981. The major difference, of course, was that much of the optimism about the possibilities of reform that the public had felt on the previous occasion was now missing.

In the beginning of his prime ministership, Jospin laid great stress on *laïcité* (factoring religion out of official life) as a major element of French republicanism. This position was easier for him than it had been for Mitterrand; in contrast to Mitterrand, who came from a traditional Catholic provincial family, Jospin was the scion of a Protestant family steeped in leftist secular ideology. Jospin emphasized his *laïcité* to compensate for the religious pomp and symbolism that had accompanied Mitterrand's funeral, and as if to demarcate his attitude from that of Chirac, who had strengthened France's formal links with the Vatican. In his first speech to the Assembly, Jospin promised to restore *laïcité*, which had been downgraded during four years of right-wing governments. Yet when Pope John Paul II came to visit France in August 1997, Jospin used scarce budgetary resources to provide official logistical support, in the form of police and army reserve forces, to coordinate the visit (Lévy and Validire 1997).

An important event that was not related to public policy but contributed nevertheless to the confusion of the French was the trial in Bordeaux of Maurice Papon, a Vichy official who had been involved in the deportation of Jews to death camps. The trial was quickly transformed into a debate about what position should be adopted with respect to trying Vichy criminals and, subsequently, about the beliefs surrounding recent French history. The Socialists of Jospin's generation, especially his cabinet colleagues, were honest enough not to be involved in scandals and young enough not to accept the myth, so carefully cultivated by de Gaulle and Mitterrand, of a France teeming with Resistance fighters, of a Vichy regime totally foreign to France, and of postwar republics representing a clean break with that regime. Unlike Mitterrand, who had blocked the prosecution of active Vichy collaborators, Jospin made no effort to prevent the trial of Papon. In 1995, Chirac had the courage to reject the thesis of a disjunction between the Vichy regime and the French people, arguing that France bore a "national responsibility" in the deportation of Jews; upon becoming prime minister, Jospin echoed that thesis, affirming that the deportation "had been decided, planned, and implemented by French people," among them politicians, administrators, judges, and police, and that "not a single German soldier was needed for that infamy." Several months later, however, after the opening of the Papon trial, he softened his position somewhat by arguing that the trial was that of a person, not a nation, and (perhaps in order to avoid antagonizing Chevènement, a leftist nationalist who shared de Gaulle's mythology about a widespread Resistance, and for whom the Vichy state was a mere "parenthesis" of French history) cautioned against "confounding the [present] republic with that state." Moreover, Jospin has done little to facilitate access to crucial documents about the Vichy regime, which are to remain classified for another generation.

Problems and Prospects

Jospin has had to face the challenge of convincing traditional Socialists and Communists for ideological reasons, and the population as a whole for practical reasons, that his redistributive impulse and progressive orientation, and those of his government, are still intact. He has gotten off to a good start, in the sense that he has been able to combine a degree of economic realism with a credible embrace of leftist orientations while conveying the impression that he has kept most of his campaign promises. These promises are ambitious; they include creating jobs; increasing family income supplements to poor families; raising minimum wages and allowances for students; granting subventions to firms voluntarily reducing the workweek to thirty-five hours; and allocating government subsidies to public transport workers and private truckers for early retirement. To this must be added the obligation to get the government deficit down to 3 percent of the GDP and the commitment to reduce the social security deficit, which in 1997 was estimated at 37 billion francs, down to 12 billion francs in 1998 and to eliminate it altogether in 1999.

The money to pay for these measures is to come from a variety of sources:

- Tax reforms, including increased corporate-profits, capital-gains, and wealth taxes; increased tobacco and gasoline taxes; selective increases in social-security deductions; and reductions in tax allowances for domestics and selected categories of professionals

- Savings on defense expenditures

- Savings in medical expenditures resulting from closer monitoring of medical expenses, especially in hospitals

- Savings in income supplements to better-off families, via a means test

- A one-time infusion of funds received from issuing shares in France-Télécom

There are those who argue that these measures are insufficient, and that the major economic policy imperatives—participation in the Economic and Monetary Union (EMU), growth of consumption and employment, and salvaging the social security funds—can be accomplished only by retrenchments in welfare-state benefits. There are others, however, who are more optimistic. They argue that neither the thirty-five-hour week nor other measures to reverse social inequities, which are said to have grown during the Mitterrand presidency, are as unrealistic as is claimed by the business community and the right-wing parties. They are convinced that France can well afford to maintain a decent level of social protections and create jobs; and they insist that in the mid-1990s many French businesses accumulated substantial profits, aided by the rise in the exchange rate of the dollar, low interest rates, and relatively low corporate taxes (Halimi 1997, 4-5).

As 1997 drew to a close, Jospin and Strauss-Kahn seemed to share that optimism. They hoped that privatization, savings on military expenditures, and the various tax increases would provide a significant proportion of the necessary funds, and that some policy aims, notably job creation, would be met by the private sector. They also hoped that a recent growth in productivity would be durable and significant enough to spur consumption and hence employment. Finally, they expected that the conditions for participation in the EMU would be relaxed and that its implementation would be postponed, since Germany, the chief promoter of a hard-line approach to the EMU, was experiencing difficulties and might itself be unable to meet the criteria for participation.

But these hopes and expectations would be—to quote Samuel Johnson's remark about a second marriage—"a triumph of hope over experience," given the increasingly insistent demands by the PCF and the more radical elements within Jospin's own party, and the hardening opposition of the CNPF. Jospin is under pressure to reconcile these demands, which are difficult, if not impossible, to resist. One thing is certain: despite continuing privatizations, the pressure of competition within the European Union, and a crescendo of rhetoric about the importance of the market, the state is unlikely to take a back seat in decision-making.[17] Furthermore, the prospects for meaningful "degovernmentalization" (*désétatisation*)—on the model of most Western European social-democratic parties—are limited, given both the nature of the French labor force and the structure of the PS leadership and electorate. The PS is essentially the same kind of etatist party under Jospin as it was under Mitterrand; at the end of 1958, blue- and white-collar workers represented 32 percent of the PS electorate and 24 percent of the registered members. Moreover, 51 percent of the PS leadership is composed of cadres and intellectuals, most of whom are tied to the state; and among the voters of the PS, 51 percent work for the public sector (Dupin 1991, 170-71).

Jospin's continued ability to govern will depend on whether his policies are feasible in terms of internal resources and his expectations realistic in the face of economic pressures, some of them external, and whether his measures will be sufficient to satisfy his leftist partners. Just as Mitterrand exploited to his advantage the uneasy coexistence between the RPR and the UDF—sometimes referred to as "the other cohabitation"—during the first episode of power sharing with a Gaullist prime minister ten years earlier, it is possible that Chirac could exploit to his advantage the cohabitation between the PS and other leftist parties, notably the PCF, in the government. Given his electoral humiliation, however, he is not in a favorable position to do so; consequently, there seems to be little incentive among members of the government to form a united phalanx to resist him.

Some years ago, Rocard had hoped for a "big bang," the implosion of the PS together with all its factions. In the eyes of observers, this hope has almost been achieved. At the party congress of November 1997, the internal factions of the PS apparently had beat a retreat, even if they had not completely dissolved, and even if Fabius, who continues to control about a fourth of the delegates to the party's national council, had not yet been neutralized. Indeed, there was such a high degree of consensus about Jospin's leadership that the congress was labeled a "consecration" of Jospin—which led some cynics to suggest that "Mitterrandolatry" had given way to "Jospinomania," a sentiment that appeared to be an echo of the popularity of the prime minister among the populace at large. The size of that popularity—Jospin's 60-percent approval rating was the largest for a Fifth Republic prime minister after six months in office—led a number of observers to suggest that the PS had been "Jospinized." Precisely what that means is unclear; perhaps it is a more systematic effort to combine the political ethics of Pierre Mendès-France with the esthetics of Mitterrand, and the retention of a firm social-democratic faith coupled with an acknowledgment of the imperatives of economics, thereby moving the PS into the twenty-first century (Favard 1997).

It is uncertain whether these developments will be followed by a recombination of all left-wing forces into a large democratic left-of-center organization. So far, the leadership of the PCF, notably Secretary-General Hue and Transport Minister Gayssot, has had such a cooperative relationship with the PS that it has given rise to speculation about a possible reunification of the Socialists and Communists, that is, the undoing of the scission between these two groups that occurred at the congress in Tours in 1920 (J.M.S. 1997, 13). Conversely, the deputies of the Green Party and a number of Communist deputies have begun to disagree with government policy on selective issues, such as immigration, environment, and the reduction of the workweek—disagreements manifested recently in selective abstentions in votes on government bills. The temptation to further disagreements is likely to grow in the face of an increasingly radical activism on the part of a mobilized mass of the unemployed. In short, given the revived electoral fortunes of the smaller leftist parties, the hope of a comprehensive structural merger of the left now seems unrealistic, and Jospin will continue to have to govern with a pluralist team, with all the inconveniences such a task entails.

Chapter 2

The Electoral Campaign

Bruno Cautrès

The campaign for the 1997 French general election was strange for several reasons. Announced "unexpectedly," the dissolution of the government on 21 April 1997 led to the improvisation of an electoral campaign that was unexpected, despite rumors of dissolution that began early that year. This campaign took place within the time limit set by the French Constitution, whose 12th article prescribes the conditions under which the president of the republic has the right to dissolve the National Assembly and stipulates that "the general elections take place at least twenty days after, but no later than forty days after the dissolution." The date chosen for the election, 25 May, was determined by constitutional constraints and by taking into account the official holidays set aside during the month of May in France. Though, at thirty-three days, the 1997 campaign was not the shortest of the Fifth Republic—there had been campaigns of twenty-one days in 1981 and 1988, twenty-four days in 1968, and thirty-eight days in 1962—it nonetheless was rather short. Jacques Chirac, whose executive popularity was wavering at the beginning of 1997, may have counted on this time factor, betting on a short electoral campaign that would leave no time for ill-prepared political adversaries to get organized.

The tremendously negative outcome of Chirac's bet was due largely to a simple factor that undoubtedly was underestimated by the government: the public grasped neither the reasons for the dissolution nor the motives behind it. Never, during the campaign, did these questions elicit convincing answers from the president of the republic, his prime minister, or anyone else in the government. On the contrary, French voters remembered the tactical aspect of the dissolution, and their discontent with the chief of state was probably underestimated. The 1997 dissolution did not, in fact, resemble any of the Fifth Republic's other dissolutions. It was not a "sanction/dissolution," like the one General de Gaulle announced on October 1962, not a "crisis/dissolution," like that declared again by the general on 30 May 1968, and, finally, it was not a "prevention/dissolution," like those announced by François Mitterand in 1981 and 1988. The 1997 dissolution was merely a political tactic. None of the elements that until then had justified the use of dissolution could be found in 1997: all that remained was the tactical intention, and that was quickly seen through by voters and the opposition during the campaign.

Could Alain Juppé, whose unpopularity is one of the factors that caused Chirac to resort to a governmental dissolution, be a "leader of government," a prime minister who could defend his record during an electoral campaign and offer voters prospects for the future? Was the moment to dissolve the Assembly well chosen, even though his popularity and that of the head of state was improving slightly at the beginning of 1997? Why was the government unable to justify the dissolution, gain the voters' favor, and offer them a framework for interpreting this sudden decision to dissolve the Assembly? The answers to these questions are found partly in an explanation of the "surprise vote" of 1997 (see Perrineau and Ysmal 1998) and are further revealed through a detailed examination of that electoral campaign. This chapter analyzes the 1997 election primarily by examining the preparation for the first ballot, because this process clearly determined the 1 June election results.

The "Juppé Problem"

The question of maintaining Alain Juppé as prime minister after the elections is undoubtedly one of the important keys to this campaign. The public tended to reject him, which made the question of his staying on central to the campaign from the very beginning. The campaign very quickly focused on the confrontation between Juppé, the head of the government and omnipresent in the media, and Lionel Jospin, the undisputed leader of the leftist opposition. By 20 April, as a guest on the televised political show *7/7*, Jospin chose his angle of attack: he denounced a "dissolution of convenience," condemned its tactical objective, and summarized in carefully selected words what was at stake in the election: "the question the French are going to ask themselves is whether or not they want more of Alain Juppé and his policies."[1] Jospin thus centered the debate on the political consequences of the dissolution around the question of maintaining Juppé in office "for five years," linking the maintaining of Juppé with the continuation and expansion of an "ultra-liberal" policy, a "hard-core capitalism" that Jospin later called "primitive capitalism."[2] Denouncing "increasing" unemployment, deficits, and disparities that the actions of the Juppé government would have caused, he concluded that he did not see "how one could untangle this crisis by reelecting the same government and by continuing with the same Prime Minister."

While Jospin focused his attacks on Juppé, some important government members let the mystery remain concerning who they would support and whether they wished to see a "Juppé III" government. On 23 April, René Monory (UDF), the president of the Senate, answered a question on a radio show about who might be prime minister, saying, "one can imagine anything. . . . Maybe Alain Juppé will get his chance? It's not automatic." The following day, François Baroin (RPR), the official representative of the French president, stated in an interview for *Le Figaro* that the dissolution should "create new dynamics, a new momentum, but also promote a new team." Even though it was not stated outright that the head of the team could change, the former Speaker of the first Juppé government obviously intended to let that be assumed.[3]

Alain Juppé himself even contributed to the confusion as to his future as prime minister: on 22 April, he stated on France 2 that he was a "candidate for no post, except for the leadership of the battle for the election and its victory." He pointed out that after the election the president would choose a new team with a new prime minister, and it would be the president's choice and his alone. This theme reappeared during a meeting in Marseilles on 24 April: stressing that one "should not mistake the elections for what they are not, for one does not choose a Prime Minister, but a majority," Juppé added that there would be many qualified men and women in the new RPR-UDF majority who could become the new prime minister (*Libération,* 25 April 1997, 2). A few days later, he confirmed during the *7/7* show on TF1 that he was "absolutely not" a candidate for his own succession.

Other statements from important members of government were more caustic.[4] Valéry Giscard d'Estaing, who voiced a "negative opinion" of the dissolution, stated on 7 May on the evening news on France 2 that he had warned Jacques Chirac about the reaction of voters who wish "to be governed differently." The former president then advised Chirac to listen to the message the French voters would send on 25 May and 1 June: "They have to be heard since it was decided to let them speak." Charles Pasqua, the former minister of the interior, stated on 26 April that the prime minister's campaign "is not up to the game."[5]

The keynote of the government's campaign was indeed the "Juppé paradox," which appeared insurmountable: "go to the battlefield" in an orderly fashion, led by a prime minister who has never known how to assert himself and whose unpopularity is one of the most visible reasons for the dissolution. Observers promptly noticed that "retired" government deputies, preoccupied with the campaign in their constituencies, campaigned weakly on the national level. Even though Juppé began his campaign as "head of government," he could not counter the effects of his poor public image and the people's lack of trust in him. His efforts to infuse the campaign with his own style and rhythm—the campaign was to be "happy but brutal"; "violent"; "sportsmanlike"; "pugnacious, united, and confident"—were in vain, even counterproductive, for they stressed the image of a leader exercising his power without sharing it.[6] Juppé's paradoxical situation in this campaign probably led the government to foster an indecisive and hesitant climate regarding his position: since the president of the republic nominates the prime minister (Article 8 of the 1958 Constitution), and nobody can be a candidate for the office of prime minister, why not let it be known that Philippe Séguin, Edouard Balladur, or Charles Pasqua (whom opinion polls showed were the three politicians the right wing favored to succeed Juppé) might be nominated after 1 June?

The perverse effects of such a tactic turned out to be more important than its advantages. The first reason for this involves the discrepancy between Juppé's theoretical role, that of a campaigning "government leader," and the credit given to him by the same government. With the latent rivalry between Juppé and Séguin lurking in the background, and Juppé trying to embody the government's "new momentum" while distancing himself from Séguin's "other policies," the climate of uncertainty and the rumors about a new prime minister put Juppé under a harsh spotlight and hindered his ability to organize and consolidate the government's campaign. Séguin finally denounced "the indecency" of "the oppressive avalanche of criticisms" that fell on Juppé (sometimes coming from the same people who once could not stop praising him): "it's the manhunt, the kill; it is unworthy of our democracy."[7]

The second reason that the government's campaign was ineffective has to do with the difficulty in convincing the public that a victory for the government would not also be Alain Juppé's political victory, which would almost automatically renew his position. This difficulty presented itself from the very beginning of the political campaign. In the IPSOS-*Le Point* opinion poll conducted soon after the dissolution, 65 percent of the people polled wanted Chirac to nominate a prime minister other than Juppé, but 41 percent of them believed he would not do that.[8] Other surveys conducted during the campaign also revealed that the electorate voting for the government thought Chirac should replace Juppé upon victory.

The final reason for the incoherence of the government's campaign is that Juppé, in spite of his ambiguous statements on remaining in office after the elections, behaved during the campaign like the future head of government. During the television show *7/7*, even though he declared he was "absolutely not" a candidate for his own position, he promised that if the government coalition won, a "new stage" would begin (with a "new team"), then offered a detailed campaign program, and even suggested a series of measures to be taken in the "first forty days" of the new legislature. The detail of those clumsily announced measures left little doubt as to who might be the person to implement them. These were the main items defining Juppé's "new momentum": controlling public spending for five years (and freezing spending for 1998), lowering taxes, adjusting working hours, establishing "universal health care," minimizing the role of the state (a maximum of fifteen departments, suppression of the École Nationale d'Administration [ENA], decentralization and deconcentration), and limiting the number of elected offices held at one time. These measures were, in fact, very similar to those Juppé was preparing to implement before the dissolution of the National Assembly was announced. Thus it appeared clearly that Alain Juppé intended to succeed Alain Juppé.

Weakness of the "Presidential Framework"

If one keynote of the electoral campaign was the "Juppé problem," another—possibly more important—may have been the "indetermination of the presidential framework," as Jacques Gerstlé[9] qualified and analyzed it. Dissolving the French National Assembly has strong political and symbolic consequences: by exercising that power, given to him by the 12th article of the Constitution, the president effectively undoes what universal suffrage decreed in the most recent general election. In this context, it is up to the president to provide a strong rationale for his decision and thus supply a framework for the campaign and elections that follow a dissolution of the government.

Such a framework for the electoral campaign that followed was oddly missing in 1997, as may be shown by comparison with previous dissolutions. In 1962 the "sanction/dissolution" acted as a means of arbitration between the chief of state and the cartel opposing the referendum on electing the president by a direct popular vote. The ensuing campaign had meaning in the context of this conflict and its arbitration. The campaign for the referendum (28 October) and that for the general elections (18 and 25 November) merged, and General de Gaulle plainly articulated the link between these ballots in his short speech on November 7: "See to it that the second decision does not contradict the first one! May you confirm by your choice of candidates the choice that by voting 'yes,' you have made for our destiny" (quoted in Viannson-Ponte 1971, 48). In 1968 the "referendum/dissolution" pronounced on 30 May was a clear example of an appeal to the people in a crisis. In his speech on that day, de Gaulle used strong words to state what was at stake with this dissolution: "France is indeed threatened by dictatorship. France would be forced to submit to a power imposed by national despair . . . a power which would be . . . one of totalitarian communism. . . . Well! Of course not. The Republic will not abdicate, the people will get hold of themselves" (quoted in Charlot 1970, 114).

In 1981 the "prevention/dissolution" was announced by François Mitterrand in accordance with his campaign promises, which were repeated during the televised debate with Valéry Giscard d'Estaing and during the first council meeting of the ministers of his presidency; the dissolution gave the president the means of enforcing his program. In 1988, lastly, Mitterrand carried out a second "prevention/dissolution" after having announced during his presidential campaign that, should he win, the National Assembly would determine the need for new elections; he stated, "The prime minister will tell me 'I can go on with the job you have put in my hands . . . [or] I cannot,' and if he says he cannot, I shall dissolve the National Assembly."[10] In this spirit Michel Rocard, who was appointed prime minister on 10 May 1988, pursued a political opening (a government coalition supported by the Socialist Party and the centrists at the National Assembly). The failure of this "opening" justified Mitterrand's dissolution of the National Assembly on 15 May, one week after his reelection: "I notice, only to deplore it, that the 'opening' I had called for did not happen, as much as I would have wanted it. I must, therefore, accept the consequences."[11]

In spite of their different circumstances, the first four dissolutions of the Fifth Republic had one thing in common: in each case the president supplied a rationale for the dissolution, and the electoral campaign was thus defined. This was not the case in 1997. The Constitution of 1958 gave the president the discretionary power to dissolve the government, the use of which is subject to the game of political constraints; in particular, the president must demonstrate that a dissolution constitutes the answer to a political crisis or to a present or impending deadlock of the system that calls for an election. The president cannot dissolve the Assembly without putting at stake the special bond that unites him to the people. President Chirac's inability to give meaning to the dissolution of 1997 weakened his entire electoral campaign, which was characterized by a discrepancy between the use of his discretionary power and the real reason for the dissolution.

Such a contradiction was first expressed in the very decision to dissolve, which was a blatant contradiction of the promises made by Chirac during the 1995 campaign and reasserted since: "The dissolution [of the National Assembly] was never done . . . for the benefit of the President of the Republic. It was done to settle a political crisis. There was not, after my election, and there is not today, a political crisis."[12] Caught in a trap of his own making, Chirac found it necessary to develop a complex but vague argument calling for the 1997 dissolution, and the tactical nature of his decision quickly became apparent.

The dominant theme of Chirac's presidential speech was "new momentum," a "new stage" for France, and his discourse tentatively justified the dissolution "in the interest of France:"[13]

> Why, *with the risk of surprising you*, did I finally come to the decision to use at this time the power granted to me by the 12th article of the Constitution, to terminate the mandate of the Assembly I retained in 1995 and whose majority has loyally supported the government? . . . I consider, according to my conscience, that the interest of the country demands early general elections. I am convinced that *the people must be given a voice, so that it can clearly state the size and rhythm of the changes to be done in the next five years.* To start this 'new stage,' we need a government with resources, with enough time for action." (emphasis added)[14]

This weak justification, a dissolution in the interest of the country, left room for covering a wide range of problems. It was rumored before 21 April that the issue of Europe would be central to Chirac's argument. But this proved not to be the case. In his address Chirac mixed together a jumble of multilevel problems that, according to him, only a "government with resources" and "enough time for action"[15] could address: reforming the state with significant cuts in public spending and taxes; changing attitudes that hinder employment; changing the education system; and maintaining necessary social security. The difference between the problems Chirac cited—which encompassed many structural difficulties—and the answer he offered—a dissolution motivated by political circumstances—was obvious. "And there is Europe," he added, almost in the middle of his speech. But when it came to Europe, the presidential discourse was no more focused, offering only a rather long list of problems: the change of currency, the reform of European institutions, the entry of Eastern Europe into the EEC, NATO reforms. Above all, he declared, "What is most dear to me is a European union in the service of people. A living social model. Joining forces against the evils that threaten our societies: unemployment and social exclusion, of course, but also the exploitation of children, drugs, dirty money, terrorism." At the bottom of Chirac's list came a call for "the values that are the foundations of our national community and that give France its unique destiny" and a reference to the "Republican ideal": "rights and responsibilities that are taken on . . . a reinforced social cohesion . . . the defense of republican order."

Chirac's speech was a strange mixture: an evocation of the country's structural problems (to be answered by cuts in public spending), a reminder of the presidential campaign of 1995 (references to the European and French "social model," to the republican ideal, and to social rights), and a lesson in current affairs ("calls for hatred have been made, and scapegoats have been designated"). The speech had no particular focus; its spectrum was too wide, and its objectives, too numerous. Dissolution, usually a symbolic act, had found its limit. The call for dissolution in this case provided no particular clue to define Chirac's ensuing electoral campaign. In a way, this dissolution recalled the unkept promises of 1995. It was announced and explained in tones suggesting referendum, even though the president, who had been elected only two years before, had the support of one of the biggest National Assembly majorities of the Fifth Republic.

Chirac's campaign was characterized by other interventions that demonstrated his will to define and control the public agenda. On 7 May he had another address, "a momentum for all,"[16] published in fourteen local newspapers. In this speech he attempted one more time to link his political objective, "a new phase, a common spirit," to the dissolution.

> If I have dissolved the National Assembly, it is precisely so that the French people have a say in the content and meaning of this new phase. It is also because our country cannot afford to have too long an election time, during which everything is idling. . . . It is also because I need to sustain the political strength necessary to defend the interests of France for the next important European commitments. Finally, it is so that our country can enjoy the stability required for effective action in the next five years.

This extremely nonspecific justification still offered voters no simple explanation for the dissolution. Chirac did allude to the spectre of a left-wing victory and a new "cohabitation," were the general elections to take place in 1998: for what other reason would the president lack political "stability" and "strength"?

The president's address was also characterized by a number of reorientations. His reference to Europe, first of all, was marginalized, and it only served vaguely to justify the dissolution and the reinforced political position that the president expected to gain from it. Characterizing the "new momentum" as "common" took it beyond its scope. The list of themes mentioned by Chirac read more like a catalog than a controlled political agenda: the public sector (its size and inefficiency), illegal immigration, republican order and safety, public debt and the role of the state, social security, the French "social model," the closeness of state and local administrations, a renewal of public life, the number of electoral mandates, and financial scandals. As Jacques Gerstlé pointed out, "his agenda has no priorities; it gets more diluted in a framework where no issue in particular stands out" (Gerstlé 1998). Chirac punctuated the evocation of issues with calls to "confidence" and "progress," thus contrasting "momentum for all" (the "new momentum" that does not renounce the "social model")[17] with those who "turn their back" on the "course of history." Finally, this address gave Chirac the opportunity to take a more sectarian tone in his discourse. He clearly took aim at the left wing, its results and ideas—"Will unemployment be reduced by decrees that always create more jobs in the public sector?"—and the stakes in the general election were narrowed down to a left wing–right wing division.

> Our country, in the past, has not always made the right choices. Too often, spending has been mistaken for efficiency, and the size of the public sector for the quality of its service. It was thought that nationalizing enterprises would guarantee their success, that multiplying debts would mean acquiring the means to take action, and that increasing taxes and social security benefits would demonstrate justice. Some thought that putting up with illegal immigration was being true to our vocation. . . . All of that in the end proved wrong. . . . It became necessary, if I dare say so, to write off the debt.

The emphasis on the specter of to-be-taken public actions and the very clear politicization of the general elections gave this public address a particular role to play in the electoral campaign, agenda, and calendar. In the middle of the campaign, when nothing seemed to mobilize the people who usually vote to the right, Chirac addressed them. The strong partisan tone of his text allowed Jospin to invoke his "right to answer," even though he focused his attacks more on Juppé than on Chirac. Publishing the presidential address gave Jospin the opportunity to use his position as leader of the opposition to place himself on an equal footing with the head of state. Qualifying Chirac's text as having "in a way, a super-Juppé style," Jospin announced on France-Inter his intention to answer the president by also publishing an address,[18] which he did on 9 May. Therein he stressed the sectarian tone of the chief of state's 7 May address: "I found it negative, partisan and unfair." The quasi-presidential tone that Jospin used to expose the main lines and choices of his program allowed him to reassert his "right to make an inventory" of the Mitterrand years: "We know how to draw lessons from the ten years when we were governing the country. I take responsibility, and the Socialist Party with me, for the mistakes of the past—without forgetting those things that I would not have liked to see done, and which will not be done again, I'll see to that."

On 21 May, a month after announcing the dissolution, President Chirac seized the opportunity of German Chancellor Helmut Kohl's visit to Paris to stress that France "will be able to defend its interests only if it is able to speak in one voice." Dramatizing the effects that cohabitation would have, the chief of state purposefully used the occasion of Kohl's arrival to assert his own preeminence in terms of foreign policy and to warn voters that calling his European policy into question would impose "irreparable damage" on both countries. Moreover, this warning was echoed by the main leaders of the right wing, especially by Juppé, who predicted "shambles over the subject of Europe" in the event of cohabitation, a situation that would lead France "into a wall."

By developing the theme that cohabitation would weaken France on the international scene, however, Chirac and the government majority chose a difficult path. On one hand, during his campaign Jospin guaranteed his commitment to Europe and refuted the hypothesis of a "fighting cohabitation." From the outset of his campaign, he tried to be reassuring about respecting the presidential role, and on the day following the visit of the German chancellor, he stated that he had no "difficulties" with the president when it came to Europe and the currency issue, unless, he added, "M. Chirac became an ultra-Maastrichian."[19] On the other hand, cohabitation, although not necessarily sought by the French, nonetheless has not been unusual since 1986-88 and 1993-95. In a survey conducted by CSA for *Le Nouvel Observateur* at the end of April 1997, 60 percent of those polled supported a cohabitation of Chirac and Jospin. The same survey showed that by refuting the possibility of a "fighting cohabitation," Jospin was in agreement with public opinion: 78 percent of those polled preferred that, in the event of a left-wing victory, Jospin and Chirac "have a cohabitation policy, where they agree on the country's main affairs," whereas only 15 percent (25 percent of left-wing voters) preferred "a cohabitation format that leaves Jacques Chirac no initiative." At the beginning of the campaign, an overwhelming majority (62 percent, according to the 25-26 April 1997 SOFRES–*Le Monde* survey) felt that if the UDF and RPR lost the election, the president of the republic should stay until the end of his mandate.

President Chirac's last intervention in the electoral campaign was on 27 May, two days after the first ballot. The right wing was already in a state of shock, as Juppé was no longer at its head, and Chirac was required to assume the leadership of the right-wing campaign. His intervention, considered by the right as its last card, was part of the tradition: the call to "make the right choice." After paying tribute to Juppé—"for his action and for his character. The day will come, I have no doubt, when the French people will agree with me on that judgment"—and after having assured the electorate that its message had been heard, Chirac returned to the theme of what needed to be done to rally France's strength: "Our country has pushed away necessary steps for too long. We are behind, and this delay has cost us dearly in terms of jobs, taxes, debts, and illusion too." His basic message can be summed up as a warning to right-wing voters, who, according to initial studies, seemed not to have been mobilized: "How could you, my fellow French, looking at the stakes, not take a stand? *Do you wish to bring back yesterday's socialist ideas?*" (emphasis added) In the remainder of his speech, Chirac made no further reference to the "new momentum" or to the "common good" but focused on the main points developed during his campaign (an economic plan of initiatives and liberties, a more efficient state, a renovated social model to protect us from the effects of globalization), adding his desire to "invent a new method of governing, closer to the people, listening to its expectations and difficulties." Europe is mentioned only at the end, in context of the theme of the "risk of destabilizing the making of Europe" (in case of cohabitation), and of the necessary "social ambition" it must give itself.[20]

In spite of repeated interventions during the campaign, Chirac managed to offer neither an interpretative framework for the dissolution, nor a strong expression of what was at stake in the general elections. Chirac's communication strategy was not, however, altogether ineffective. In addition to stories directly linked with his campaign were numerous reports in the media of his presence and actions connected with other matters, especially in mid-May: the European summit, Chirac's visit in China (14-18 May), a statement on pedophilia on 12 May, and many other events reported on and given television time. That strategy did not mask the president's difficulty in setting the electoral agenda, however, a difficulty that may be explained by the obviously tactical use of the dissolution and the difficulty of justifying it.

Projects and Programs: Unclear Alternatives

Although the campaign was constrained due to its short duration, it gave the parties an opportunity to present their projects and programs. Despite rumors of the dissolution preceding its announcement, most parties had to rush to clarify and present their projects and programs in the few days following 21 April. Since the beginning of the year, each of the major political organizations had had a basic program plan, prepared with a 1998 general election in mind. The smaller political groups, however, Philippe de Villiers's *La Droite indépendante* in particular, had greater difficulties and were unable to find their rhythm in the 1997 campaign, which both came too fast and was too short for them.

The government, first of all, agreed rapidly on an RPR-UDF union platform ("a new momentum for France"), whose first statements justified the dissolution ("a brave decision, in order to offer the country, after an effort to bring back order, the new momentum, confidence, stability, and prospects for the future") and accused the left wing of writing off the debt: the Socialists had "left the country in a recession, in a state of collapse. Under Mitterrand's two terms, disparities grew even wider. The French are still paying the price of those mistakes." The government platform[21] had four major points: (1) to create an "efficient state" that was "thrifty, refocused on its essential missions" (lowering taxes, stabilizing public spending, making justice more efficient, modernizing political life, reforming schools, and decentralization); (2) "to liberate initiatives for more jobs" (reduction of social security contributions for low-paying jobs, federal and local tax cuts, creation of jobs in small- and middle-sized enterprises, involvement and participation of workers, privatizations); (3) "to renovate our social pact" (preserving our social model, enacting major law on public health while integrating the environment policy, offering a second chance to those having dropped out of the school system, aiding unemployed people and workers who wish to retrain, stepping up the fight against social exclusion); and (4) to bring about "a Europe close to its citizens" (change to a standard currency on 1 January 1999, reinforcement of the cooperation between countries' different police and courts, creation of a genuine European society, inclusion of Central and Eastern Europe in the European Union after the reform of European institutions). If the main points of the platform match those articulated directly following dissolution, they nonetheless are in keeping with a continuation of policies rather than with a "new momentum." Indeed, a comparison of this platform with that presented by the Union for France (the union of the UDF and RPR) in the 1993 general elections reveals many similarities between the two, sometimes even in the titles of chapters. As *Libération* (30 April 1997) pointed out, "the right wing gets its 1993 program out again," with a program very close to that of Alain Juppé between 1995 and the 1997 dissolution. The electoral calendar, strangely enough, probably did not allow the right to add the finishing touches to its 1997 program, with each of its two party formations (UDF and RPR) having prepared its own program for the 1998 elections. The right wing's paradoxical situation in this electoral campaign was at its peak here. As noted in *Libération* (30 May 1997), "a number of deputies who have been in the National Assembly for the past four years are going to have a hard time explaining to their voters that their project today is to put in place what it is they were elected to do four years ago, which is also partly why Jacques Chirac was voted in the Elysée two years ago."

As for the left wing, the program presented by the Socialist Party (PS) definitely urged change.[22] Its general theme, "let's change our future," had three aspects: (1) "let's change the social and economic policy" (fairer distribution of wealth, without increasing the public deficit and without sending inflation up; the creation of 700,000 real jobs for youth; the reduction of the workweek from thirty-nine to thirty-five hours, with no pay cut; a national conference on employment, salaries, and workload; a policy aimed at research and training; a fairer tax system); (2) "let's change the daily life of the French" (defending and renovating social security, creating universal health coverage, keeping pension benefits in line with distribution, creating public housing, ensuring neighborhood safety, promoting education as a first budgetary priority, controlling immigration and making social integration a success, developing long-term economic development, protecting the environment, promoting culture, renovating the public sector); and (3) "let's change Europe" (saying yes to one currency "but on certain conditions,"[23] adhering to the Maastricht criteria for convergence).

The Communist Party's program "for another policy" in five points was presented by Robert Hue at the National Council of the French Communist Party (PCF) on 25 April. It stipulated (1) "more money and purchasing power for more jobs" (raising the minimum wage by Fr 1,000 effective immediately, to be brought to Fr 1,500 later; quadrupling taxes for the very rich; repealing the Juppé plan; creating 1.5 million jobs in two years, 700,000 of which would be for young people); (2) "a development plan for the long term" (reopening the question of privatization; national and regional development and planning; strong measures in favor of the public sector); (3) "money for jobs and social development" (general overhaul of taxes and credit); and (4) "a republic for the people, transparent and honest" (giving workers more rights; reforming political life; repealing the Pasqua-Debré laws). The Communist platform further stated (5) that "France should show initiative in Europe and in the world" (acknowledging the impossibility of changing the currency under conditions bearable by the people; initiating another discussion to reorient the establishment of a united Europe toward social goals and progress; presenting the French people with a new treaty that opposes the idea of one currency; refusing the continuation of austerity measures imposed for the single currency; and stopping the process of reintegrating France in NATO).

Once the 1997 dissolution was announced, the Socialist and Communist Parties moved beyond their respective programs and hurriedly focused on a joint strategy, in the form of a single declaration, seven pages long, prepared by two Socialist negotiators (Jean-Christophe Cambadélis and Dominique Vaillant) and two Communist negotiators (Pierre Blotin and Jean-Claude Gayssot) and made public on 29 April.[24] Neither a common platform nor a governmental program, this declaration remains nonetheless an important act: for the first time since the 1977 local elections, the Socialist and Communist Parties joined forces before the first ballot. The declaration came into being in that way not only because the dissolution sped up political agendas, but also because there had been meetings and reconciliations within the left wing in the months prior to the dissolution. At the time the dissolution was announced, the Socialist and the Communist Parties had been working for months (since the fall of 1996) in an effort to move closer and reach agreement before the legislative elections expected in 1998.[25] Their common declaration expressed the desire to "join forces and unite against unbearable policies." It acknowledged the "well-known differences" in the projects of both parties, with each one standing up before the voting public with its own identity and program, while alluding to "being conscious of (their) responsibilities." The common goals of the PS and PCF addressed and reaffirmed certain important points in their respective programs: creating 700,000 jobs for young people, reducing the workweek to thirty-five hours "without a pay cut," reforming the tax system, stopping the privatization process of France-Télécom and Air France, defending and renovating the public sector, substituting a real immigration policy for the Pasqua-Debré laws, restoring the "right of the land." Europe was the topic of the last paragraphs of this declaration: deemphasizing the extent of their differences (talking about "well-known respective positions, and their evolution"), the PS and PCF stated that they wanted to "go beyond the Maastricht treaty to construct a social Europe . . . nationalistic withdrawal is not the answer . . . we say no to a liberal Europe, to a Europe where money would be king, and to submission to monetary markets." This declaration did not mention the question of whether there would be Communist ministers in the government in the event of a left-wing victory.[26]

Other political groups also presented their proposals or programs. On 23 April Bruno Mégret presented "in a few simple words" the content of the National Front (FN) program, centered around immigration policies: "social justice, the French first, republican order." The denunciation of "euro-globalism" and of the single currency, and the assertion of "national preference" (especially when it comes to welfare) made up the rest of this brief program. On 1 May, during his traditional celebration of Joan of Arc's feast day, Jean-Marie Le Pen explained his program in detail, reasserting its outlines and bringing forward the "social window" of its proposals.[27] On 4 May the Independent Right (LDI), made up of the Movement for France (MPF) of Phillippe de Villiers and the CNIP, presented the three points of its program: (1) "against the Europe of Maastricht"[28] (abandoning the convergence criteria objective, stopping "the race for the euro," asserting a "European preference," the Europe of Nations); (2) "the defense of moral values" ("one has to teach young people to love France, to remind all Frenchmen that they don't have only rights, but also duties, and any politician who has been sentenced for a crime must then be ineligible for public office for the rest of his life"); and (3) "for an economic liberalism" ("massive cuts in social security contributions and taxes, cutting down the number of government employees). The Greens, finally, presented a program organized around four themes: (1) the environment; (2) unemployment (reduction of the workweek to thirty-five hours right away, and cutting it down to thirty-two by the end of the century, helping the needy, making jobs less precarious); (3) Europe ("inventing an environmental and social Europe, making it a model of eco-development"); and (4) citizenship (repeal of the Pasqua-Debré laws, institution of the proportional ballot, parity of representation of men and women in politics, voting rights for resident aliens who have resided in France for more than five years, European citizenship).

The projects presented by both the government and the left wing offered beyond any shadow of a doubt exclusive, well-contrasted perspectives. The right wing had a program whose main points were cutting public spending, lowering taxes, and lowering employers' contributions to employees' benefits in order to "free energies." A mixture of economic liberalism and references to the "ideal of the Republic" or the French "social model," this program attempted to reflect the "organized and shared liberalism" evoked by Edouard Balladur or the "corrected, moderate, legitimized liberalism" of Philippe Séguin. This somewhat hybrid synthesis tried to reconcile liberalism and social values, whereas the time period before the dissolution had been labeled a "liberal turn" inspired by Alain Madelin, an impression that Chirac had, in the end, not chosen.[29] The references to the "social" aspect of "moderate liberalism" probably indicated the desire to make the connection with Chirac's presidential campaign of 1995 (but in a watered-down, expurgated tone) as well as the desire not to give the left wing an easy angle of attack.[30] At the very beginning of his campaign, Alain Juppé pushed aside the idea of a "liberal turn" along with the idea of the moderate right wing going back to its liberal credo of the mid-eighties: "The selfish individualism, the hardcore capitalism, the simplistic hyperliberalism of the eighties are also over," he said during a meeting to launch his electoral campaign the day after the announcement of the dissolution (*Le Monde*, 24 April 1997, 6). The left nonetheless condemned the "hardcore capitalism" embodied by Juppé and suggested very different measures to fight unemployment, based on an economic intervention by the state (jobs for young people and reduction of working hours in particular). From this point of view, the campaign did not fail to bring out the right-left difference, especially when it came to the economy: Jospin's campaign theme was "the choice of civilization," whereas Chirac, in his 21 April speech, called for voters "to say clearly in which society we want to live." On 24 April François Léotard succinctly summed up the prism through which the right wing would like the campaign to be viewed: "every time M. Jospin says we are capitalists, we will say that socialists are Marxists" (*Le Monde*, 26 April 1997, 6).

The reemergence of the left-right division alone did not guarantee the clarity of the parties' programs and the stakes involved. The vague way in which proposals were cast, the imprecision of the conditions proposed to implement a number of proposals, and the changes expressed during the campaign did not inform voters of the full force of the real differences between the left and right wings presenting themselves in meetings and on television. This reemergence had another limitation: the many internal false notes sounded within each side about programs, about how to conduct the campaign, and about some issues (Europe in particular). On the right, if the measures presented in the UDF-RPR platform were not subject to much criticism, the general orientation of the campaign and platform was more targeted. Criticisms came separately from the "pair" who, along with Juppé, had supported Chirac in 1995: Alain Madelin and Philippe Séguin. The former criticized the lack of a liberal turn, regretting that "new momentum" was not a "soaring liberty." In a meeting on 28 April, Madelin reacted to Juppé's proposals for the forty days after the elections by stating that "in political life, it is better to offer a vision than a program" (*Le Monde*, 30 April 1997, 8). On 29 April Séguin remarked that he was sorry that unemployment was not at the heart of the right's campaign, and he defended his "conception of a new momentum," especially the Europe of Maastricht, which, according to him, had too often been portrayed as serving the good pupils of ultraliberalism.[31] Séguin's stance on Europe went through several variations during the campaign. If the question of Europe was the main theme of the National Assembly president's campaign[32] ("the reason at the heart of the dissolution decision," which also should have been "at the heart of this campaign"), his discourse combined a softening of his position with an acceptance of European deadlines: "In 1992 the French people, whether they said yes or no . . . all said in their way that they wanted Europe. . . . Our big change is and remains Europe. . . . On the condition that, of course, Europe be designed accordingly." In the period between the two ballots, Séguin maintained his distance from the right-wing program concerning Europe, stating at the same time that "for France, there is no other subject than Europe." On 29 May he noted that "after the big hope of 1995," Chirac's answer to the alternative of "seeking a third route, a liberal and social one, for the construction of Europe, remains to be heard" (interview, *l'Express*, 29 May 1997).

As far as the Socialist Party was concerned, the question of privatizations, first of all, turned out to be "not so clear." Whereas the party's program and the joint PS and PCF declaration called for stopping privatizations that were currently in the works, François Hollande (Speaker of the PS) let it be understood that, once back in power, the Socialists could consider new privatizations: "When it comes to enterprises in the competitive sector that do not serve activities in the common interest, where the role of the state is not needed anymore, we must be guided by pragmatism. We must remain flexible. What we call 'breathing.'"[33] Martine Aubry later stated that she would consider "an evolution of the public sector" and that she saw "enterprises that must remain public." These statements caused Jospin to clarify the matter: "There will not be any new privatizations and it is not the order of the day to make lists of possible privatizations." This, in turn, allowed Juppé to assert that "it is better to wait for the final version [of the Socialist program] before settling on criticisms." The question of creating jobs for young people, especially the 350,000 jobs to be created in the public sector, gave rise to other discordant opinions within the PS: Michel Rocard said in an interview for *La Croix* that he would have "set not so high a goal," and in another conversation, in *Libération* (14 May 1997), that he regretted that, compared to his 1995 presidential campaign, Jospin was, in 1997, "a little less bound by the traditions and routines of the party." Finally, when Jospin stated that the PS refused to "absolutely respect" the criterion of 3 percent of the gross domestic product (GDP) as an acceptable public deficit, Elisabeth Guigou pointed out immediately that renegotiating the Maastricht Treaty criteria was out of the question.

Internal debates in the left were not restricted to the PS. In spite of the Socialists' and Communists' common declaration on 29 April, and in spite of changes made by the PS, the question of Europe continued to be viewed differently by the two main partners of the "plural left": the PCF maintained, among other things, its suggestion of a referendum about the single currency. In addition to such differences, partly acknowledged in their common declaration, the PS and the PCF continued to sound their traditional false notes regarding the union of the left wing; these were linked to the balance of power between them. The main source of tension focused on the "single orientation" that a leftist government would present following the election. As early as 29 April, Jospin stated that "if we have a government representing the forces of change, that government will follow one orientation only," based on the balance of power after the first ballot, that is to say, based on the "central position" of the PS within the left. Faced with this position, which Jospin reasserted on several occasions ("If the left turns out to be the majority in Parliament, the number of socialists will by far outnumber the communists . . . there will be only one orientation" [declaration on France Inter, 7 May 1997]), Robert Hue stressed on 9 May that the PS would need the PCF to form a majority, and that "it will be necessary to discuss our orientation . . . without trying to line up this one or that one or the other one" (conversation on France 2 on 9 May, quoted in *Libération*, 10 and 11 May 1997, 9). Such tensions between the PS and the PCF are traditional, as well as specific to the particular context of the 1997 elections. The campaign quickly became centered on the confrontation between Juppé and Jospin, who rejected the principle of a "televised debate of the four" (UDF, RPR, PS, and PCF), while advocating a debate with two protagonists, in the period between the two ballots.[34] Several leaders of the left, not only from the PCF, stressed that the 1997 elections were not to be considered the "third ballot" of the 1995 presidential election (Fabius), and they sometimes seemed to fear the "presidential drift" of the PS leader. The answer given by Jospin in the media, in reply to the address Chirac had in the press on 7 May, had, for that matter, a quasi-presidential style ("My dear fellow citizens . . . "). From this viewpoint, it would seem that the 1997 electoral campaign allowed Jospin to take advantage of an echo effect from the 1995 presidential campaign.

Faced with abundant programs presented in a rather short period of time, programs that were a little blurred by changing attitudes and the differences within the two major coalitions, how could the voters react? Were they able to face "an overloaded agenda to be dealt with in a specific time limit" (Gerstlé 1998, 66)? Analysis of opinions in the context of the main themes of the campaign allows us to venture an answer to that question. As the SOFRES survey in the period between the two ballots shows (see table 2.1), there was strong support for several of the left's propositions: raising the minimum wage by Fr 1,000, creating 350,000 jobs for young people in the public sector, and reducing the workweek to thirty-five hours with no pay cuts were widely favored. The proposition to reduce the number of government employees was rejected, but maintaining the Pasqua-Debré laws and reducing social security contributions were widely accepted. People polled tended now to trust the left wing, now to trust the right, depending which problems France must face. As Gérard Grunberg and Pascal Perrineau (1997, 10-11) pointed out, "to them the right wing seems more credible when it comes to modernizing the country, fighting against illegal immigration or constructing Europe. On the other hand, they would rather trust the left wing when it comes to social protection and fighting disparities."

TABLE 2.1. OPINIONS ABOUT CAMPAIGN THEMES AND PROPOSITIONS (IN PERCENTAGES)

	Totally in favor or somewhat in favor	*Totally against or somewhat against*
Reduction of the number of government employees	43	57
Raising minimum wage by Fr 1,000	81	19
Maintaining the Pasqua-Debré laws	60	40
Lowering social security contributions by enterprises	82	18
Creating 350,000 jobs in the public sector	71	29
Reducing the workweek to 35 hours without pay cut	64	36

SOURCE: Telephone survey between the first and second ballots, conducted by SOFRES for *Libération*, CEVIPOF (Paris), CIDSP (Grenoble), and CRAPS (Lille). It consisted of a national sample of 3,010 French people 18 years old or older.

Voters' perceptions of these programs and projects represent only one aspect of how they viewed the electoral campaign. Analyzing the interest and attention it received, the voters' exposure to an overloaded agenda within an especially short campaign, and people's voting rationales enables us to grasp one powerful characteristic of the 1997 campaign: it seemed to take place in a climate of voter indifference and indecisiveness.

A Lackluster Campaign

The first dimension of public opinion during the 1997 campaign that we examine deals with the dissolution itself. First of all, this dissolution did not correspond with the wishes of the French. The IPSOS survey, published in the *Journal du Dimanche* on 13 April, eight days before the dissolution, shows that 65 percent of those polled wished the electoral calendar to be respected. Public opinion would accept scenarios other than a dissolution: Alain Juppé's resignation (40 percent), or a reshaping of the government (21 percent). Once decided on, however, the dissolution nonetheless was well accepted: the SOFRES–*Le Figaro* survey, conducted two days before the dissolution was announced, shows that public opinion favored it (53 percent of those polled thought that "it will be a good thing"; 33 percent disagreed). But once the dissolution was announced, it did not cause the "shock" that Chirac had anticipated. The president was not convincing: 57 percent of the people polled by CSA the day after his speech on 21 April considered that he was not, and only 44 percent expressed their satisfaction following the announcement of the dissolution.[35]

The dissolution announcement's failure lay in its interpretation by public opinion, as shown by the same survey (see table 2.2, page 62). Although the dissolution, in its general principle, was well accepted (72 percent of those polled saw it as "a good way to give the French a way to express themselves"), Chirac's use of it was seen as "an acknowledgment of a failure on the part of the right wing" (58 percent agreed with that statement, among which 32 percent were right-wing sympathizers). Foremost, however, it was seen as an especially "political maneuver": 81 percent of those polled were of that opinion, among which 75 percent were UDF and 62 percent were RPR voters. One reason for the dissolution submitted by Chirac, the need to get ready for the European deadlines, did not seem a convincing way of justifying it (although 40 percent thought it was, among which 50 percent were right-wing sympathizers). On the other hand, public opinion did incline toward using the dissolution as a means of changing the incumbent government (79 percent were in favor, among which 80 percent were right-wing sympathizers!) and changing economic policies (48 percent agreed, among which 51 percent were right-wing sympathizers). Thus, the dissolution did not modify public opinion, which by far favored replacing the prime minister and changing economic policies, even before the dissolution was announced. At the end of February 1997, the IPSOS–*Le Point* survey showed that 43 percent of those polled called for a new prime minister along with a change of policies, and if not that, a change in economic policies alone (23 percent). If one adds Juppé's unpopularity with the public, which did not fluctuate during the campaign, one can better understand how the right wing's strategy, and the president's choice of a program of continuity for the campaign, backfired.

TABLE 2.2. PUBLIC OPINION ON THE DISSOLUTION (IN PERCENTAGES)

	Agree	*Disagree*	*No opinion*
It is foremost a political maneuver.	81	14	5
It is a way to change the governmental team.	79	14	7
It is a good way to give French people a voice.	72	25	3
It will allow the future government to enforce more austere policies.	68	20	12
It is an acknowledgment of failure for the current majority.	58	37	5
The dissolution will not change anything in France's situation.	51	40	9
It will allow a change in economic policies.	48	40	12
It is a way to get out of social deadlocks.	46	44	10
Getting ready to meet European deadlines justifies the dissolution of the Assembly.	40	43	17

SOURCE: CSA for *Le Parisien, Adjourd'hui/France, Inter-France Info,* a national survey conducted on 22 April 1997 on a sample of 1,002 people 18 years old or older.

The second dimension of the analysis of public opinion during the campaign deals with indecisiveness and indifference, and many of those surveyed before the first ballot expressed these feelings. Half said they had no interest in the campaign, according to the SOFRES survey. The interest in the campaign diminished as it went on, which is uncommon: whereas 49 percent of the people polled by SOFRES said they were interested in the electoral campaign at the beginning of May, only 43 percent reported interest one week before the first ballot. There are several reasons that could explain why the electoral campaign did not mobilize people's enthusiasm and only moderately interested voters. Gerstlé (1998, 69) indicated that the electoral campaign was "a hotchpotch of a vague agenda, disorganized promises, and a limited amount of time." The comprehensibility of the campaign, in spite of important program differences, was weak: interest in the campaign declined, while at the same time the percentage of people who stated that it failed to make clear what was at stake in the election was increasing (58 percent on 28 April and 64 percent on 10 May, according to surveys conducted by CSA).

On top of voters' lack of interest for the campaign came their indecisiveness, which several signs made clear. First, how sure were the voters of how they would vote? All the surveys done during the campaign indicated that the proportion of undecided people, defined as voters who could change their minds before the first ballot about whom they would vote for, represented about a third of all voters. This rough estimate was fairly close to that shown before the announcement of the dissolution (actually 40 percent in the SOFRES–*Le Figaro* survey of 18 and 19 April 1997). The announcement of the dissolution did not sway undecided voters one way or another, nor did the campaign, at least until the first ballot. As table 2.3 shows, the percentage of undecided voters as measured by the BVA institute is rather stable throughout the campaign.

TABLE 2.3. INDECISIVENESS IN VOTING INTENTIONS (IN PERCENTAGES)

		Undecided among . . .				
	Total undecided	*Communists*	*Socialists*	*RPR-UDF*	*Ecologists*	*National Front*
27 March–5 April	44	27	36	38	61	31
24–26 April	38	31	34	29	40	25
30 April–3 May	37	28	37	32	45	27
9–10 May	35	33	29	33	53	19
15–16 May	36	19	35	30	61	33

SOURCES: Preelection surveys, BVA, Legislative Elections Barometer, conducted on samples of French people registered to vote (http://www.bva.fr/sondages/fermete.htm).

NOTE: Undecided respondents answered "Can still change my mind" or "Have absolutely not decided yet" to the question "Would you say that your choice is made, could still change, or is absolutely not decided yet?"

The degree of voters' indecisiveness is related to their political affiliation (highest among those favoring the Greens, and among ecologists in general), but it remained generally high nine days before the first ballot. This was confirmed by surveys: the last CSA survey, published eight days before the first ballot, indicated that 40 percent of those polled stated either that they could still change their minds, or that they had not decided how they would vote. Voter mobilization is another sign that helps gauge the continuing indecisiveness: 70 percent of voters stated they definitely would vote, according to a BVA survey done on 15 and 16 May; this was four points lower than in BVA surveys done at the end of April and the beginning of May. Once again, far from mobilizing voters and reducing their indecisiveness, the campaign seems to have had the opposite effect.

Indifference and indecisiveness seemed to characterize the voters' attitude toward this campaign. Its lack of dynamism was expressed in how stable people's voting intentions remained despite the potentially chaotic situation projected by the media, considering the impact one percentage point difference might have in terms of Assembly seats.[36] As table 2.4 indicates, the campaign seemed to have almost no effect on the way people intended to vote. The final result, on 25 May, was very close to what the polls measured two days before the dissolution, with the exception of the RPR-UDF votes (which can be accounted for within the margin of error).

TABLE 2.4. VOTING INTENTIONS DURING THE CAMPAIGN (IN PERCENTAGES)

	18–19 April	*25–26 April*	*2–3 May*	*9–10 May*	*16–17 May*	*20 May*	*23 May*	*25 May*
Communist Party	10	9	10	10	10	9.5	10.5	9.9
Extreme left	2	2.5	2	2	2	2	2	2.5
Socialist Party	27	28	28	27	26	26	25	25.7
Diverse left	1	1.5	2	2.5	2	2	2	2.2
Ecologists	6.5	5	5	2	6	5	5.5	6.9
RPR-UDF	34	35	34	35	34	33.5	33	31.5
LDI + diverse right	5	5	4	4.5	6	6	6.5	4.7
National Front	14.5	14	15	14	13	15	14.5	15.3
Other	—	—	—	—	1	1	1	1.2

SOURCES: Preelection surveys conducted by SOFRES on samples of registered voters.

A study of all the surveys of voting intentions published during the campaign (SOFRES, BVA, IFOP, IPSOS, CSA) shows a few differences, which, nonetheless, fit the model of fluctuations with no particular tendency. In analyzing those fluctuations, which brought both good and bad news to the right and the left, Daniel Boy and Jean Chiche averaged the numbers published by the different polls from April through 7 May, and discovered only minor changes: +1.0 for the left, -0.5 for the right. They concluded that the fluctuations in voting intentions show that "there is almost nothing happening in the campaign, at least as far as swinging opinions are concerned" (Boy and Chiche 1997, 13). Assessing the whole of the electoral campaign, Jérôme Jaffré (1998, 44) came to the same conclusion and noted the lack of electoral dynamism in voting intentions.

In terms of public opinion, the electoral campaign was particularly lifeless. This phenomenon was a factor explaining the right wing's defeat, especially since there seemed to be little support for the "new momentum," whether "for the common good" or not. Generally speaking, neither the right nor the left elicited high expectations during the campaign: in a SOFRES survey conducted on 25 and 26 April for *Le Monde*, 38 percent of those polled considered that "it would be a good thing" if the Socialists and their allies were to win the elections, but 33 percent thought the same for an RPR and UDF victory. A third of those polled said they expected nothing from either the right or the left.

As table 2.5 shows, voters seemed to expect (with no enthusiasm) a victory for the right, while preferring (without being entirely convinced) one for the left. The left wing benefited from some positive expectations, and a slight preference for a win by the left developed beginning in mid-May. The 25 April forecast that the right would win also predicted the "sluggish mobilization," common to moderate right-leaning voters despite a foreseeable victory (see Dupoirier 1997, 11; Bréchon and Cautrès 1997).

TABLE 2.5. PREDICTIONS AND WISHES OF VICTORY DURING THE CAMPAIGN (IN PERCENTAGES)

	22–23 April	*29–30 April*	*6–7 May*	*13–14 May*	*23 May*	*27–28 May*	*30 May*
Predictions							
The left	20	17	23	18	18	39	43
The right	47	56	45	50	49	26	25
Neither	1	2	1	1	1	1	1
No opinion	32	25	31	31	32	34	31
Wishes							
The left	35	38	37	38	38	37	41
The right	38	42	38	37	35	36	38
Neither	8	7	7	9	7	7	7
No opinion	19	13	18	16	20	20	14

SOURCES: Preelection surveys by IPSOS–*Le Point*, conducted on national samples of French people 18 years old or older who registered to vote.

In this context of indecisiveness and uncertainty, where the dissolution did not reflect a vision shared by the people, where a short campaign may have exposed voters to a confused and overloaded agenda, where the political groups' platforms were being touched up along the way, and where expressed expectations only seemed vague, all was in place for early judgments to prevail over other considerations.

Examining what motivated the vote, as measured by the SOFRES–*Le Figaro* surveys (see table 2.6) clearly shows the retrospective prism through which the voters viewed the campaign: at the time of the vote, the actions taken by the Juppé government were judged, and that is what counted, even if other factors were taken into account. The actions of those Socialists in power counted less, which demonstrates that Chirac's partisan discourse in his 7 May address, and in two other interventions, had a limited effect. The people polled ranked the topics that determined their vote, with unemployment first (mentioned by 81 percent on 9 and 10 May),[37] followed by social disparities (mentioned by 39 percent). The right wing received less credit than the left when it came to those issues. In the SOFRES–*Le Monde* survey at the beginning of the campaign, 61 percent of those polled said they saw no difference between the RPR-UDF and the left wing concerning unemployment (19 percent trusted the left wing, and 19 percent trusted the party in power on this particular question). On the other hand, insecurity and immigration (for which voters credit the right to the detriment of the left) are only ranked third and sixth in the order of voter motivations.

Juppé's and Chirac's images affected voters' precampaign judgments, of course. In spite of a slight rise at the beginning of 1997 at the time the dissolution was announced, their popularity was at a very low level—Juppé, in particular, had reached in October and November 1996 the "historic" low level of 21 percent of people satisfied.[38] Although surveys conducted in late 1996 and early 1997 grant the prime minister courage and integrity, his image a few weeks before the dissolution was very bad: insensitive to people's expectations, not supporting good social and economic policies, incapable of reforming the country—such is the portrait that a *Gallup–l'Express* survey drew of Juppé in autumn 1996.[39] Two weeks before the announcement of the dissolution, the president of the republic was severely judged on his 1995 presidential campaign promises, which until then he had not kept. Sixty-eight percent of the people polled by CSA for *Le Nouvel Economiste* on 7 and 8 April 1997 thought that a president "should keep the promises he made during the electoral campaign"; a vast majority thought at the same time that Chirac had abandoned the main promises of his 1995 campaign: to boost wages (75 percent), to fight long-term unemployment (64 percent), not to limit health costs (59 percent), and to cut taxes (55 percent).[40] His actions were deemed disappointing by 65 percent of those polled by the SOFRES on 23-25 April 1997, which was the worst score ever recorded for a president since the SOFRES created a barometer of presidential action in 1975. This survey confirms that in most cases, his record was judged to be negative, especially in the fight against

TABLE 2.6. VOTE MOTIVATIONS IN THE 1997 NATIONAL ASSEMBLY, FIRST BALLOT (IN PERCENTAGES)

Q: Among the following elements, which are the two or three that will count the most for you when it is time to vote?

	Total		*Left-wing sympathizers*		*Right-wing sympathizers*	
	25–26 April	*23 May*	*25–26 April*	*23 May*	*25–26 April*	*23 May*
Your judgment of the results of the Juppé government	46	44	54	54	39	38
Your judgment of the program and propositions of political parties	35	29	36	33	31	25
Your opinion of the personalities of the candidates in your constituency	35	33	33	35	36	32
Your judgment of the results of the Socialists when they were in power	23	26	19	22	30	34
Your opinion on Jacques Chirac's personality	23	27	14	22	36	38
Your support for a specific political party	24	22	29	29	22	16

SOURCE: SOFRES for *Le Figaro:* preelection survey conducted on national sample of 1,000 voters.

NOTE: Surveys were conducted on 25–26 April and 23 May 1997. Another survey of voters' motivations was conducted by SOFRES on 9–10 May 1997; its results varied little from the results of the surveys conducted at the beginning and end of the campaign.

unemployment (87 percent), social policies (74 percent), reducing socioeconomic disparities (73 percent), introducing morality into the political sphere (64 percent), and immigration (64 percent).

In the absence of a framework for the future that matched public expectations, the dissolution pronounced by Chirac established a set of conditions that brought about an "election linked to past results" rather than an "election for future momentum."[41] A short campaign with an overloaded agenda, a vague message concerning whether to dismiss or maintain Juppé in the event of a right-wing victory, a campaign that voters "suffered" through, unclear programs and propositions—all these considerably handicapped Juppé and his government in this campaign and in the process of shaping voters' preferences.

Dissolution to Election: The Outcome

On 25 May 1997, the RPR-UDF coalition and Jacques Chirac paid a very high price from those accumulated factors that influence the voters' choice. The campaign never enabled voters to understand, and thus accept, Chirac's decision to dissolve the National Assembly. The short campaign of the second ballot (one week) changed nothing: neither Chirac's final intervention nor Juppé's getting "in touch" right after the first ballot, nor the Séguin-Madelin comeback (which Jospin called "a baroque yoking") was of any consequence. The week between the first and second ballot was marked by the question of whether to maintain National Front candidates in some constituencies; by the departure of Juppé, making him no longer the "chief of the majority"; and by Séguin's strong comeback. The voters were given the sight of a sinking right wing, "in ruins."[42]

Begun in a climate of political and social ill-will, "of anguish for the future,"[43] the dissolution and the ensuing electoral campaign caught voters off guard and could not eradicate the disappointments and disillusions Chirac had created by turning his back on the promises of his presidential campaign. The right undoubtedly made many mistakes during the 1997 campaign, and the left, Jospin in particular, knew how to spend the capital of expectations stored up for this occasion. A good interplay of alliances, unity in diversity ("the plural left wing"), a well-chosen angle of attack (the threat of Juppé for another five years, "hardcore capitalism"), seem to have been the main qualities of the campaign of a candidate who, in facing Chirac in the presidential run-off of 1995, had been able to obtain 47.3 percent of the votes.

In spite of mistakes by the right, and the left's well-managed campaign, one might ask if, in the end, all had not been decided as early as 21 April, the evening the dissolution was announced. By proclaiming a purely tactical dissolution "for his own convenience," and then being unable to give it meaning, President Chirac failed in a major way to give his term a second wind. The dissolution's meaning was articulated as early as 20 April by Jospin: did the French wish to give Juppé and Chirac a "second wind" for five years, with no foreseeable change of direction? By asking this question, Jospin defined the electoral campaign. By associating the dissolution with a vote of confidence for Juppé, and by activating the fear of "a turn of the screw" among voters once Juppé was again settled in the Hôtel Matignon, Jospin provided the framework for the campaign that Chirac could not.

Chapter 3

The National Front and the Legislative Elections of 1997

Martin A. Schain

For the National Front, the legislative elections of 1997 were a considerable, though not an unqualified, success. The elections provided one more indication that just because the FN could provide voters with little prospect of gaining government power, this was no deterrent to its ability to increase its electoral support. Moreover, even though it won only one seat in the end, the electoral impact of the party within the party system has clearly grown. Finally, the growing electoral strength of the party has augmented its long-term electoral and governing prospects, as well as its impact on the political agenda. The party has built on the electoral breakthrough that it achieved over a decade ago, has stabilized its electorate, and is now building on its strength in electoral and political terms.

Breakthrough and Electoral Gains: Why Continued Gains?

Since its electoral emergence in 1983-84, the increasing successes of the National Front have been well documented and analyzed: from the sudden breakthrough in the European elections in 1984 with over 11 percent of the vote, to the 14.4 percent of the vote that Jean-Marie Le Pen attracted in the first round of the presidential elections in 1988, to the record 15.1 percent vote for Le Pen in the first round of the presidential elections in 1995, to the 15 percent of the vote in the 1997 legislative elections (see Schain 1987; Mayer and Perrineau 1989). The number of voters supporting the National Front in national legislative elections has grown steadily (see table 3.1 on page 70).

During the past decade, the National Front has not only increased its electoral support but has also developed a "normal vote" that has grown by about 50 percent.

TABLE 3.1. NATIONAL FRONT VOTES COMPARED TO OTHER PARTY VOTES, FIRST ROUND LEGISLATIVE ELECTIONS, 1986–97

	1986		*1988*		*1993*		*1997*	
	Millions of votes	%	*Millions of votes*	%	*Millions of votes*	%	*Millions of votes*	%
National Front	2.7	9.7	2.4	9.6	3.1	12.6	3.8	15.0
RPR	7.6	27.2	4.7	19.2	4.9	19.7	4.3	16.8
UDF	4.4	15.7	4.5	18.5	4.7	18.8	3.7	14.7
Socialists	8.6	30.7	8.9	36.4	4.4	17.6	6.5	25.6
Communists	2.7	9.8	2.8	11.3	2.3	9.1	2.5	9.9

SOURCE: All results are from *Le Monde, Dossiers et documents,* various issues.

More than half the voters who supported Le Pen's list in the European elections in 1984 had "converted" from one of the two major political parties of the established right (as measured by whom these voters had supported in the 1981 presidential elections), while another 19 percent had been mobilized from the ranks of new voters and abstainers; most of the rest had supported Mitterrand in 1981.[1]

Between 1984 and 1986 this electorate gradually solidified, as measured by voter loyalty rates. Surveys indicated that 65 percent of those who had voted FN in 1984 voted for the party once again in the 1986 legislative election. Although almost 30 percent of this electorate did "return" to the RPR/UDF, the FN continued to attract a proportion of former abstainers and new voters that was larger than the proportion of its party vote in the election, and its "loyalty" rate was far higher than that of other protest parties of this period, such as the Ecologists (20 percent). It was argued at the time that the temporary impact of proportional representation had encouraged voters to support the FN in this "serious" election (as compared with the European elections four years earlier, which were deemed to have no serious consequences). When proportional representation was abandoned for the 1988 legislative elections, the percentage of the vote remained about the same as in 1986, but the proportion of voters remaining loyal between 1986 and 1988 rose to that of the established parties. Moreover, the FN continued to attract a disproportionate share of new voters and former abstainers.

These new recruits, combined with defectors from the established parties of the right, made up for those who had returned to the established right. Some softness in FN electoral support was signified by the fact that Le Pen, as a candidate for the presidency in 1988, had attracted 5 percent more than National Front, his party, with most of the difference in the legislative elections going to support candidates of the established right. Nevertheless, by the 1993 legislative elections, FN candidates (none of whom won a seat—indeed, the FN lost the one seat it had won in 1989) attracted 89 percent of the voters that had voted for the National Front in the legislative elections of 1988, as well as a significant number of voters from both the right and the left, plus new voters and former abstainers, to increase its legislative showing by 25 percent. The loyalty rate among FN voters greatly exceeded that of all established parties in 1993, as it did again in 1997. Perhaps the best single measure that we have of who will vote FN is whether a voter supported the party last time (see table 3.2.).

TABLE 3.2. VOTER LOYALTY IN FIRST-ROUND LEGISLATIVE ELECTIONS, 1988–93 AND 1993–97 (IN PERCENTAGES)

	Communists	*Socialists*	*RPR-UDF*	*National Front*
1988–93	78	50	74	89
1993–97	78	75	87	91

SOURCES: J. Jaffré, "Législatives, 93 . . . ," SOFRES, *L'État de l'opinion 1994* (Paris: Seuil, 1994), 145. CSA, "Les Élections législatives du 25 mai, 1997," sondage sortie des urnes (exit poll) pour France 3, France Inter, France Info, et *Le Parisien*, 18.

The National Front thus built its breakthrough largely on voters of the right who were disappointed with their former parties, then increasingly on new voters who emerged from the traditional working-class constituency of the left. One of the most striking aspects of the electoral growth of the party has been its spread to current and former "bastions" of Communist strength.

If we consider twenty-three towns (each having a population of more than 30,000) in which the Communists dominated from at least 1947 until the early 1980s, in all of them the National Front has attracted a percentage of the electorate well above its national average, and in some it has become the party second in popularity to the Communists (PCF). In 1986, when the FN gained less than 10 percent of the vote nationally, it attracted more than 13 percent in these bastions. In 1993, with 12.5 percent of the vote nationally, the party attracted 17 percent of the vote in these towns. In the 1995 municipal elections, the FN demonstrated its ability to field attractive local candidates by gaining 11.6 percent of the vote in the 226 cities with more than thirty thousand people, and a record 19 percent in the PCF bastions. Therefore, it is hardly surprising that the National Front vote in these former PCF bastions in 1997 averaged 18.7 percent.

There is no evidence of which I am aware that there has been any substantial direct transfer of votes from former Communist voters to the FN, although there is evidence of a transfer of Socialist voters to Le Pen in the first round of the 1995 presidential elections (see Perrineau 1995a, 243-61; *Le Monde*, 1 February 1996). Perhaps more important, the FN seems to have succeeded in mobilizing the *kinds* of voters that used to be mobilized by the Communists: young (mostly male) and working class. This is probably what accounts for the sharp rise in the proportion of working-class votes going to the National Front, as well as for the FN becoming the number two party in about a third of the old PCF bastions (see table 3.3).

TABLE 3.3. BLUE-COLLAR AND WHITE-COLLAR WORKERS VOTING FOR THE NATIONAL FRONT, 1984–97 (IN PERCENTAGES)

	1984[a]	*1986*[b]	*1988*[c]	*1988*[b]	*1993*[b]	*1995*[c]	*1995*[a]	*1997*[b]
Blue-collar	10	11	18	11	15	27	25	25
White-collar	11	12	13	10	16	17	16	16

SOURCES: Elisabeth Dupoirier, "L'Électorat français, le 17 juin 1984," in SOFRES, *Opinion publique 1985* (Paris: Gallimard, 1985), 209; SOFRES, *Les Élections du printemps 1988*, 4 and 34; Jérôme Jaffré, "Législatives 93: l'alternance inéluctable," SOFRES, *L'État de l'opinion 1994* (Paris: Seuil, 1994), 144; *Libération*, 25 April 1995, 8; CSA, "Les Élections législatives du 25 mai, 1997," sondage sortie des urnes (exit poll) pour France 3, France Inter, France Info, et *Le Parisien*, 18.
a. European elections.
b. Legislative elections.
c. Presidential elections.

Thus, as measured by the level and stability of its electorate, the National Front has become an established political competitor, and this role has been stabilized not only at the national level, but also within the constituencies and in subnational politics. In its competition with both the right and the left, the FN is seeking to expand its influence by competing for similar voters.

This process of developing a stable electoral following appears to have been built first—in the early years—on voter response to the core issues of the party: immigration and law and order (*securité*). After its initial breakthrough, the very success of the party seems to have had an impact on political priorities, not only for those who have voted for the National Front, but for those who have supported other parties, thus changing the terms of political conflict to those most favorable to the National Front. This process is indicated by the priority that voters have given to various issues from election to election. In 1984, what most clearly differentiated National Front voters from those of the more established right (as well as other parties) was the priority they gave to the issue of immigration. Of the subsample who voted for the FN, 26 percent cited "immigrants" as their primary concern, and 30 percent cited "law and order," compared with 6 percent and 15 percent for the entire sample (see table 3.4). By 1986, as the FN electorate began to solidify, the priorities of party voters did so as well, with 50 percent giving priority to law and order and 60 percent to immigration (several responses were possible).

TABLE 3.4. PERCENTAGE OF PARTIES' SUPPORTERS MOTIVATED BY VARIOUS ISSUES

Issue	*1984*	*1988*	*1993*	*1997*
Law and order				
Communists	9	19	29	28
Socialists	8	21	24	29
Established right	17	38	37	43
National Front	30	55	57	66
All voters	15	31	34	35
Immigrants				
Communists	2	12	16	15
Socialists	3	13	19	15
Established right	3	19	33	22
National Front	26	59	72	72
All voters	6	22	31	22
Unemployment				
Communists	37	59	77	85
Socialists	27	43	71	83
Established right	20	41	67	72
National Front	17	41	64	75
All voters	24	45	68	75
Social inequality				
Communists	33	50	52	46
Socialists	24	43	40	47
Established right	7	18	23	21
National Front	10	18	26	25
All voters	16	31	32	35

SOURCES: Exit poll, SOFRES/TF1, 17 June 1984, *Le Nouvel Observateur,* 22 June 1984; and SOFRES, *L'État de l'opinion, clés pour 1987* (Paris: Seuil, 1987), 111; Pascal Perrineau, "Les Étapes d'une implantation électorale (1972–1988)," in Mayer and Perrineau 1989, 62; Perrineau 1993, 155; CSA, "Les Élections législatives du 25 mai, 1997," sondage sortie des urnes (exit poll) pour France 3, France Inter, France Info, et *Le Parisien,* 5.

NOTE: Because several responses were possible, annual issue totals may exceed 100 percent. The 1988 percentages represent supporters of presidential candidates nominated by the voter's party.

What is more striking, however, is how the issue priorities of the National Front and its voters appear to have influenced those of people voting for other political parties. In 1984, relatively few voters, aside from those who supported the National Front, considered either immigration or law and order to be a strong priority. By 1988, the importance of these issues ranked with such issues as social inequality, and far higher than concerns about the environment, corruption and the construction of Europe; only concern with unemployment ranked higher (see Perrineau 1993, 155).

We can look at the relationship between the rise of the National Front and the evolving priorities of voters in a somewhat different way. In 1993 fewer than half the voters who identified themselves ideologically as "centrist" said that they had voted for a candidate of the established right—RPR-UDF—(most of the others had voted for the left), compared with 63 percent in 1986; on the other hand, 63 percent of those who were identified as "extreme right" voted for the established right in 1993, compared with 55 percent of what was a smaller group in 1986. By 1993, "We find ourselves . . . in the presence of a political radicalization of the moderate right electorate [that is, those who vote for the moderate right], probably linked to the increase of its audience among working-class categories" (see Chiche and Dupoirier 1993, 133).

I have argued elsewhere that the emergence of the National Front in electoral politics in the early 1980s at first reflected the preceding weakening of the party system, as well as conflict about the political agenda on integration and incorporation among political actors involved in the policymaking process across the political spectrum. Later, the ability of the party to build an electoral following, and its increasingly important role in the political debate, had an impact on the priorities of all voters (see Schain 1996, 169-99).

However, in the 1990s the growth dynamics that I have analyzed here gradually leveled off. The percentage of National Front voters (indeed, of all voters) who gave priority to issues of immigration and law and order stabilized, as did the proportion of working-class support for the party (see tables 3.3 and 3.4). In addition, the presence of immigrant communities seems to be less important as a dynamic for FN electoral growth than it was for electoral breakthrough. Recent surveys indicate that more than two-thirds of the voters who identify with the National Front live in communes in which the immigrant population is less than 10 percent.

Table 3.5 shows that there is an "advantage" for the National Front where there is an immigrant population, but this advantage tends to level off when the proportion of immigrants rises above 5 percent. While identification with the party usually rises with the presence of immigrants, it appears to do so at a relatively low threshold, rather than in a linear fashion.[2] On the other hand, identification with the established right tends to be far higher in communes where there is no immigrant population, and then falls sharply even where there is a small proportion of immigrants. Although there is no way to demonstrate a direct shift from the established right to the FN at the commune level, the tradeoff merits further investigation.

TABLE 3.5. PARTY SUPPORT AND THE PRESENCE OF IMMIGRANTS

	Immigrant percentage of commune population			
	None	*1–4*	*5–10*	*Above 10*
Communist	4.7	2.7	6.5	6.3
Socialist/MRG	23.6	29.9	24.9	29.2
UDF	9.4	8.0	4.4	4.3
RPR	15.6	10.7	10.9	11.0
National Front	5.5	5.9	8.5	8.3
Not identified	27.3	31.6	30.4	31.1

SOURCE: CSA survey 9662093, November 1996, RS10/RS12.

Although the breakthrough sources of National Front support seem to have stabilized, the party has continued to attract large numbers of new voters. In the legislative elections of 1993, and again in 1997, the National Front increased its support by 700,000 votes. Thus it appears that if we account for voters lost to other political parties, in each case about a million new (or former) voters had to be recruited to account for the total. It would seem, then, that other dynamics can help us to account for the party's ability to mobilize new voters, even while it retains its existing clientele.

The Dynamics of Mobilization Capacity

Party Position

The continuing growth of the National Front electorate is perhaps best explained by the party's enhanced mobilization within the party system. Although we have been looking at electoral support nationally, the mobilization capacities of the party have been gradually increasing at the constituency level. In 1993 the National Front gained in every French department except the Bouches du Rhone (the Marseilles region), where it was already very strong, and the Haute Corse. In 1997 it gained in every department except Paris, Mayenne (Brittany), and the Alpes Maritime (the Nice region), where it nevertheless remains the primary opposition to the established right. The party has significantly increased both the number of districts in which it is the "first" party of the right and the number in which it is the "second."

TABLE 3.6. NUMBER OF ELECTORAL DISTRICTS IN WHICH THE NATIONAL FRONT PLACED FIRST OR SECOND AMONG PARTIES OF THE RIGHT, IN THE FIRST ROUND, 1993 AND 1997

	1993		*1997*		*Total electoral districts,*
Region	*First*	*Second*	*First*	*Second*	*1993, 1997*
France	11	430	44	456	555
Île de France (except Paris)	2	68	10	61	78
Provence–Alpes–Côtes d'Azur	5	29	12	27	40
Nord–Pas-de-Calais	1	30	8	27	38
Rhône-Alpes	1	37	3	44	49

SOURCE: *Le Monde, Dossiers et documents,* various issues.

The key contest, as defined by Le Pen, is within the right, and the National Front made considerable progress in this contest in 1997, when even a small increase (2.5 percent) in overall support had important consequences for the relative standing of the party at the constituency level (see table 3.6). In well over three quarters of the districts in metropolitan France, the FN had become the second party of the right by 1993, and in 2 percent (11) it was the first (in terms of votes). In 1997 the relative position of the party within the right improved considerably. The National Front scored better than other right-wing parties in 8 percent (44) of the districts and came in second in 82 percent. This is consistent with the results of a CSA survey in 1996, which indicated that among respondents living in towns with populations greater than 100,000, the National Front attracts more support than any other party of the right (indeed more support than any party except the PS).[3] Thus, by 1997 there were almost no areas of the country in which the National Front did not present a significant political challenge to the right in the arenas in which political conflict occurred. Most of these gains were concentrated in the old industrial suburbs of Lyons, Marseilles, Paris, and the old industrial areas of the Nord–Pas-de-Calais, as well as in a growing network of towns between Marseilles and Nice, and in Alsace, where the party had not progressed in 1993.

This local success against the *frères-ennemies* (rivals within the same camp) of the right also has implications for the more traditional enemies of the left. Most striking is that in many of the old concentrations of Communist strength, even where the PCF still dominates, the National Front has become the main party of the right: in the Seine-St. Denis, the FN was in first position on the right in 8 out of 13 districts. These are the areas in which the ability of the extreme right to mobilize young working-class men is best demonstrated.[4] Here the National Front has undermined the parties of the right by mobilizing the *constituency* of the left.

Postelection surveys indicate (once again) that only a relatively small percentage of voters who voted for the left in 1993 transferred to the FN in 1997 (4 percent from the PCF and 4 percent from the PS, according to the CSA postelection survey).[5] This is small consolation to the left, however, if we consider that 25 percent of blue-collar workers now vote for the party, far more than for the PCF, and just a shade fewer than for the Socialists. Moreover, even a small transfer vote from the left (which has a relatively large pool of voters) results in a considerable increase for the FN: the SOFRES/CEVIPOF survey indicated that 12.4 percent of FN voters in 1997 had voted for the left in 1993, and 19 percent had voted for Jospin in the second round of the presidential elections in 1995 (see Mayer 1997).

The capacity of the party to maintain candidates in the second round of legislative elections demonstrates the evolving positioning of the National Front as a party challenger to both the right and the left at the constituency level (see table 3.7). This capacity has improved considerably since 1988, when the FN maintained its candidates in only 14 districts, compared with 132 in 1997. What has also changed is the growth in the number of direct confrontations between an FN

TABLE 3.7. NATIONAL FRONT CANDIDATES IN THE SECOND ROUND OF FRENCH LEGISLATIVE ELECTIONS, 1988–97

	1988		*1993*		*1997*	
Contest	*Number*	*%*	*Number*	*%*	*Number*	*%*
National Front vs. left	9		5		25	
National Front vs. right	1		83		31	
National Front/right/left	4		12		76	
Total	14	3.2	100	20.7	132	24.1

SOURCE: Ponceyri 1997, 7–8.

candidate facing a candidate of the left, as the standard bearer of the right, the capacity of the party to play the spoiler in triangular contests, and thus potentially to blackmail the right, has also increased. One analyst has calculated that the established right has lost thirty-five seats, and therefore a majority of one, because of the presence of the National Front (see Jaffré 1977).

Organizational Capacity

This competitive position of the National Front at the constituency level has been enhanced by the deeper roots the party has been sinking in the space that it occupies. Although it governs in only four cities, the party now has about two thousand municipal councilors elected in 1995, as well as 239 regional councilors elected in 1992 (concentrated in Île de France, Provence–Alpes–Côtes-D'Azur, and the Rhône-Alpes). A quick reading of the electoral results of 1997 indicates that the FN is succeeding by using the traditional building blocks of French politics: local offices linked by *cumul des mandats.* With its many subnational officeholders, it is not surprising that the party had little difficulty presenting a full range of candidates in 1997, and that many of these candidates already had at least one local mandate. Although the National Front has consistently presented itself as an antiestablishment party against "the gang of four," at the constituency level its candidates increasingly are already known and established officeholders.

Social concentrations of National Front supporters are also an important base for building greater electoral support, and they have been growing in unexpected ways. Almost a third of those who claim to be close to the party also claim to be close to a union organization; most of these are affiliated with the CGT, the CFDT, FO, and the FNSEA. Among union backers, FN voters represent a small but significant percentage of supporters, especially among those with the FO, for whom the National Front is the right-wing party of choice (see table 3.8).[6] Given the growing working-class support among FN voters, this is not entirely surprising. What makes the situation striking is an indication that established trade unions—organizations that historically have most intensely opposed the ideas and political priorities of the National Front—have been unable to resist penetration and mobilization by the party. National Front beachheads within the unions provide receptive arenas for party expansion, particularly since there is evidence that over half of trade union supporters feel that immigrant workers are a "charge" on the French economy.[7]

National Front successes at the subnational level have meant that in particular localities the party has bargaining, if not governing, power. In the French polit-

TABLE 3.8. PARTY PREFERENCES OF UNION MEMBERS AND SYMPATHIZERS, 1997 (IN PERCENTAGES)

	Union					*Not union members*
	CGT	*CFDT*	*FO*	*CFTC*	*FNSEA*	
Communist Party	23.6	—	7.1	—	—	1.6
Socialist Party	36.6	52.6	34.1	29.4	6.7	19.2
UDF	4.9	7.0	7.1	29.4	6.7	5.2
RPR	4.1	14.0	7.1	23.5	46.7	12.7
National Front	4.9	3.5	8.2	5.9	6.7	7.8

SOURCE: CSA survey 9662093, November 1996, RS10/RS12.

NOTE:
CGT = Confédération Générale du Travail.
CFDT = Confédération Française Democratique du Travail.
FO = Force Ouvrière.
CFTC = Confédération Française des Travailleurs Chrétiens.
FNSEA = Fédération Nationale des Syndicats des Exploitants Agricoles.

ical system, subnational positions have traditionally proved important in nurturing national influence and power. While in federal systems such as the United States, local electoral successes by a "third party" have been contained within local and even state structures, in the French system, local success tends to become a springboard for regional and even national success. The system of *cumul des mandats* directly links the subnational influence of the National Front to the national political arena in two ways: it provides its elected officials a subsidized springboard to other elective offices, and representatives of other parties who occupy national office inevitably are influenced by National Front pressure in their home constituencies.

The inability of the governments of either the right or the left to derail the electoral support of the National Front appears to be related to the expanding organizing abilities of both the party and its elected representatives, and these have been growing. In the early months of 1996, the National Front sought to capitalize on widespread worker disaffection (as well as the weakness of established trade union organizations) by establishing its own police unions, a union of Paris transport workers, a union of transport workers in the Lyon region, a teachers' union, a student organization, and its own association of small and medium enterprises (see *Le Monde*, 13 February, 24-25 March, and 3 April 1996). These initiatives have provoked successful court challenges by the CFDT and the CGT (see *Le Monde*, 9-10 June 1996), but they have also accentuated the FN's growing (though not always successful) organizing abilities in unexpected and unanticipated arenas.

In this French context, such social organization provides the party with additional modes of mobilization through a widespread network of elections for local office. So, for example, a newsletter of the CFDT reported that in December 1995, in elections for bilateral commissions, the two FN police unions gained only 5.8 and 7.5 percent of the votes nationally, but picked up 20 percent in Metz, 16 percent in Lille and Marseilles, and 15 percent in Paris.[8] The party has also presented rosters of candidates for other professional elections, as well as for public housing offices, with mixed success.[9] In December 1997, the National Front made a small but significant breakthrough in elections for labor court councilors (*conseils des prud'hommes*), gaining eighteen councilors.[10] Since almost all of these local elections are organized according to some form of proportional representation, even minimal success ensures that the National Front will force its opponents to deal with its issues and may leave its representatives in place to create additional pressure in favor of its agenda. Moreover, success in local elections often means additional subsidies for potential candidates for public office, as well as direct and continuing contact with, and the possible patronage of, a potential electorate.

Thus, I would argue that it is important to consider not only the level of electoral support for the National Front, but also the spatial and social distribution of its following, and the impact of this distribution on the party system as a whole as well as on the future growth of FN support. What differentiates the National Front from most other parties of the extreme right in Western Europe is not simply its level of electoral support, but its ability to dominate a space within which it can stabilize and then build additional support (see Martin 1996, 13-14). The party has set in place a machine to increase support. The mobilization of electoral support no longer depends simply on voter sympathy for FN-backed issues, nor on the priority voters give these issues. Thus, as table 3.4 (page 73) illustrates, even when the priorities given to "immigration" and "law and order" have diminished, the National Front has increased its electoral support, mostly in areas where it is already strong.

The distribution of the immigrant population has related in important ways to the National Front's electoral breakthrough. Beyond this, however, what sets the party apart is how it has used this breakthrough to enhance its position, molding and defining the immigration issue to sustain and solidify its electoral support.

Agenda Setting

Issue Definition

The story of immigration politics after 1983 is less about policy orientation than about the struggle by political parties on both the right and the left to undermine the National Front's ability to sustain the initiative in defining these issues. In competing with the FN for voters who are frightened by the problems of a multi-ethnic society, the RPR has been deeply divided between those who advocate cooperating with the FN and taking a moderate approach to their issues, and others who wish to destroy their rival on the right through isolation and total rejection of its views. Each time the RPR feels it has succeeded in outmaneuvering the National Front (the legislative elections of 1988, the municipal elections of 1989, and the immigration legislation of 1993), the party is reminded that the challenge will not disappear (the by-election victories of the FN in Marseilles and Dreux in December 1989, the legislative elections of 1993, the presidential and municipal elections of 1995, and the legislative elections of 1997). More and more, the electorally weak parties of the right frequently need the 10 to 15 percent of the electorate that has voted FN.

As for the Socialists, through 1993 they struggled to defuse the rhetoric of the National Front with a variety of approaches: by offering policy initiatives (strengthening border controls while trying to develop a policy of integration) when they controlled the government; by agreeing with the established right when they were electorally threatened by the opposition (as did Socialist Prime Minister Fabius, debating with Chirac in 1985 that "the National Front poses some real questions"); and, more generally, by alternating between the pluralist rhetoric of a "right to difference" approach to immigrants and an individualistic "right to indifference" approach (see *Le Monde*, 11 February and 7 December 1989; Vichniac 1991). Despite the confusion, the dynamics of party competition have resulted in redefining the issue of immigration in national politics from a labor-market problem, to an integration/incorporation problem; to a problem that touches on national identity; to problems of education, housing, law and order; to problems of citizenship requirements.

It is hardly surprising that the National Front's electoral success has defined and driven the agenda formation of successive governments. What has been more surprising is how shocked established political leaders always seem to be when the FN is successful in elections. One conclusion we might draw is that portrayals of immigration/integration issues that are meant to mobilize broad support for either the right or the left seem only to increase FN support. Governments driven by the dynamics of party competition, however, seem unable to resist recapturing what they see as a volatile electorate by engaging with the National Front.

The difficulty of the FN challenge was well demonstrated by the end of the 1995 electoral cycle. Immigration themes played almost no role in the presidential election campaign. Both Balladur and Chirac apparently presumed that the legislation passed in 1993 would defuse the issue, while Jospin, in a brief paragraph in his election program, indicated he would ease requirements imposed by the 1993 legislation on children born in France to immigrant parents. Only Le Pen spoke of going further (*Le Monde*, 20 September 1994).

After Le Pen's impressive showing in the first round, however, both Chirac and Jospin attempted to attract FN voters without making obvious overtures to Le Pen. Jospin spoke approvingly of proportional representation, while both Chirac and Juppé (who would be named prime minister) spoke darkly of problems of law and order and "the confiscation of the maintenance of order by ethnic or religious groups" (see *Le Monde*, 27 April 1995; Shields 1995, 34-35).

The campaign and results of the municipal elections in June 1995 once again focused attention on immigration issues. Le Pen promised to use the FN's new local power to emphasize "national preference" in all policy areas. Clearly, this new angle on the immigration issue posed a challenge for Chirac. The president created a full ministry to deal with questions of immigration and integration, with the awkward name Ministry of Integration and the Struggle against Exclusion. In a series of dramatic moves, the government rapidly moved against undocumented immigrants and announced a program to move "delinquent families" (generally considered a codeword for immigrant families) out of slum neighborhoods, presumably into other slum neighborhoods.[11] Then, in reaction to National Front victories in the municipal elections, as well as to a new wave of bombings by Algerian dissidents, the president suspended the implementation of the Schengen Accords in July.[12] In an interview with a German newspaper, one of Chirac's chief aides argued that "Europe works for Le Pen," and he suggested that the Le Pen challenge might be met by derailing Schengen and returning to a hard-line Gaullist definition of the nation-state (*Le Monde*, 26 March 1996; *The European*, 28 July-3 August 1995).

A now forgotten incident in April 1996 illustrates well how regionally concentrated support for the National Front may serve as a springboard for its national influence over policy. Thirty members of a National Assembly committee recommended new immigration legislation that would limit undocumented immigrants' access to hospitals and schools, and facilitate expelling minors from

French territory. These recommendations were widely opposed, even by the majority—the opposition included the former hardline interior minister, Charles Pasqua—and the proposal never gained government support (*Le Monde*, 17 and 19 April 1996). Nevertheless, immigration legislation was now back on the political agenda, placed there by committee members who were particularly vulnerable to FN pressure. The National Front had emerged from the 1993 legislative elections as the second party in the districts of nine members of the committee, and in twenty-two of their thirty districts, the FN vote was well above the 1993 national mean for the party (*Le Monde*, 19 April 1996).

In a number of respects, the Jospin government's reactions to the National Front's electoral success in 1997 were an impressive result of the FN's ability to set priorities for the national political agenda. Because of pressures from its own constituency, as well as the weight of the FN, the government could not avoid dealing with the immigration issue. In one of its first moves, the government announced that it would appoint a commission to study the broad question of immigration legislation and then quickly decide what action to take regarding new legislation on immigration and nationalization. Within a month of its appointment, that commission issued its report, which recommended that the government try a bold new approach to the immigration issue: to accept with modifications the changes in immigration and naturalization legislation that had been made by the right since 1993, and to develop an explicit centrist approach that would tend toward consensus and isolate the National Front.[13] In the short run, this centrist approach was largely rejected by the opposition, and it created emotional divisions within the left as well. Its long-run impact on the growth of the National Front remains to be seen. Nevertheless, in the debate on the minister of the interior's immigration and naturalization proposals, concerns about how these bills affect the strength of that party frequently were expressed explicitly, and were never far below the surface (*Le Monde*, 30 November 1997, 6).

Alliance Formation

The dynamic of alliance formation at the subnational level also has promoted the National Front's agenda. Alliance formation in regions, departments, and communes takes place at two levels: that of electoral alliances, and that of governing. In general, established political parties would prefer not to engage with the National Front in forming either explicit or implicit alliances. Nevertheless, from the very earliest days of the party's electoral breakthrough, this position was almost impossible to maintain. In the municipal elections of March 1983, local

RPR and UDF politicians in Dreux decided to form a joint roster with the FN, a decision approved by the national leadership of both parties. That decision was reversed when irregularities forced a second election in September. Unable to secure an absolute majority in the first round of the election, the RPR-UDF would have been forced to pay an unacceptable price for continuing to ignore the FN in the second round. In the end, they decided to form a joint list with the FN, which then was victorious. As a result, three National Front councilors were named assistant mayors in the new local government (see Schain 1987).

Since then, the party's ability to win elections at the subnational level, where there is some proportionality, has increased with its ability to field candidates, and its ability to field candidates has increased with success in elections. In 1986, FN lists were presented in each of France's twenty-two regions. Winning almost 10 percent of the vote, the party elected 137 (out of 1,682) regional councilors; not many, but enough to exert strategic influence over coalition formation on twelve of the twenty-two regions. In six regions their votes were needed to elect a council president from the established right. In Languedoc-Roussillon the Gaullist president reached a formal accord on a "Program of Action" with the FN; in five other regions the FN was able to negotiate important positions in the regional government, and in five additional regions it gained some lesser positions (see Birenbaum 1992, 79-80). Six years later, the FN increased its regional representation to 239, with representation in every region. In fourteen of the twenty-two regions, the right now depended for its majority on FN councilors, who carefully demonstrated their ability to arbitrate in the election of regional presidents and the selection of regional executives (see Patrait 1992, 311). The influence of FN-elected representatives on agenda formation is still unclear, but the expanding implantation of the party at this level will probably have an impact on the day-to-day operation of government, and on the construction of alliances for future elections.[14] We find a similar pattern at the local (commune) level.

With little presence at the local level (despite the victory in Dreux), the National Front benefited from the conversions of some local notables from the established right during the 1980s. By 1989, the FN was able to present lists in 214 of the 392 cities with more than 20,000 people. In other cases, candidates of the FN joined with others in lists simply dubbed *divers droite* or *extrême droite.* Well over a thousand FN municipal councilors were elected in 143 towns with more than 20,000 people, 478 on lists with the FN label and 621 on alliance lists or as individual candidates. Here too, the agenda-setting role of these municipal councilors was unclear. What has been clear is that, at least in the larger towns in

France, the National Front has been engaged in day-to-day politics and has been in a position to build support on the basis of its local *notabilité* in much the same way that it did after its success in Dreux (see Birenbaum 1992, 162-70).

The 1995 municipal elections, therefore, both confirmed the effective presence of the FN at the local level and demonstrated its ability to build on that presence. For the first time, the party won outright victories in three large towns and expanded its presence (thanks to proportional representation) in many others. Of particular importance was the victory in Toulon, where the FN captured 41 of the 56 municipal council posts. In Marignane, the party won control from the UDF, gaining 27 of the 39 council seats; and in historic Orange, the FN won 24 of the 35 seats by edging out Socialists in the second round. In at least four other towns—Vitrolles, Noyon, Dreux, and Mulhouse—only "republican front" (left/right) alliances in the second round prevented the FN from taking control, and in Vitrolles the FN would take control in a special election in February 1997. In all of these towns, however, the National Front had been building support for a decade, and, in this sense, the breakthrough was the result of a long and successful effort.

All in all, the National Front fielded almost 25,000 candidates in 1995, which enabled it to more than double the number of municipal councilors directly or indirectly affiliated with the party.[15] Perhaps the best measure of its growing influence was that, with almost 12 percent of the vote in towns with a population of more than 30,000, the National Front gained sufficient support to remain in the second round in more than half of them (119) and then to win seats in most of the towns (101) in which it had run. The FN became the key arbitrator of the second round. Although it certainly failed to provoke the parties of the established right to form common coalitions (despite some initial successes that were later withdrawn [see *Libération*, 1 and 4 June 1995]), its presence in the second round had a strong influence on outcomes for both the left and the right.[16]

The results of the municipal elections of 1995 (and the special election in Vitrolles in 1997) are most important because, as noted earlier, local electoral success in France is frequently the key building block for national success. These results are also important because thousands more elected FN officials are now in place, prepared to trade their votes for influence over policy agendas. Finally, they are important because they influence policy at the local level. By November 1995, mayors from the parties of the conservative majority reported that they were cutting back on programs against "exclusion" and in favor of immigrant integration. Voter distrust of such programs, they argued, "explains the rise of the National Front" (*Le Monde*, 12-13 November 1995).

Some Concluding Comments: The Strategic Dilemma

The 1997 legislative elections have further confirmed that the National Front has stabilized in terms of the party's increased importance in shaping electoral terms and agendas. This clear success has also brought the party to the brink of a strategic dilemma, however: whether to remain a party—an effective party—of opposition, or to move toward governing power at the national level by employing a more sophisticated coalition strategy. This conflict has set the traditional Catholic wing of the party organization, which has rallied around its secretary-general, Bruno Gollnisch, in opposition to its modernist wing, led by the general delegate, Bruno Mégret.

Not surprisingly, conflict has become more open and more bitter as the party has achieved broader electoral success. In the autumn of 1995, Le Pen brokered a balance between the two sides (*Le Monde*, 17-18 September 1995, 6; and 11 October 1995). By 1997 Le Pen had tilted clearly toward the traditionalists, in opposition to Mégret's continuing pressure for a strategy that would give priority to "seduction to conquer" the voters, militants, and local organizations of the established right, particularly those of the RPR. In contrast to Mégret's seductive alliance approach, Le Pen's dialogue and strategic approach increasingly have toughened toward the established right (*Le Monde*, 16 June 1997, 6; and 20 January 1998, 8). Despite the party's considerable electoral success in recent years, Le Pen sees the National Front as "the hard core of the opposition," as opposed to Mégret's vision of political participation: "Our calling is not to remain in the opposition as a force of protest" (*Le Monde*, 20 January 1998, 8).

Thus, the success of the National Front has carried the party to a classic turning point, one often faced by radical parties. Under Le Pen's leadership, the organization seems destined, in the short run, to support a stance of opposition. In the long run, however, party recruitment appears to favor Mégret. In the volatile world of the French right, the National Front is a seductive, growing political force that very well may pursue a coalition strategy resulting in power at the national level.

Chapter 4

Europe Becomes French Domestic Politics

George Ross

The French electorate never allowed European integration to go forward in a state of "permissive consensus." Few should have been surprised, therefore, when the question of Europe divided the French electorate in the 1990s, in particular after the 1992 Maastricht referendum. Deep partisan and electoral cleavages over European integration had existed in France since the European Union's (EU) beginnings—the 1954 vote to shelve the European Defense Community, for example, was no accident. It was surprising, however, that persistent differences over Europe, in which strong minorities persistently opposed the forward movement of European integration, indeed often the idea itself, had so little direct practical effect until very recently. The reasons for this are complex, lying mainly in the workings of partisan coalitions and institutional logics, as the first part of this chapter shows. It is important, however, to characterize the changes that occurred in the 1990s. Roughly from the election of Jacques Chirac to the presidency in 1995 through to the present (after the surprise Socialist victory in the 1997 legislative elections), European integration ceased being external to French domestic politics and became a central structuring factor. France's "internalizing" of European integration is the subject of the second part of this chapter.

Past as Preamble: The Myth of Consensus on European Integration

From its beginnings, European integration divided French public opinion and party politics. In the EU's critical early years in the Fourth Republic, the Communists (who held over 25 percent of the vote until the late 1950s) judged European integration to be a capitalist plot against "existing socialism," their project and ideal. General de Gaulle and the Gaullists, with voting strength similar to the PCF, drew upon deep nationalism to advocate a "third way" against Cold War dualism and interpreted first steps towards European Union as an American strategy to undercut French sovereignty. Even among the Socialists (SFIO) there were misgivings, shown by the defection of half of the SFIO's parliamentary votes over the EDC in 1954 (Griffiths 1993).

Europe by Stealth?

Coalitional settings and institutional contexts in the later Fourth Republic, not "permissive consensus," fostered the beginnings of European integration. The parties of the political center—Socialists, Christian Democrats, and Independents (plus the steady trickle of Gaullists who refused de Gaulle's injunction to steer clear of the republic's parliamentary games)—were the pivot point. Their Europeanism was facilitated by a setting where Communists and Gaullists, despite their strength, were *hors jeu.*[1] At this point, as in much of the EU's later history, the French were key leaders of the new Europe. But this was not because the French population really desired European integration; rather, the workings of a multiparty system, as well as particular constitutional settings, pushed anti-Europeans to the margin.

The play of political coalitions and institutions in the 1960s and 1970s, although changing (largely because the constitution changed in 1958)—continued to neutralize anti-European opinion. Ironically, the success of Gaullism after 1958 allowed the first "Common Market" period of European integration to happen (Zorgbibe 1993). The rules of the new Fifth Republic and the circumstances of its birth combined to give its first president, General de Gaulle, immense power, particularly in international affairs. The General's reconsideration of his earlier anti-EEC views was decisive. De Gaulle concluded that Europe, provided that it subsidized French agricultural modernization, could be a useful tool to promote his "third way" alternative to either the United States or the Soviet bloc, in particular through the astute cultivation of Franco-German relations. He did insist, however, that Europe not be supranational. The veto of British entry in 1963, the Fouchet Plan, the "empty chair" episode, and, finally, the "Luxemburg Compromise" of 1966 successively promoted strong intergovernmentalism.

In domestic political terms, the General's change of mind on Europe obliged anti-European Gaullists to accept European integration on Gaullist conditions. One source of opposition was thus quashed, even if quiet, but serious, Gaullist political differences about Europe persisted throughout the Pompidou and most of the Giscard presidencies (Burban 1993). The PCF did not cease its opposition, but coalitional changes in the new republic caused the party to mute its stridency. Early in the 1960s, Communist leaders concluded that *Union de la Gauche* was one possible outcome of the new political setting. To make this happen, however, the PCF had to downplay the issues that divided it from the non-Communist left. European integration was among the most important of these.

A pattern had emerged. When opposition to European integration presented barriers to a party's participation in a potentially powerful coalition, the issue was placed in the background. When, in contrast, coalitional unity came under strain because of internal conflict, Europe might become one of many bludgeons to be used against rival coalition partners. Two durable multiparty coalitions were created in the 1960s, but when these began to disaggregate in the later 1970s, Europe reemerged briefly as a divisive issue. Until it realized that Left Unity was benefiting the Socialists more than itself, the PCF muted its position on Europe, which nonetheless remained unchanged. After Left Unity broke down in 1977, however, the Communists spoke their anti-Europe piece loudly in the hope of cutting the Socialist vote down to size, particularly in 1979 in the first direct elections to the European Parliament. On the other side of the aisle, as long as the Gaullists dominated the ruling center-right coalition, they could see the possibilities for Europe to expand France's international position and trade. But when their domination of this coalition was threatened by Giscard d'Estaing after 1976, Jacques Chirac, the new Gaullist leader, with the 1981 presidential election in the offing, ran a separate anti-European slate in some Euro-parliamentary polls (see Flood 1997; Chirac 1978).

Mitterrand's Magic?

Given this background, what happened during the period from the early 1980s through Maastricht in 1991 was remarkable. During this period France took the lead in promoting major leaps forward in European integration, in particular the 1985 Single Market Program and movement toward the Economic and Monetary Union (EMU). The logic of the entire process marked major steps away from intergovernmentalist caution and implied very large shifts of economic sovereignty away from France to the EU. One would therefore have thought that anti-European feelings would have come out in force. But they did not. Why not?

Coalitional and institutional circumstances again provide most of the answers to this question. François Mitterrand's domestic politics marginalized and diminished partisan sources of anti-Europeanization. *Union de la Gauche* weakened the Communists to the point that they participated without much influence in Mitterrand's government until 1984. Then, their vote having dropped below 10 percent, they began wandering the political wilderness fighting with one another. The Gaullists, in opposition for the first time since 1958, were concerned primarily with reestablishing their position. The most profitable way of doing this was to mobilize around the "misdeeds" of the left in power, its *dirigisme* (state economic planning), its attempts at redistributive policies, its economic policy roller coaster, and its educational reform goals. Mitterrand's renewed Europeanism was low on this list. The emergence of the anti-immigrant *Front National* in the mid-1980s provided another reason for the Gaullists to focus on domestic matters, since the FN, with origins in France's traditional extreme right, gained its first converts in Gaullist electoral territories (Fieschi, Shields, and Woodes 1996).

There were other reasons why renewed European integration was not taken unduly seriously in French domestic politics. The state of the EU itself helped prevent it. The EU had reached a "Europessimistic" impasse in the early 1980s, and despite many new proposals made by the European Commission, the European Parliament, and others to change this, nothing much happened. Thus, in 1985, renewed European integration looked unlikely, even though Mitterrand's leadership of the 1984 French EU presidency had begun to reveal more ambitious plans.[2] The 1985 Commission White Paper on completing the Single Market and the Single European Act held great potential for change, but whether much would come of them was initially obscure. Even after it had become clear that things were indeed happening, these things did not much touch the lives of voters. From the point of view of ordinary French people, the first years of the "1992" program mainly involved producing piles of paper. Before the Single Market could become a reality there first had to be years of intense Euro-legislative activity. This meant that renewing European integration was cost-free for a time, a bonus for those who wanted to keep it off domestic political screens.[3]

Mitterrand's deeper strategy was barely understood below the elite level. After the left's "nationalize and plan" program failed, Mitterrand envisaged renewed European integration as a substitute with comparable mobilizing strength. France could, with clever politics, play a predominant role in shaping the destiny of a more unified Europe. The French had a skilled administrative corps, key military assets, and a determination that the Germans, the other likely leaders of a new Europe, clearly could not match. The British might become fellow travelers because of 1992's liberalism, but they could not lead, given their ambivalence about Europe in general. The road seemed open, therefore, for France to plan a new Europe. Building it could provide a renewed mission for the left. The new Europe, because it seemed to promise economic growth and job creation (Mitterrand's biggest mistake was believing this) might also bring new prosperity to sustain the left's electoral fortunes.[4] The hidden dimension of this situation was an effort to "exogenize" economic and social reforms that would have been impossible to promote otherwise.[5]

Europe's chronic "democratic deficit" was yet another reason why all of this complex maneuvering was not picked up in French domestic debates. In most EU member states, the processes set in motion after 1985 were largely obscured by the EU's institutional workings. The treaty base of the EU, which organizes debate on EU policy, is difficult even for insiders to understand. The Commission, which produced voluminous "Eurospeak," was appointed, and thus was politically inaccessible. The Single European Act (1986) did make the Commission more responsible to the European Parliament, but the Parliament itself was difficult for ordinary Europeans to comprehend.[6] The real legislative arm of the EU was a Council of Ministers that conducted its business in secret—neither its votes nor its debates were made public.[7] The member state side of the "democratic deficit" was also important. There was little European political culture, and issues of European integration were rarely foregrounded in national political debates, particularly in France. Parties and interest groups continued to work according to their traditional national focus. Elections for the European Parliament were almost always fought around national political debates.

Mitterrand's Mistakes

Mitterrand began to lose control of the "Europe option" with the end of the Cold War.[8] The emergence of the United States as the only superpower rendered decades of expensive and complicated French maneuvering for a European "third force" superfluous, devaluing French military assets in the process.[9] The Gulf War and U.S. efforts to reconfigure NATO proved that these assets were not much use in regional conflicts either—as warfare in the former Yugoslavia also showed. Unification made Germany the largest EU member, endowing it with more economic and political clout and giving it new domestic preoccupations, particularly given the politically astute but financially reckless tactics used by Helmut Kohl to ensure rapid unification.[10] These events occurred as Mitterrand was moving forward the biggest pieces in his European game. Plans drafted by Jacques Delors for the EMU were approved by everyone but the United Kingdom at the Madrid EU summit in 1989. Through the EMU, the French hoped to take back some of the control over money and banking that the Germans had come to hold over other members of the European Monetary System (EMS). This, in turn, would make different monetary policies in Europe possible and perhaps bring an end to the compulsive quest for price stability that the Bundesbank enjoined upon everyone.

In the immediate context of German unification, the French and Germans led the EU in calling for the Intergovernmental Conferences (IGCs) that resulted in the Maastricht Treaty. Maastricht did not turn out the way the French had hoped, however. The EMU was negotiated, but on critical matters it followed German, rather than French, purposes. Problems in financing unification meant that the Germans were unwilling to hand their monetary policy over to the EU as rapidly as the French had hoped, and they also insisted, through "convergence criteria" for monetary policy, that potential members of the EMU follow strict price stability and budget balancing guidelines.[11]

Difficulty in ratifying Maastricht, and Mitterrand's domestic political miscalculations, eventually brought the issue of Europe to the fore in France. The Danes, constitutionally enjoined to hold a referendum on the treaty changes, voted against the treaty in June 1992. The French, however, could choose between two ways of ratifying Maastricht. They could invoke stringent parliamentary procedures and require a three-fifths majority of both houses of Parliament meeting together. But it was also within presidential prerogative to submit the issue to a referendum, even if, in 1992, the almost certain success of the parliamentary route made it unnecessary. But earlier electoral competition and initial discussions of the treaty revealed that the center-right opposition was divided. In the Gaullist camp, Chirac, who was concerned about his presidential future, had to come out in favor of Maastricht, but Charles Pasqua and Philippe Séguin, both of whom had recently rebelled against Chirac's RPR leadership, were opposed to it. Opposition also appeared in the UDF, the other center-right partner, in particular from Philippe deVilliers, an aristocratic neoliberal. Moreover, the left had been soundly beaten in regional elections in early 1992 and could expect similar results in the 1993 parliamentary elections that would set the stage for the all-important presidential elections in 1995 (Habert, Perrineau, and Ysmal 1992). In the meantime, a sense of *fin de règne* had turned the Socialist government into a flock of lame ducks.

It was in this context that Mitterrand decided on the Maastricht referendum of September 1992. A French "yes" might reestablish momentum for European integration, which the Danish vote had helped to diminish. More important to Mitterrand, the referendum campaign might further divide the center-right and help the left in 1993, at the risk of allowing differences over European integration to take center stage. Mitterrand discounted this risk, since early polls gained 60 percent for "yes," but he was quite wrong. Over the summer the electorate, perhaps the majority, mobilized strongly against Maastricht (Habert 1992-93). The PCF and the National Front, able to mobilize faithful voters around a "no," hoped to exploit the vulnerability of the more "legitimate" parties of left and right. Jean-Pierre Chevènement and the remains of CERES in the PS came out for "no." The RPR, divided, abstained from giving its supporters any official instructions, but both Séguin and Pasqua spoke their anti-Maastricht pieces strongly. De Villiers also campaigned for "no," arguing that his position would prevent Le Pen from making major new inroads.

Mitterrand's tactics backfired. Elite consensus to keep quiet about European integration was broken, obliging Europeanist factions of the political class to pull together, left and right, to save the day. Raymond Barre, Giscard d'Estaing (who had become a leading Euro-parliamentarian), and other center-right leaders joined prominent Socialists barnstorming the country for "yes" votes. Even Chirac, as usual worried about his presidential future, came out personally for a "yes," despite the free vote he had allowed RPR supporters. The campaign deepened divisions on the center-right, as Mitterrand had foreseen. But it also divided the left.

The de facto center-left coalition that emerged to save the day neutralized Mitterrand's hopes. The ways in which the electorate divided over the referendum were striking. Farmers, workers, small businessmen, and white-collar employees tended to oppose Maastricht. "Educated" France favored it. "Cosmopolitans" wanted European integration and "locals" did not (Habert 1992-93). The *petit oui* of 51 percent for Maastricht allowed the treaty to go forward but did little to reestablish European momentum. It also did nothing to rekindle the left's electoral fortunes. The center-right headed toward a huge victory in the 1993 legislative elections.[12]

The Single Market program and, to a greater degree, Maastricht's proposals for the EMU, were designed to reconfigure the policymaking environment in France and elsewhere in the EU. Both involved major pooling of sovereignty. The Single Market transformed important issues that had earlier been politically determined into market decisions. Once a genuine Single Market existed, national states would lose most of their individual capacities to regulate inter-EU trade. Moreover, as market actors restructured around the Single Market, emerging economic patterns would constrain these same states in new ways. The EMU was somewhat different. It would dilute sovereignty over monetary policy by removing the national government's ability to revalue national currencies, manipulate interest rates, and use deficit finance to stimulate growth.

EMU also would impinge indirectly upon other national prerogatives. Monetary adjustments to shocks and/or shifts in relative competitiveness would no longer be feasible. Labor costs (wages plus the "social wage") and industrial relations regulations would become adjustment mechanisms. Rather than dissolving national regulatory capacity into market flows, the EMU would delegate it to an independent European Central Bank. These changes would inevitably provoke political struggles. There would be tough dealing among EU member states about the powers, prerogatives, and procedures of the new monetary authority. And within potential EMU member states there would also be tough dealing about adaptation to the new EMU setting.

Maastricht, and Mitterrand's referendum, set both processes in motion for France. Maastricht's timetable for moving toward EMU projected three stages. The first was retroactive to the full liberty of capital movement in 1990.[13] The second, which began in 1994 (after member states all had made their central banks independent), established the European Monetary Institute (EMI) to pressure potential members toward meeting convergence criteria and to promote greater cooperation among central banks. Movement to the third stage would begin by identifying the eligible members who met the convergence criteria, at the earliest in 1996 or 1997, but more likely on 1 January 1999, based on the 1997 and 1998 budgets. It would proceed by locking eligible currencies and establishing the new European Central Bank (ECB) and the banking apparatus, the European System of Central Banks (ESCB). Then, after a transition period of three years, the single currency, eventually named the "euro," would replace national currencies.

The 1996-97 date was quickly ruled out by events. Difficulties in ratifiying Maastricht demonstrated that there was considerable public resistance to the new treaty, making it prudent to go slowly. Beyond this, the financial world and the business cycle created new problems. Beginning with the United Kingdom's Black Wednesday in September 1992, and continuing through summer 1993, there was a rage of speculation against EMS currencies, causing many devaluations and (usually temporary) exits from the EMS Exchange Rate Mechanism (ERM). This rolling process ended only when, with the French franc threatened, the structure of the ERM fluctuation bands was broadened. By this point, deep recession had settled in across most of the European Union, pushing unemployment levels in key member states to postwar highs. In this context, EU credibility dipped. The Single Market, promoted as an economic magic bullet, had cost jobs and created insecurity without stimulating new growth and job creation.

Setting January 1999 as the date when the EMU third stage would have to start, no matter how many member states fit the convergence profile, was a bargaining victory for the French during the very last stages of the Maastricht negotiation. Early in 1998 the account books of EU member states would be scrutinized to decide who satisfied the convergence criteria. This would make 1996 and 1997 very tough budget years for everyone, since, as of 1993, a few EU members, in particular, France and Germany, had a distance to go. France's performance on four of the five criteria—currency stability, interest rates, inflation level, and government debt—was within range. The real issue was getting a nearly 6-percent budget deficit down to 3 percent. To begin with, unemployment at Great Depression levels inevitably increased budgetary costs. Squeezing the budget would raise unemployment even more, lower consumption, increase pessimism, and make it more difficult to get out of recession. In effect, the Maastricht budget deficit criterion, seemingly plucked out of the air by German negotiators, made serious countercyclical macroeconomic policies impossible.

Chirac and Jospin

Mitterrand's mistaken referendum tactic on Maastricht had introduced a new logic into the relationship between European integration and French politics. It would be necessary to find ways of bringing Europe into the daily life of French politics instead of burying it. The search for such ways would be far from straightforward, however. If the EMU movement were not to collapse of its own accord, as some expected in the mid-1990s, French governments would be compelled to cut back severely to meet the convergence criteria. Given high unemployment and low growth, the French electorate would almost certainly desire these governments to create jobs and expand the economy. The old levers of the Keynesian "political business cycle" could, of course, no longer be used as electoral tools. Further, EMU meant that even very limited fine-tuning would be extremely difficult.

Chirac's Mistakes

In the short run, however, after the Maastricht referendum, every effort would be made to rebury the Europe issue in the interplay of coalitions that earlier had kept it in the background. This was inevitable because of the logic of the electoral cycle. Prominent politicians would do almost anything to prevent a split in their coalitions in the period leading up to the all-important 1995 presidential elections. According to this perspective, the 1993 legislative elections, which gave the center-right a huge parliamentary majority, handed all the cards to the neo-Gaullist leader Chirac. In 1995 Chirac, who had already lost two presidential elections in a row, had only one more chance to win. With bitter memories of cohabiting with Mitterrand after 1986 and then losing the 1988 presidential campaign, Chirac decided not to run for prime minister in 1995, but he wagered on making his "friend" Edouard Balladur premier, leaving him to deal with the dying president, while keeping himself "in reserve."

The problem with Chirac's gamble was that it tempted Balladur to become a presidential hopeful himself. Still, with a presidential election in the offing, the Balladur government had to be very careful to avoid initiatives that might lose votes for the center-right, whoever its candidate might turn out to be. This implied that actions to meet the Maastricht demands, in particular the 3-percent budget deficit criterion, would be postponed until after the 1995 poll and that, more broadly, the Europe issue would be removed from discussion as much as possible.[14] Balladur was an astute politician. The left, and in particular Pierre Bérégovoy, the last Socialist prime minister, had pursued stringent monetarism to tie the franc to the DM in anticipation of EMU. This created a space from which Balladur could benefit, while carrying on the same policies. Balladur thus did nothing to hurt France's EMU prospects, but neither did he do much to signal what measures would be necessary after 1995 to make EMU happen. His success, which ironically was enhanced by his elitist, aloof manner, lay in soothing the French between storms. The only European crisis that impinged on French domestic politics during his watch was the confrontational conclusion of the GATT Uruguay Round. Its central issue was the liberalization of European agriculture, for which French farmers had little enthusiasm. There were demonstrations and a lot of ill will, but controversy over the European Commission's earlier astute reform of the Common Agricultural Policies (CAP) took the edge away from the GATT flashpoint (Ross 1995). Moreover, the negotiators' final choice to agree to disagree over audiovisual trade provided French nationalists with the feeling of having "stood up to the Americans."

From the point of view of keeping the European body buried, the spring 1995 presidential election campaign came at a critical moment. Chirac faced his last chance of winning the job he had sought for most of his adult life. If the scandals and bungled policies of the last years of Mitterrand virtually guaranteed that the Socialists would lose, nothing guaranteed that Chirac would win after Balladur shot up in the opinion polls. Chirac had to find ways to cut Balladur down. Balladur presented a guarded, dignified version of how his Socialist predecessors had left France with 12-percent unemployment and growing problems of ghettoization and social exclusion. Chirac's strategy, cooked up by Séguin, centered on populist themes and promised to heal France's "social fracture" through job creation and economic growth (Gaffney and Milne 1997). Chirac's promises tapped real anxieties and desires. In order not to spoil that effect, he was carefully vague about France's fundamental commitment to European integration, in particular about the EMU.[15] This tactic was necessary, since for France to fulfill EMU criteria, austerity policies would have to be intensified and Chirac's pledges about job creation and growth could not be honored. On the other hand, if a Chirac presidency acted on the campaign's populist pledges, France would not meet the criteria and there could be no EMU at all. Pulling back from the EMU would mark a fundamental break with half a century of French advocacy of European integration. When questioned about the clashing ingredients in his political soup, candidate Chirac responded that political will could overcome all obstacles.

Chirac's first months were marked mainly by a buccaneering Gaullist style in foreign policy.[16] While the new president strutted the world stage, his prime minister, Alain Juppé, stayed home to mind the store. Juppé made few moves initially to redeem Chirac's campaign pledges; indeed, he did very little at all except to muddle along according to the lines set by Balladur.[17] Without a rapid policy shift, the EMU would be placed in jeopardy. The way in which Juppé engineered the shift was almost surreal. At the end of October 1995, the *Plan Juppé* was announced. Its biggest item was the introduction of a .5-percent addition to income tax for thirteen years to pay off the accumulated Social Security debt (which the government estimated at $60 billion). The Juppé Plan aimed primarily to raise taxes to make Social Security solvent, and to reduce France's broader budget deficits and longer term debt. It also proposed many more controversial changes, the first being a significant alteration in public-sector pension arrangements, requiring everyone, including civil servants, to contribute a full forty years to pensions before retiring. Taxes would also be imposed on family allowances, with exceptions for those in the poorest economic conditions. There would also be changes in, and a certain broadening of, the "generalized social contribution" (CSG), a general tax introduced by the Socialists in 1991 to cut Social Security deficits. Juppé's plan included cost-controlling changes to existing health-care programs plus increased user fees. Paris would replace local government in running hospitals, which was an indication that hospitals would be shut down. Finally, direct appointments by "social partners" (unions and other representative organizations) would replace long-standing parity procedures for workers to elect administrators to Social Security *caisses* (pay boards). Parliament, rather than the paritary Social Security bodies themselves, would get final say on levels of Social Security spending—in effect ending "paritarism" in Social Security administration.

The plan thus contained plenty to upset different groups and coax them toward an alliance for protest, perhaps to join the students who were already marching. The prime minister's personal approach to politics proved very helpful in forging such an alliance, however. Juppé suffered from the chronic professional malady of France's elite technocrats, believing that he was wise enough to judge what was best for the French and that they themselves should recognize this. His authoritarian approach and inept plans greatly assisted French unions—themselves often inept and always divided—in welding a coalition of different groups of angry workers and feuding union organizations into one of the most significant strikes in recent French history.[18] It began in mid-November 1995 when civil servants in Paris called a "day of action" against the plan. Then Paris transport and railroad workers went on strike. It took five weeks, nearly until Christmas, to get things back in order. The strike probably never deserved the rejoicing that greeted it from the left—"the first great movement against globalization"—but it was a shock to the Chirac presidency.[19] To quote *The Economist* (9 December 1995, 11), "strikers by the millions, riots in the street; the *évènements* in France . . . make the country look like a banana republic in which an isolated government is battling to impose IMF austerity on a hostile population."

The strike's cost was great. Juppé had projected reducing the Social Security deficit from $13 billion to $3.2 billion in 1996 and eliminating it altogether in 1997, but the 1996 deficit turned out to be about $10 billion, with projections of $7 billion for 1997. The price of the prime minister's clumsiness also included delaying French progress toward meeting the EMU convergence criteria. Indeed, from the EMU point of view, the Chirac administration achieved little in its first months other than making the situation worse than it had been under Mitterrand. In political terms Chirac, in trying to be all things to everyone and projecting ersatz Gaullist voluntarism, was exposed for his false promises. It was obvious that Chirac's pledge "to create 700,000 new jobs by the end of 1996" was a mirage. Juppé had demonstrated that writing memos and plans better than anyone else was not enough if one was politically clueless. Both paid dearly. Chirac's and particularly Juppé's opinion poll ratings dropped precipitously: by the end of 1996 the prime minister was the most unpopular in the history of modern opinion polls.[20]

Chirac had tried to handle the new dimensions of European integration by avoiding its issues rather than confronting them. His approach made things worse and wasted precious time. Unemployment rose to unprecedented levels: 12.8 percent by early 1997. Economic growth was even slower than what had been projected (0.9 percent as opposed to 2.2 percent in the first quarter of 1996, partly because of the strikes). Under such circumstances the budget deficit still had to be reduced from 5 percent of the GDP in 1995 to 3 percent by the end of 1997. Therefore it became evident that growth and job creation would have to be drastically curtailed if France were to reach the Maastricht goal, and the countercyclical policies Chirac had brandished in his campaign were out of the question. Indeed, there were precious few ways to save money other than new cutbacks and job losses in public services and public employment.

There were other reasons for the Chirac team to worry. European integration was forcing deregulation and greater competition in France's unusually large public sector. Europe also obliged France to deregulate and perhaps even to privatize public utilities such as telecommunications, electricity, gas, and postal service, which raised hackles among defenders of the *services publiques.* The EU was not the only external agent at work. The end of the Cold War had left France with a bloated defense sector. In the new security setting, where arms sales depended more on competitiveness than on financial backing from governments, France had to act urgently, in particular because the Americans were ahead in reconfiguring their own defense sector. French arsenals had to be rationalized quickly, for example, which put many more jobs on the block. Large nationalized French defense contractors, such as Thomson, had to be privatized, again putting jobs at risk.[21]

The EMU made Juppé's 1997 budget a stern affair. Public spending levels were frozen at 1995 levels, which meant an actual 1-percent budget cut. Civil service and public-sector jobs were eliminated. Creative accounting found money hidden in the Social Security system, and the government also charged off a one-time windfall of $8 billion from the state's takeover of some pension funds of France Télécom, which was to be privatized—another triumph of creative accounting that lowered the deficit by 0.5 percent.[22] Juppé also pledged to continue Social Security reform, announcing that certain benefits henceforth would be taxable, in particular subsidies for employment. The final item was a promise to lower taxes in 1997, which, in the context of the EMU, would have made the budget deficit problems worse. The budget made it clear that the Chirac presidency had run out of smoke and mirrors. If a creative "third way" or "other politics" existed between retreating from European commitments and experiencing EMU as a forced march toward compulsive monetarism, lowered growth, and higher unemployment, the Chirac presidency did not know what it was.[23]

On the other hand, Chirac's emergence from the demagogy of his campaign to embrace the EMU was a pleasant surprise for other EU member states, in particular the Germans. Only close Franco-German collaboration would make the EMU possible, and there remained significant disagreements between the two countries. The biggest issue was faced at the December 1996 Dublin European Council, as part of the Maastricht II Intergovernmental Conference deliberations (which would eventually produce the Amsterdam Treaty in 1997). The French wanted to make space for an "economic government" to gain influence over German monetary policy. The Germans wanted to lock EMU members into restrictive monetary policies reflecting German goals (which would amount, in effect, to a German-dominated "economic government").[24] Theo Waigel, the German finance minister, proposed a new "growth and stability pact," which would include automatic financial sanctions on EMU members failing to keep budget deficits below 3 percent.[25] There would be provisions in the rules for economic emergencies and recessions, but the pact's logic was something akin to a "balanced budget amendment," and it would dictate austerity to the French and others for years to come. Kohl and Chirac had failed to agree on the issues twice prior to the Dublin summit, but very tough negotiations there reached a deal. The result, though not quite as austere as the Germans had wanted, was much more demanding than almost anyone else desired. Chirac thus failed as much diplomatically as he had domestically.

What Chirac really believed would happen after his election is difficult to know. He was undoubtedly not prepared to confront the rest of the Maastricht signatories with policies that would have made the EMU impossible. But he may have thought that the Germans could be persuaded to give in somewhat on the EMU convergence criteria so that a few of his campaign pledges of job creation and growth could be enacted. On the other hand, he may have concluded that winning was all, and that French voters would forget his promises after election day. In any event, Chirac's maneuvering resurrected the Europe issue, which, however, could no longer be perceived as abstract and distant. Henceforth it would be a pervasive day-to-day constraint on French politics. This meant that the French had to be persuaded that they could live with it and that their politicians could deal with it.

Jospin's Turn

Jacques Chirac was caught. The year before the EMU decision point in 1998 had to involve brutal budgetary compression. But it was also a year in which Chirac needed to prepare for the parliamentary elections to be held by springtime 1998. With an abysmally unpopular government that could look forward to accomplishing little other than becoming even less popular, the outlook was bleak. Barring miracles, the 1998 elections would eliminate most, if not all, of the huge center-right majority won in 1993. This was so obvious that some of Chirac's majority had already begun the unruly behavior that politicians adopt when their seats are threatened, second-guessing and criticizing the government from all directions. In the midst of this cacophony, a queue was forming to succeed Juppé, whose ministerial career was presumed finished.

Chirac knew that something dramatic needed to be done. He decided that his immediate choice was either to name a new prime minister or to call new elections (using Article 12 of the Constitution) before they were officially due. The first option was the most conventional. The second, which Juppé and Chirac's chief advisor Dominique de Villepin urged, and which Chirac chose in late April 1997, was riskier. The electorate, already in a foul mood, might interpret a snap election call as more of Chirac's cynicism. Moreover, it was certain to receive Chirac's announcement for a new mandate for "reform" as an early warning that even greater austerity was on the way.

What did Chirac think he might win? Possibly more order in his own camp. A campaign would oblige the majority to unite to retain governmental power. The center-right was bound to lose a considerable number of seats, and if it won a new majority, this would tighten up parliamentary discipline. Next, calling a snap election would allow a new government to prepare for the EMU without having the shadow of elections over its head. Finally, and perhaps most significantly, in the spring of 1997 the opinion polls, strongly against Chirac and Juppé for months, began to shift slightly. This was important because Chirac saw that the Socialist leader, Lionel Jospin, whose party had its own internal divisions, was saying little or nothing. The president interpreted this to mean that the left was unprepared to fight an election, especially one with an unusually short campaign.

The polls quickly settled into a dead heat between right and left, making Chirac's gamble look more dangerous by the day. His tactic of allowing Juppé to lead the campaign, thus giving the impression that the unpopular prime minister would be reappointed were the majority to be reelected, appeared plainly suicidal. The EMU was central in what followed. Jospin understood the people's depth of frustration, in particular about Europe, much better than Chirac did, and he knew that voters had to be given some reassurance. It made tactical sense for him, then, to advocate "softening" the approach to the EMU to give France more budgetary space. This might allow for the creation of 700,000 new jobs, almost exactly what Chirac had promised in 1995. Jospin also pledged to reduce the workweek to thirty-five hours and to stop privatization, promises that made it easier to consolidate working relationships with the Communists and the Greens, with whom the PS formed electoral alliances. These pledges also quite shrewdly provided incentives for National Front voters to vote left in the second round. In all, however, Jospin's campaign, promising new efforts against unemployment and what sounded like moderate Keynesian stimulation of the French economy, sounded remarkably like that of candidate Chirac in 1995.

The election results were shocking, particularly for the president (Perrineau 1997a; Jaffré 1997a), who had repeatedly intervened in the campaign to promote his side, and this made it all the more evident that he himself would be targeted and lose credibility if the center-right collapsed. After a disastrous first round, Chirac even agreed to oust his friend Juppé, and he rather pathetically appointed Séguin and Madelin to run the last week of the campaign, which was viewed as yet another transparently cynical Chiraqian gesture.[26]

In all, the moderate right lost over 2 million votes from its 1993 high, down to 36.1 percent of those voting (from 44.1 percent in 1993), its worst numbers in the history of the Fifth Republic. If one compares the 1995 presidential results with the 1997 results, Chirac lost more than 4 million votes. The Socialists did much better in the first round than they had done in 1993—25.7 percent vs. 19 percent—but nowhere near as well as they had done in the 1980s. The *Front National* won 14.9 percent, its best score ever in a legislative election. Indeed, the ratio of RPR-UDF votes (i.e., excluding independent and nonaffiliated candidates of the center-right) to those of the FN was 51 percent, by far the highest ever.[27] What the electorate did, therefore, was to send the Chirac team and majority packing without giving a majority to the Socialists. Jospin became the first Socialist prime minister of cohabitation through a "left pluralist" alliance with the Communists and the Greens (Le Gall 1997; Ponceryri 1997).[28]

Europe posed by far the biggest challenge to Jospin, as it had to Chirac and Juppé. EMU was closing in and bringing with it strong new constraints on French policy capacities. The new prime minister could reflect upon a variety of past approaches. Europe's forward movement had initially been kept distant from domestic French politics by the play of coalitions and institutions. For a decade Mitterrand had proceeded by stealth, in the process stoking fires of anxiety that he himself had allowed to burn fiercely hot in 1992. Balladur had returned briefly to stealth after 1993, mainly to prepare for the presidential elections. Chirac had tried to finesse the issue in ways that were either naive or cynical, and Juppé had miscommunicated it. But by 1997, if there were to be an EMU—and most of the French elite was committed to it—there seemed no way around convincing the French to accept it. This meant a strategy that would let the EMU happen and convince the French who were wary of it that it would not turn out to their detriment. Long-standing cleavages among the French, which did not follow partisan lines, made this complicated. Segments of public opinion on both right and left favored Europe while others feared its consequences. In rough terms, the 1997 polls once again drew the line between "cosmopolitans and locals."[29]

The new prime minister's first months showed that he had reflected on his predecessors' mistakes. Jospin's strategy had both diplomatic and domestic dimensions, as theirs had. But the specific contents of his strategy were quite different. His diplomatic manner was much less regal and opaque. It was now essential to persuade the French that EMU was a negotiable process that France could influence over time, and not simply a constraint imposed from outside. On the domestic side it was important to show that in EMU and Europe there were margins of maneuver and, more important, real space for adjustment and for distributing costs and benefits.

Chirac and Juppé had left Jospin an extremely unhappy setting for his left government. Moreover, many on the left regarded the EMU as a test of Jospin's reformism. "Change the future," the Socialist election program exhorted, putting "changing Europe" high on its list of priorities.

> A Euro, yes, but for what? The answer to this question will determine the future of Europe and France. . . . Faithful to all of the history of building Europe, we are opposed to its liberal deviation. We want a political and not a technical vision for Europe. We want a dynamic approach to Europe, not one of accounting. . . . For Socialists, making the Euro succeed involves building a Europe which is turned towards growth, employment and democracy (Parti Socialiste 1997, part III, author's translation).

In campaigning, Jospin used strong rhetoric about working toward an EMU that would serve the interests of "people rather than bankers." But simple renunciation, which some on the left desired, was unrealistic, and not only, or even mainly, because French Socialists had been the major architects of the EMU. Without the EMU, France's situation would become even worse. Shorter-term perturbations on financial markets could damage already hurting EU economies, that of the French included. More important, EU morale could collapse, setting the entire project of European integration back for years. Renunciation of the EMU could trigger a set of disasters, even the smallest of which could be more costly than going ahead with the EMU (see Aaronovitch and Grahl 1997, for the case).

Jospin's choice—made under severe pressure at the Amsterdam EU summit in June after but two weeks in power—was to accept the EMU timetable. His choice came with strong critical words, however. France wanted an "economic government" to give economic policy guidelines to the new Central Bank in its monetary policy duties. It also wanted revision of the Dublin "stabilility and growth pact," such that the pact would allow explicit EMU commitments to growth and employment and the creation of a "European growth fund," following the recommendations of a European Commission White Paper from 1993 (EU 1993). Jospin and his team were stared down in Amsterdam, however. This particular European Council was a bad occasion to force a showdown. EU members were desperately trying to conclude a difficult Intergovernmental Conference (leading to the Amsterdam Treaty), and what Jospin and Dominique Strauss-Kahn, his finance minister, said that they wanted to do would have caused serious trouble for agreement on treaty changes. Moreover, the complexities of cohabitation hindered the effort, for President Chirac could not be persuaded to be as helpful as Jospin might have hoped.

Jospin thus "changed his Europe" (Mauduit 1997b) by accepting the arrangements for the EMU that he had castigated in his campaign. But at the same time he was also able to influence the future course of Europe.[30] The new government's agitation ensured that the Amsterdam Treaty contained a new clause on employment policy.[31] Employment thus became a new "priority" on the EU agenda. In one paragraph of the preamble to follow the paragraph on the EMU, the union committed itself to "promote economic and social progress and a high level of employment"(EU 1997a, 7). A new Article 109 added that member states and the Community should work toward a "common strategy for employment and particularly for promoting a skilled, trained and adaptable workforce and labour markets responsive to economic change," and that they should regard promoting employment "as a matter of common concern and shall coordinate their action" (p. 33).[32] The new clauses also allowed "measures to incite" employment and established an official "Committee for Employment" modeled on the EU Monetary Committee.

These changes to treaty wording were significant, even after being watered down by the Germans and discounted for their relative lack of compulsion. In the short run they gave new notice to citizens, particularly French citizens, that the

EU might not be a completely neoliberal affair. In the words of another amendment, the union should be "determined to promote economic and social progress . . . and to implement policies ensuring that advances in economic integration are accompanied by parallel progress in other fields" (EU 1997a, 7). The medium-term consequences were difficult to predict, given the powerful liberal valence of EMU, but the inclusion of words on employment in the EU treaty signified a more serious emphasis on employment policy.[33]

The Amsterdam summit also promised an extraordinary European Council in November 1997 to discuss employment policy. It decided that the treaty's new "employment guideline" procedure should go into effect immediately, even before its ratification. It also recognized the need for a "coordinated macroeconomic policy" (a soft bow to the French desire for "economic government"), plus a more systematic harnessing of various community instruments to help employment growth. Moreover, the summit approved the use of a new 10 billion *ecu* loan from the European Investment Bank to promote targeted job creation, a move that the European Council had systematically refused earlier (EU 1993; 1997b). The "Jobs Summit" did not produce spectacular results, but it did send signals that the EU recognized the employment problem in more pressing ways than it had earlier. Behind this was a deeper message. Perhaps the EU could be reconsidering the desirability of a serious "social Europe."

In terms of integrating the EMU into French politics, Jospin's first months of diplomatic effort were a work in progress. He hoped to communicate that the EMU was an interactive process, rather than a fixed object, that could be influenced by resolute French action.[34] His efforts also sent the message that there was a left position, as well as the French position, to be defended within the EMU. How convincing such messages will turn out to be remains to be seen. In fact, the full implications of the EMU are not yet clear to anyone. The worst scenario, from the French point of view, is that a central bankers' EMU, in the absence of employment and social protection, will lead to a situation in which the cost of change in the relative competitiveness within the EU's new single currency zone must be borne by wage earners and welfare states. Regions (including nations) whose wage costs are too high will have no choice but to cut them. Likewise, those nations whose social wages are set too high to meet budgetary constraints will have to make large cuts as well. The potential for serious social and political problems in worst-case scenarios should be evident. Jospin's wisdom has been to recognize that in such a context important matters must be, first of all, genuinely negotiable, and second, visibly so to citizens.

Jospin's diplomatic choices on Europe and the EMU placed the domestic policies of his government under the same constraints that had limited its predecessors. Moreover, he had made campaign promises that were similar to theirs. The biggest problem was the Maastricht 3-percent budget deficit target.[35] The Juppé government had reached only 3.7-3.8 percent when it was forced to vacate the premises. Jospin had to find ways to apply more pressure. The French were tired of being squeezed, however, and had concluded that squeezing, unprecedented unemployment, and Europe were connected. In short, they had caught on to Mitterrand's astute trick of "exogenizing" reforms to a European level that the experts believed the French needed but would otherwise refuse. Jospin's initial problem was how to reduce the deficit without betraying his promises. The larger challenge was to carry out domestic policies within the EMU context such that the French would understand what was happening and why it might make sense.

The government's first steps involved job creation. The PS had pledged to create 700,000 jobs over five years, particularly for young adults under the age of twenty-six (one in four of whom were unemployed). This pledge was redeemed, in part, in late summer 1997. There have been a succession of youth employment programs in France over recent decades, mainly subsidized hiring in the public and private sectors. Employment Minister Martine Aubry's plan was different, however. It proposed hiring for "jobs of a third type" to "facilitate the progressive emergence of a new model of growth and development." These jobs, subsidized to 80 percent of cost under the budget, would employ younger people at minimum wage to accomplish tasks that, according to the program's line, were socially needed but were not ordinarily performed by either the private or public sectors.[36] Hiring for these jobs could only be done by local government and nonprofit associations (not by private-sector employers or the national government). Finally, those hired would receive five-year nonrenewable contracts.

The government's insistence upon targeted and decentralized hiring was meant, in part, to stimulate reflection, capacity, and flexibility in local government and nonprofit associations. An additional purpose was to nourish the development of "civil society," in response both to an obvious need for more substance in decentralization and to repeated claims by parts of the left that France lacked sufficient local solidarity and democratization (Aubry 1997). The five-year limited contracts, which prompted union anxieties about precedents that could undermine the labor code, fit well into contemporary notions of struggling against "social exclusion." Giving young people meaningful employment with a future, plus a chance to make a real contribution, could lessen the risk of alienating much of an entire generation. The hope was that five years would be enough time to socialize young people to labor-force participation and enable them to find new work at the end of that time.

There were many "ifs." The first was obvious. Did the novel notion of "jobs of a third type" make sense, and in particular was there a genuine demand for them? If they turned out to be public sector "make-work," as had so many of the jobs from earlier youth unemployment programs, the government would fall short of its purpose. The other major "if" was what might happen to participants at the end of their five years. Would they find jobs with dignity on the market? Aubry's proposals were experimental, therefore, but underlying them was some tough logic. The government knew that in the short run, even if French growth were to increase more than anyone expected, there would not be enough new employment to make much difference for young people. Whatever else it might be, the Aubry plan was an add-on to anything the market could conceivably do. The government thus was sending another and deeper message: something could be done about a chronic problem such as youth unemployment, despite Europe, only if a collective commitment to do so were made.

The next initiative, also closely associated with Martine Aubry, was the October 1997 national conference on work-sharing (officially on "employment and wages"). The government's goal was to persuade France's "social partners" to agree to reduce the legal workweek from thirty-nine to thirty-five hours by the year 2000 and to transform this shorter workweek into more jobs. Unions, it hoped, would be willing to bargain on work time "flexibilization" (in particular on an "annualization" of hours). Employers might then accept the shorter workweek and pledge to create new jobs.[37] The "partners" would be prodded together toward such goals by government good will, negotiating tenacity, and incentives such as tax breaks, job-creation subsidies, increased taxation on overtime, and a *loi cadre* (outline law) fixing a date for concluding branch and firm negotiation.[38] Once again the government's intention was to stimulate as much decentralized negotiation as possible, even though it started with a splashy national event and insisted on national legal compulsion to promote such bargaining.

The conference turned out to be difficult. Getting labor and its market adversaries to behave like "social partners"—the vocabulary was itself interesting—had often been a pious, but rarely realized, hope. French employers and French unions are weakly organized and divided. Whether French unions would behave intelligently was a huge question, for example. France has the lowest level of union membership of any major capitalist society. Despite this, each confederation behaved as if its most important job was to steal an advantage over the others, even if they all suffered in consequence. At the October event, however, the unions turned out not to be the problem, despite considerable preliminary jockeying among them for position.[39] It was the employers who did not want to play.

French employers, like their colleagues elsewhere, have had the upper hand in recent times. Getting them to cooperate, and persuading them to make genuine promises to create jobs, was the government's largest problem. French employers' recent strategy has been to shed labor to increase productivity with no new hiring, hence helping to create much of the new French unemployment. Other things being equal, cutting four hours off the workweek was likely to be used in the same way if the government could not bind the bosses to do otherwise. This would be particularly true if pay were not reduced to levels more or less commensurate with the reduction in hours. The government's proposal caused divisions in the CNPF to explode. Jean Gandois, CNPF president (a friend and former boss of Martine Aubry), tried to bargain for employer cooperation in exchange for government rejection of a *loi cadre* and time limits.[40] The government ultimately refused. Gandois was forced to resign, leaving the door open, as he himself noted, to "the killers."

The thirty-five-hour story is far from over, however. It is not clear whether the union front will hold when it comes to negotiating at the branch and firm level about adjusting salaries downward, if only briefly, in exchange for shortening the workweek.[41] Major union players such as the CGT and FO are balking. Finally, many employers may simply refuse to cooperate, which could lead to shows of force. The new president of the CNPF, Ernest Seilliere, announced that he intended to use the thirty-five-hour issue to "destabilize" the government, while Chirac himself, coming out of postelection shellshock, denounced the plan. Moreover, no one knows whether moving to thirty-five hours would create jobs at all.

Once having backed away from an immediate confrontation with those negotiating the EMU, Jospin's biggest policy problem became meeting the 3-percent EMU deficit criterion. The first decision he made was that roughly two-thirds of the total projected deficit reduction in 1997 and 1998 would come from raising taxes (with the other third coming from budget cuts, much from the defense budget). Raising taxes remains something that French governments, whether right or left, can still do, as Alain Juppé had demonstrated. What distinguished the Jospin tax raises was that their brunt fell on business. Corporate tax rates were "temporarily" boosted by 5 percent, with the biggest hits taken by the biggest companies. This came at a moment when corporate profits were quite high and in an international setting in which French companies are taxed slightly less than many others.

This set a pattern: the new budget would be strongly redistributive. Finance Minister Strauss-Kahn described the philosophy underlying it as a quest for "new equilibria." The first such equilibrium involved shifting tax burdens from wage earners to capital income. This move was based on the principle that the better-off should assume more of the EMU burden—50 percent of new revenue—than those less well-off. The second new equilibrium was established between indirect and direct taxation. This involved shifting the bulk of health care contributions tied to employment (payroll taxes amounting to 5.5 percent of gross wages) onto the Contribution Sociale Géneralisée (CSG), which everyone paid at tax time. Here the principle was that, in the interest of competitiveness, labor should be made cheaper to employers, and the taxpayer should help bring this about. Another, shorter-term goal for both adjustments was to stimulate consumption by putting more take-home pay into wage earners' hands. The budget also was designed to shut down tax loopholes for the better-off (Strauss-Kahn 1997). Finally, the early outline of tax reforms for a post-EMU setting underlay many of these changes. Payroll taxes penalized job creation because they provided a disincentive for employers to hire new workers and raised the cost of employment. Shifting the burden toward general taxation would redistribute the costs of social services away from the employment contract.[42]

Jospin's approach has been consistently accused of being "old fashioned Socialist"—as opposed to Blair's new liberal New Labour, for example—and, very recently, it was debunked for its alleged "doctrine of global glut" (Krugman 1997). In light of these criticisms, the broader conceptual context of Jospin's policies merits consideration. Jospin pledged to promote new relationships between state and market, thus announcing his acceptance of the market, of course. But what kind of role did he envision for the state? The guiding concept was redistribution—"solidarity." The state's job was primarily to nourish and stimulate creation of those types of solidarity that would allow France to function in new surroundings, particularly in the new Europe. Despite market constraints, different French interest groups had responsibilities to, and for, one another. Those who had steady work should contribute to providing work and resources to those who had none. Wage earners and employers should work toward greater flexibility for the general success of the French economy. The better-off should assume more of the fiscal burden than those who were less well-off. Taxpayers in general should help maintain universal social services in order to give wage earners more take-home pay and lower the cost of employing labor. The accusation of left archaism seemed misplaced, therefore, except for those who believed that the market should make all essential decisions and the state should wither away. Despite some nostalgia, to be expected from a left that only very recently had ceased citing Marx in public, slogans such as "nationalize and plan," "breaking with capitalism," and "changing life," along with the rest of the old left package, were mostly gone. Moreover, the new concept of solidarity was not based on the idea of class. Indeed, "class" is not part of the current vocabulary at all.

Despite having one of the highest percentages of *Énarques* in the history of the Fifth Republic, the Jospin team has been aware of the dangers in traditional French statism. The state should not decree solidarity, it has repeatedly announced. Instead it should stimulate decentralized solidarity movements and promote discussion, debate, and, eventually, agreement among different groups. The state should exhort "social partners" to be responsible. French "civil society" should be moved toward decentralization. Citizens, through associations and local networks, should take more responsibility for the decisions that count most to them. Solidarity is not a euphemism for what the hard-liners of the old French left used to call "class collaboration," with all that this term connoted in terms of social warfare. Instead, it refers to a national moral community composed of individuals belonging to different groups. Group interests vary and often conflict. Despite this, groups can and should sort out such differences in the broader interests of the community. All of this recognizes France's problem of group affiliation. The "space" between public and private, which one might call civil society or community, is insufficiently occupied in France, partly because Jacobin political culture has discouraged it. Thus leftist governments must make special efforts to nourish it.

In this Jospinist vision, the market is acknowledged as one important way among others of making distributive decisions. Such recognition does not lead to liberal antistatism, however. There remains a significant public sphere where the state's role is important. Some of what the state must do is classical—providing "public services," security, order, and social services. Beyond this, however, the state's job is not to decree, but rather to stimulate, organize, and bring together others to sustain the national moral community.[43]

It is too early to tell whether this ideological context will become permanent for the left. Given that the pluralist contentiousness of the French left draws upon a veritable museum of left ideas whose origins range from the fifteenth to the twenty-first century, one never knows for sure what will emerge. Its complex breaking of ranks around the significant movement of the unemployed in early 1988, which was the Mitterrand government's first really difficult moment, may be a sign. But if the Jospin experiment turns out to be more than a brief interlude, and its early success supported this possibility, the old ideas will be replaced by a redistributive and technocratic communitarianism. Far from being archaic or a retreat from contemporary reality, these new ideas, albeit very French, would bring the French left closer to many of its European counterparts. The degree to which the French ideological shift has been tied to the unfolding of European integration is, however, distinctive.

Toward a Europeanized Polity in France?

The Jospin government achieved high levels of popularity in its first months, indicating that its policies, ideas, and personnel—particularly Jospin himself—responded to the French public's expectations. This is very important because the left did not win a resounding vote of confidence in the 1997 elections and its popularity has had to be earned. Short-term success does not permit bold conclusions, however, as the movement of the unemployed underlined. Jospin's policies may fail, his ideas may appear naive, and the government's popularity may prove evanescent. Time will tell.

The issues that should concern us most, however, are neither the future of the French left nor that of the Jospin government. What matters is that the "Jospin experiment" represents the first concerted effort, in France at least, to incorporate Euro-level processes, via the coming of the EMU, into the day-to-day life of French democratic politics. European integration has always moved forward on two levels: "international relations" and "national politics." In most, if not all, EU member states until very recently, the first level of negotiation, with the secrecy and regal trappings of "high politics" conducted by heads of state and government, has worked to insulate the second from serious confrontation with the profound implications of change. This situation became politically untenable in the late 1990s, however. Lionel Jospin and his team thus have tried to redefine the French approach and to engage the French much more deeply in unfolding processes.

At the transnational level, the Jospin government has moved to renegotiate parts of the EMU bargain with its EU counterparts. It has not achieved its stated goals, but it has had successes. Given the political situation of 1997 (particularly the domestic situation in Germany) it was unlikely that a spectacular institutional breakthrough toward an "economic government" to frame the EMU would occur. It was also unrealistic to expect any major moves toward a new, highly targeted, neo-Keynesianism (best argued in Fitoussi 1995 and, in different ways, Muet 1997). The nature of the EMU process is long-term. Negotiations about its ultimate nature and shape will continue for years, and there already is considerable evidence that this process will include the kind of institution building favored by Jospin and his government, but it will be incremental.[44] The Jospin team thus must pursue its diplomatic mission vigorously for the rest of its time in office in order to achieve lasting success. Equally important, however, the new administration has begun to make the French people aware of the efforts that are underway. At the national level, the Jospin government has sought to define and implement policies that redistribute the EMU's costs and benefits across the population. Such activities, too, will need to continue as the EMU becomes ever more real. Once again, public knowledge of the government's efforts and the logic behind them is as important as their results. The experiment's content matters less than its general nature. What is at stake in the long term is whether European-level politics can be articulated more adequately with the various dimensions of French political life.

The relative quiescence in France during the earlier years of European integration masked real and continuing differences of opinion among parties, and presumably, voters. From its beginning, the new Europe was a controversial issue in France. It was consistently masked, however, by the workings of multipartisan coalitions and the constitutional settings that fostered them. In addition, during this earlier period and continuing into the 1980s, the issue of Europe had no marked impact on the day-to-day lives of the French, with the exception of particular groups, such as farmers. Moreover, the institutional processes that came to be called the EU's "democratic deficit" helped immeasurably in masking any impact that did occur.

In contrast, the most recent period of integration, which began in 1985 with the declaration of the Single Market Program and continues with the EMU being put into place, has greatly changed the situation. The Single Market and the EMU have brought Euro-level regulatory mechanisms into the daily lives of virtually everyone in the EU, including the French. Matters such as employment, regional competitiveness, taxation levels, international trade policies, what national governments can or cannot do, the levels and nature of social protection programs, the shape of industrial relations, and even the nature of member states' culture are all profoundly touched, even when they are not primarily shaped, by what "Europe" does.

Were "Europe" to continue to affect people's daily lives without their greater active understanding and participation in European processes, the situation might become dangerous. European politics would become less democratic as member state governments lost the capacity to respond effectively to citizen needs; this is the "democratic deficit" nightmare that continues to haunt European integration (see Weil 1997 for a discussion). One extreme outcome of this could be EU citizens taking to the streets to protest the effects of a Europe over which they have no control, perhaps even to the point at which nations become unstable.

This chapter tracks the timid beginnings of an answer in France. Despite the change in French-European relations after Maastricht, and despite the 1992 referendum, French governments did not really begin confronting the problem of Europe seriously until 1997. The 1995 presidential elections led those in power to rebury the Europe issue, despite the urgency of preparing the EMU. The Chirac presidential campaign worsened things by promising to make the consequences of the EMU disappear. The Jospin government has proceeded differently, articulating a two-level strategy for confronting the EMU and European problems and, perhaps for the first time, helping citizens to connect with European changes.

On the diplomatic level, Jospin thus far has carried on a persistent and public struggle with the European Council and on other European occasions to bargain about dimensions of the EMU that some French citizens feel are prejudicial; quite as important, he has been seen by these citizens to be doing so. French presidents, and sometimes prime ministers, consistently have engaged in European-level politics in the past. More often than not, however, they have acted in quasi-secret, hiding behind the opacity of European institutions and the discretion allowed executives in foreign affairs. Jospin's approach has been distinctive in that he has connected domestic concerns with European-level decisions in a more open way, and thereby communicated to the French that European arrangements are negotiable and not immutable *faits accomplis.* The domestic arm of Jospin's strategy has opened up discussion about different ways the costs and benefits of European constraints might be distributed. The particular content of Jospin's policy goals are less important than is the prospect that his general strategy could set a precedent for new ways of integrating European matters into French political life. It would not be difficult to conceive of other governments following these general strategic lines, even with very different policy agendas. If they do, then important steps will have been taken to rectify the "democratic deficit."

A final remark is in order. Specialists in European political development argue endlessly between "functionalist" and "intergovernmentalist" explanations. The process discussed here resembles neither but partakes of both. The French outcome—if it turns out to be durable—does appear "functional" at a stage of European development when extensive transfers of sovereignty to the market and to Euro-instances of power risk substantially diluting national democratic processes. Jospin has acted to integrate French democracy and European-level changes. Such a view of "functionalism" is much too simple, however. Virtually all the major decisions about Europe that have led to the present situation were taken without the French people having much real control over them. The 1992 referendum brought matters to the fore abruptly, but for domestic political reasons. That it exposed deep and long-standing public differences over Europe was an unintended consequence. Those in power after the referendum then very quickly tried to sweep this consequence under the political rug: Balladur by soporific inactivity, and the ill-starred duo of Chirac and Juppé by smoke and mirrors. It was only Chirac's profound mistake in calling a snap election in 1997 that created the political space for a new strategy. Functionalism, if that is what it is, thus has worked in strange and indirect ways. "Intergovernmentalism" is quite as tenuous. If successive political leaders have sought to impose French preferences upon Europe, and in the 1990s have usually fallen short of real success, their definitions of French preferences have changed quickly. Only with Jospin have the important democratic determinants of these preferences been introduced. Pursuing this debate, however, is another matter.

Chapter 5

Why Did the Right Lose?

Gérard Grunberg

The defeat of the right in the legislative elections of 1997 constituted one of the most surprising political events in the history of France's Fifth Republic. For the first time since 1958, the dissolution of the National Assembly was decided by the president of the republic, at a time when he had the advantage of an overwhelming parliamentary majority and when the country was not being rocked by any political crisis. For the first time, a dissolution was the occasion of the president's political defeat, a defeat that was all the more surprising because three years earlier, the Socialists—who had been in power between 1981 and 1986 and then again between 1988 and 1993—had suffered an even bigger defeat in the European elections than they had in their electoral disaster during the legislative elections of 1993. The Socialist Party had seemed nearly dead as an opposing force. So how can one explain the defeat of the right in 1997?

First of all, there is a paradox. When President Chirac announced the dissolution of the National Assembly on 21 April 1997, the majority of political observers and poll-takers foresaw an easy victory for his party. During his traditional address on 14 July 1997, however, six weeks after the left's victory, the president of the republic declared that even if the elections had taken place at their normal time (in the spring of 1998), the right would have lost. Was this simply Jacques Chirac's attempt to justify an unfortunate decision, or did his declaration truly translate the mindset of those still in control of the majority the night before the dissolution? Was the defeat of the right really inevitable in 1998? There is no certain response to this question, and it is not our intention here to engage in political fiction. The very scenario of dissolution and political conjecture from 21 April to the second round of political elections on 1 June may have furnished numerous elements that explain the defeat of the right. Even if this is the case, however, we must also examine the reasons for the defeat that emerged in the period preceding the dissolution.

The Situation of the Right since the Referendum of 1992

Since the end of the 1960s, the French right has been divided into two political organizations that are both allies and rivals: the Rally for the Republic (RPR), or Gaullist party, which is the most powerful; and the Union for French Democracy (UDF), which consolidates non-Gaullist, moderate, Christian-democrat, and radical sentiment. In the first round of each presidential election since 1981, the RPR candidate Jacques Chirac successively faced Valéry Giscard d'Estaing in 1981, Raymond Barre in 1988, and Edouard Balladur in 1995, each supported by the UDF. These internal divisions of the right were a constant weakening factor. In 1995, the candidacy of Balladur—the prime minister since 1993 and a former minister under Chirac between 1986 and 1988, at the time of the first cohabitation—did more than perpetuate the major division between Gaullists and moderates. By aligning himself against the leader of the RPR, Balladur, himself an RPR member and former member of Chirac's inner circle, added a deeply personal and moving breakup between the two major RPR personalities to the already divided organization of the right; this weakened the RPR and made subsequent reconciliation and unification more difficult. Several eminent RPR figures, most notably Charles Pasqua and Nicolas Sarkozy, supported Balladur, while Alain Juppé and Philippe Séguin, members of the RPR who had competed for control of the party, supported Chirac's candidacy.

Disagreements of a political nature also deeply divided the right during the ratification proceedings of the Maastricht Treaty in 1992. The UDF and RPR experienced internal upheaval. While Giscard d'Estaing and Chirac voted in favor of the Maastricht measures, two members of the RPR, Séguin and Pasqua, and Philippe de Villiers, the UDF representative from La Vendée, voted against them. During the European elections of 1994, de Villiers broke with the UDF by presenting an "anti-European" roster, which obtained 12.4 percent of the vote, versus 25.4 percent for the UDF/RPR "union" roster.

Finally, since the mid-1980s the National Front—a party of the extreme right headed by Jean-Marie Le Pen—has had considerable election success, obtaining 15 percent of the vote in the presidential election of 1995. The National Front's gains have been attained to the detriment of the moderate right in particular, notably among small business owners and factory workers. This new menace is of utmost importance for the moderate right. The strategy of the National Front has in fact been to weaken and break the moderate right in order to play a central role in the eventual regrouping of the different right factions. Furthermore, the electoral law, which requires a high level of success in order for a candidate to be able to continue to the second round of voting (12.5 percent of registered voters in the first round), ceases to benefit the right when the National Front's results allow it to pass on to the second round in a large number of districts, thus putting it in a position to defeat the right in these areas. By making the themes of security and immigration the major election issues, the National Front has forced the moderate right to harden its own position on these issues, at the risk of dividing its own ranks.

The presidential election of 1995 presented a synthesis of these multiple divisions on the right. Chirac won in the second round of voting with 53 percent, versus 47 percent for the Socialist candidate, Lionel Jospin. Given the left's catastrophic situation of the previous two years, however, the relative narrowness of this victory revealed obvious potential weaknesses. During the legislative elections of 1993, the moderate right had carried 57 percent of the votes in the first round, and after the second round it had won 470 out of 577 representative seats. In the first round of the 1995 presidential election, Chirac came out on top of the candidates on the right, but with only 20 percent of the votes, versus 18.5 percent for Balladur, 4.8 percent for de Villiers, and 15.3 percent for Le Pen. Chirac's electoral and political base thus was a narrow one on which to form a government. Believing that Balladur and his partisans had betrayed him, Chirac did not choose a single leader favorable to Balladur for the government to be led by Juppé. Chirac also refused to admit into the government any supporters of Séguin, who, although he had supported Chirac, seemed unreliable because of his position on Europe and his ambitions within the RPR. And a few months after the formation of his government, Chirac dismissed the new minister of finance, Alain Madelin, who was one of the rare UDF leaders to have supported Chirac, but who Chirac felt was too liberal. Thus, the foundations of this government were extremely shaky because Chirac rejected both the National-Statist Séguin and the liberal Madelin, as well as the majority of the UDF leaders and the supporters of Balladur. These rejections constituted one main point of the new government's potential weakness.

The second point of weakness emerged during Chirac's 1995 presidential campaign. Threatened by Balladur, who represented a moderate political conservatism, Chirac was forced in the first round to defend a political stance that on many points seemed to the left of the Socialist candidate. Crushing the liberal "unique and single thought for Maastricht," while promising a voluntaristic action by the state in favor of jobs for the young and an increase in buying power, Chirac declared that it was time to "renounce renouncing." This speech undeniably paid off, as it allowed Chirac easily to outdistance Balladur among the younger generation and the popular classes and to end up leading the right. His promises, however, brought about repercussions in public opinion as early as the fall of 1995. Between 1995 and 1997, Juppé had the highest scores for unpopularity; his realist politics, far removed from the discourse of the presidential campaign, was quickly rejected by a large majority of the public. Afterward, the government was unable to recapture the trust of the French. Juppé's personality, as well as his conception and practice of power, adversely affected the government's popularity. Juppé was characterized by public opinion as uncompromising, authoritarian, abrupt and arrogant, unmethodical, more technical than political, surrounded for the most part by mediocre administrators, monopolizing governmental communication, and committing serious errors such as reorganizing his administration so that the majority of women in the government were let go. He was rejected by the public, which reacted as though it had been tricked. The image of the president was also greatly weakened. Unemployment, especially among the young, had not diminished. In spite of a slight rise in government popularity at the beginning of 1997, Chirac's government seemed worn out and at the end of the line the night before the dissolution. In March 1997 a SOFRES poll showed that 64 percent of the French no longer trusted Juppé to solve the problems of France. Thus one can imagine that the government's situation would not have readily improved in the eyes of the public had it remained in power for another year.

Faced with a weakened moderate right, the left experienced a surprising comeback between 1994 and 1997. In 1994, after the Socialist defeat in the European elections and Michel Rocard's forced surrender of control of the party, the Socialists seemed considerably weakened and deeply divided. Three years later, Jospin was able to reverse this tendency. As the Socialist candidate nominated by a large majority of militants during the presidential election of 1995, he had come out on top after the first round of that election and attained an admirable portion of the vote in the second round (47 percent). Jospin then reunified the Socialist Party, took over its guidance, and made it into a credible opposing force. He pursued the work, begun by Rocard, in bringing the Communists and Ecologists closer, and he pushed for renewal and for more female Socialist candidates in the next legislative elections. At the moment when Chirac was getting ready to dissolve the National Assembly, Jospin was the uncontested leader of his party, having reconstructed a broad system of alliances and embodying a renewed and determined opposition. The Socialists' nightmare of the years 1993-94 was well on its way to being forgotten.

All these elements combine to show that the government's position of power was greatly weakened by April 1997, without going so far as to affirm that it was desperate. The dissolution and the legislative campaign were what transformed this precarious situation into a clear and stupefying failure.

Dissolution and the Legislative Campaign

Why this dissolution one year before the normal date for elections? Several explanations have been given, and an investigation by journalists from the daily newspaper *Libération* is particularly illuminating (*Libération* 1997). The main reason for the dissolution is linked to Juppé. Chirac did not want to separate himself from his only truly faithful follower, who held both the office of prime minister and that of president of the RPR. A number of elements contributed to Chirac's view of Juppé as his undisputed choice to direct the government: Juppé's intellectual strengths, his closeness to the president, his middle-of-the-road political stance (lying between the Gaullist-Statists, such as Séguin, and the liberals, such as Madelin), his commitment to Europe, his humanistic convictions, and his ability to complement the president as chief of staff. Chirac saw no one in his entourage who might succeed Juppé, but Juppé was very unpopular and his government was moribund. No single reorganization would have brought about a change sufficient to alter public opinion, with the exception of bringing back into his government some of those who had "betrayed" Chirac in 1995, and whom he still distrusted greatly. In addition, the necessity of producing a single currency and respecting the Maastricht criteria was putting increasing pressure on the state of public finances. Juppé estimated that the restrictions weighing on governmental action would not allow him to achieve these European objectives and win in 1998. He would have to acquire a new legitimacy.

Chirac's refusal to replace his prime minister therefore left him only one possibility, dissolution. Moreover, the president and his prime minister thought dissolution would allow them to take the Socialists and the National Front by storm, having surprise on their side and taking the offensive in the campaign. In the event of victory, Juppé could be reappointed prime minister for five years (the period of time remaining until the end of the presidential mandate in 2002), at the head of a government widened politically to include the UDF and some of Balladur's supporters. Lastly, most of the poll takers, taking into account the majority party's extraordinary parliamentary domination, estimated that in spite of probable losses of important seats, the UDF/RPR alliance could retain the majority until the new elections. These are the reasons that Chirac, after several months' hesitation, decided on a dissolution that would prove to be disastrous.

The False Advantage of Surprise and Initiative

Burdened with an unpopular government, Chirac could legitimize a dissolution only on certain conditions: replacement of the prime minister, a change in the government's political line of thought, a dramatization of the issues at stake, the president's strong personal commitment, and the nullification of political alternatives. Not one of these five conditions was met.

We have seen that replacing the prime minister was, from the beginning, excluded as a possibility; on the contrary, the decision to retain Juppé was at the heart of the dissolution. Any change in political thinking also was excluded. The president and prime minister both believed that there was no alternative to their line of political reasoning and that the only possibility was carrying it out to its conclusion. This line of thought meant accepting a reduction in social services, a reduction that had already destroyed medical professionals' confidence in the government. Also, the government already having decided to support the creation of a single European currency, there remained the issue of the European Union; the government's demonstration of support for the EU could not be strong, because an important segment of the public regarded its establishment with fear and even hostility. In his announcement of the dissolution on 21 April, Chirac therefore devoted an important part of his allotted time on television to this question, declaring that in order for him to undertake difficult negotiations concerning Europe from a position of power, French cohesion and support was essential. In the middle of the campaign, however, the European issue was neither placed in the foreground nor strongly emphasized.

As for the personal commitment of the president, since he left his prime minister to direct the campaign, he was not seen to be completely involved. Indeed, Chirac's posture seemed more like that of Mitterrand than that of de Gaulle. General de Gaulle, in dissolving the National Assembly in 1962 and 1968, and in calling for the referendums of 1961, 1962, and 1969, had announced each time his decision to resign in the case of political defeat, thereby greatly dramatizing the issues at stake. But Chirac, like Mitterrand, had decided he would stay in office no matter what, and thus he could not devote himself completely to the campaign, contenting himself instead with emphasizing the disadvantages of cohabitation by insisting it was necessary for France to "speak with one single voice." He declared that answers would not be found "in archaic solutions founded on still more State control, still more expenses, still more taxes"; this attack on the Socialists was indirect, however, as they were not even named. He addressed the French only one time during the entire campaign, by way of an article published in the provincial press before the first round. Between the two rounds, when the Socialist victory seemed certain, rather than dramatizing the issues at stake, Chirac thanked Juppé for the work he had done, thus implying that the two were no longer together, and indicated that he would accept cohabitation. Juppé also played his part immediately following the first round by resigning his post as prime minister effective the day after the second round, no matter what happened. In this way the campaign rested until its end upon the shoulders of a prime minister who was completely discredited and who had virtually resigned.

Between the two rounds, Séguin and Madelin—the Gaullist Jacobin and the liberal—who had decided to take control of the RPR and the UDF, respectively, after the government's defeat, met and shook hands, adding confusion to the uncertainty of France's leadership. At that point the ruling majority was like a ship adrift with no one at the helm. Finally, contrary to the hopes of the president and prime minister, there existed a political alternative to that ruling majority in power.

The Credibilities of the Left and the Right

The day before the first round of legislative elections, the left was able to rid itself of its believability handicap, and moreover it presented certain advantages that the majority was lacking. First, the left had a leader. In April the BVA Survey Institute announced a very important gap in public opinion, showing that more trust was placed in Jospin than in Juppé, with a difference of 42 percent to 25 percent. On election day, BVA reported that while some voters said that they voted to keep the left from coming back into power, 38 percent had voted to express their dissatisfaction with Juppé's government. The poll carried out for the Center for Studies of French Political Life (CEVIPOF) by SOFRES between the two voting rounds showed that only 23 percent wished to see Juppé play an important political role in the future. The showing for Jospin on the same issue was 47 percent. The Socialist leader's credibility at this time was still mediocre, but compared to that of Juppé, it was quite satisfactory. This same poll showed that 70 percent of the French were disappointed by Chirac. Twenty-eight percent of the French said they had confidence in the left to govern, 26 percent preferred the right, and 44 percent had confidence in neither party. With more or less equal, though weak, credibility shown by both sides, the question of leadership would make all the difference.

Once again, as in 1995, the French expected change from the vote, and we must remember that since 1978, no established government had won the legislative elections. This time the French wanted to sanction Juppé, and the existence of a more or less credible opposition gave them the possibility of doing so. Jospin's presidential candidacy in 1995 had supplied the French with a replacement leader. Furthermore, it was evident that there was a unity of authority on the left after agreements had been reached among the Socialists, the Communists, the Ecologists, and the leftist radicals. Jospin appeared clearly to be the head of a unified opposition; it was the first time since the beginning of the 1960s that such unity had occurred. In the other camp the situation was very different. Juppé owed his leadership in the right completely to Chirac's support, and the other leaders of the right were beginning to question Juppé's presence. The Socialist Party was more unified than the Gaullist RPR, and it benefited once again from greater popularity.

Moreover, faced with the need for change expressed in the French polls, the Socialists and the left presented an electoral platform that at least concerned itself with French preoccupations, even if it did not entirely win them over: the creation of public jobs for the young, the reduction of the workweek, the safeguarding of the social aid system, and the decrease of inequality. These propositions were welcomed very favorably by the voters. At the same time, the government's proposal to reduce the number of civil servants met with more hostility than favor in public opinion. The only proposition of the left that the public clearly rejected was the proposal to repeal the laws of the Balladur and Juppé governments concerning nationality and immigration, laws that made it more difficult for immigrants to visit, stay for long periods, or obtain French nationality. Table 5.1 compares the credibility of the majority to that of the opposition on the principal issues at stake. The right had the edge on issues concerning the European Union, immigration, and economic modernization; public opinion favored the left regarding social aid and inequality; and the right and the left came out even concerning unemployment. These last three issues were to become priorities in the minds of most French people.

Finally, the Socialist Party also knew how to respond to the French desire for renewal by presenting a majority of new candidates (nearly 60 percent), including far more young and female candidates, while the right brought back the same old candidates, among whom women were nearly nonexistent and young candidates were rare. Thus, while the Socialist Party presented 133 women candidates (28

TABLE 5.1. CAPABILITY OF THE LEFT AND THE INCUMBENT MAJORITY TO SOLVE PROBLEMS (IN PERCENTAGES)

Problem	*Majority RPR-UDF*	*Left*	*Both*	*Neither*	*No answer*
Unemployment	34	33	4	25	4
Social aid	29	51	4	12	4
European unification	49	30	8	9	4
Immigration	57	23	5	11	4
Economic modernization	47	31	10	8	5
Inequality	25	57	5	9	4

SOURCE: Survey by SOFRES for CEVIPOF conducted between the two ballots.

percent of its total number of candidates), the RPR and UDF presented only 22 and 24 women, respectively—7.7 percent and 8.9 percent of the total number of candidates in each party (Mossuz-Lavau 1997, 458).

Thus, at the time the French were getting ready to vote, one could have said that the left had a better chance of winning than the right did. While the right had the initiative and the choice of timing, the left rapidly gained the offensive with a leader who was confident and had a fighting spirit, which quickly reduced Juppé to a defensive posture as the discontent of the French polarized around him. With the right unable to define clearly the issues at stake in the dissolution, the French discovered one with the help of the left: the defeat of the head of the government. By launching the slogan "Victory for the right means five more years of Juppé," the left found its voice to be in unison with the voice of public opinion. Even among the electorate of the right, half the voters wanted the prime minister out of the picture. In this way, dissolution functioned like a boomerang against the majority party.

The First Round and the Conditions of the Second Round

The first round was disastrous for the moderate right (see table 5.2, page 124), which did the worst it had ever done during the Fifth Republic, with less than 36 percent of the declared votes. The UDF and RPR candidates received a total of only 31.4 percent of votes, with the rest going to various candidates of the right and those presented by de Villiers. Never before had the National Front's proportion of the electorate been so high with respect to that of the UDF and RPR, reaching nearly 50 percent of their vote total.

The global results of the first round were poor for the right, and the configuration of candidates in the second round contributed strongly to its defeat (see

TABLE 5.2. RESULTS OF THE FIRST ROUND OF LEGISLATIVE ELECTIONS, 1988, 1993, AND 1997 (METROPOLITAN FRANCE) (IN PERCENTAGES)

Parties	*1988*	*1993*	*1997*
Left, including Ecologists	49.4	42.1	46.2
Moderate right	40.5	44.1	35.8
Extreme right	9.9	12.9	15.4

SOURCE: *Le Monde, Dossiers et documents,* various issues.

table 5.3, page 125). The comparison with the second round in 1993 is particularly illuminating from this point of view. In 1993 seventy-two candidates for the right were elected in the first round, as were seven in 1997. The method of voting in force for legislative elections makes it necessary for a candidate to receive votes from at least 12.5 percent of registered voters in order to proceed to the second round. Moreover, if a single candidate receives this percentage, only that candidate and the one in second place may go on to the second round. In 1993, taking into account the poor results for the Socialist Party, the left was eliminated in numerous areas immediately following the first round, and in 81 races the National Front became the opponent of the right in bipartisan competition. All of these races were won by the right. In 1997, inversely, the right was eliminated as often as the left in the second round, with 31 two-way races (dual races, or "duels"), in which the National Front opposed the right, and 25 two-way races pitting the left against the National Front. There were 399 two-way races between left and right in 1997, versus 335 in 1993. Especially in 1997, three-way races (triangular races, or "triangulaires") took place among the left, the right, and the National Front in seventy-six districts, versus twelve in 1993. Lastly, fourteen candidates for the right found themselves passing to the second round in 1993 with no competitors, while no candidates for the right found themselves in this position in 1997; three candidates for the left were in the same situation in 1993, as were twelve in 1997. Thus, from any perspective the second round promised to be more difficult for the right in 1997 than in 1993.

In 548 races, the left (including the Ecologists) picked up 48.2 percent of the votes in the second round, versus 46.1 percent for the right and 5.7 percent for the National Front. In the 369 two-way races between the Socialist Party and the right, the Socialists obtained 51.5 percent, and the right 48.5 percent. Thus the left had a clear advantage over the right. In these races, the Socialist Party won in 210 cases and the right in 159, which was the result of the quality of the left's carry-over (see table 5.4). In fact, the Communist voters, and to a lesser extent the Ecologist vot-

TABLE 5.3. CONFIGURATIONS FOR THE SECOND ROUND IN THE 1993 AND 1997 LEGISLATIVE RACES (IN THE 555 DISTRICTS OF METROPOLITAN FRANCE)

	1993	*1997*
Elected by the right in the first round	72	7
Configuration for the second round		
Left/right two-way races	335	399
Left/National Front two-way races	3	25
Right/National Front two-way races	81	31
Within-the-right races	31	2
Left/right/National Front three-way races	12	76
Other three-way races	3	3
Unopposed left candidates	3	12
Unopposed right candidates	14	0
Other	1	0
Total	555	555

SOURCE: *Le Monde, Dossiers et documents,* various issues.

TABLE 5.4. CARRYOVER OF VOTES FROM FIRST ROUND TO SECOND ROUND IN TWO-WAY RACES BETWEEN SOCIALIST PARTY AND RIGHTIST CANDIDATES (IN PERCENTAGES)

	Party voted for in the second round		
Party voted for in the first round	*Socialist Party*	*Right*	*Abstention, blank, or no response*
Communist Party	84	5	11
Socialist Party (or diverse left)	96	2	2
Ecologists	62	14	24
Right	1	93	6
National Front	21	59	29
Abstention, blank, or no response	21	23	56

SOURCE: Postelection survey by SOFRES.

ers, voted heavily for the Socialist candidates in the second round. Supporters of the National Front voted only 59 percent for the right, and a fifth of its supporters voted for Socialist candidates. Finally, contrary to its hopes, the right had no more influence than the left over those who had abstained in the first round, because those who voted in the second round divided nearly equally between the Socialist Party and the right.

Some observers also have estimated that the high number of three-way races in the second round was the decisive factor in the left's victory, which would mean that the left possibly owed its victory to the National Front. It is true that the left won 47 out of 76 three-way races, versus 29 won by the right and none by the National Front. To the extent that the right obtained thirty-three seats less than an absolute majority, such a hypothesis seems plausible. In the interest of a complete and rigorous study, we must ask ourselves, as did Jérome Jaffré (1997a, 434), what the results would have been for two-way races between the right and the left. The simulation he carried out showed that in this scenario the former majority would have carried 54 of the races, instead of the 29 it won in the three-way races. The right thus would have captured twenty-five more seats, which would not have thwarted the left's victory but would have noticeably reduced its margin. Table 5.5 shows the extent of the right's defeat, a loss of nearly half its seats. The balloting method of majority voting over two rounds generally amplifies the effect of political movements, working in favor of the right in 1993 and of the left in 1997.

TABLE 5.5. CHANGES IN NATIONAL ASSEMBLY SEAT DISTRIBUTION AFTER 1997 ELECTIONS

Parties	*Seats held prior to election*	*Seats held after election*	*Seat change*
Left and Ecologists	99	320	+221
Right	478	256	-222
National Front	0	1	+1
Total	577	577	

SOURCE: *Le Monde, Dossiers et documents*, 1997.

Weaknesses of the Right's Sociological Foundations

The right's electorate is very different from those of both the left and the National Front (see table 5.6). First of all, it is mainly an older electorate. Less than one-fourth of those younger than fifty years old voted in the first round in favor of a moderate right candidate, versus nearly half of those older than sixty-five. In the 1995 presidential election, Chirac had succeeded in attracting an important portion of the eighteen-to-twenty-four age group by promising to reduce unemployment among young people: 29 percent of young voters had voted for him, versus 21 percent for Jospin and 11 percent for Balladur. In 1997, 28 percent voted for

UDF and RPR candidates together, and 28 percent voted for Socialist candidates. Such "backing-off" indicates that the young people who deserted the majority felt deceived by it (Jaffré 1997b, 139).

TABLE 5.6. SOCIOLOGICAL PROFILE OF VOTERS IN THE 1997 ELECTIONS

	Percentage of respondents who voted for the moderate right
Sex	
Male	34
Female	39
Age	
18–24 years	32
25–34 years	28
35–49 years	28
50–64 years	41
65 years old and older	52
Occupation	
Farmer	60
Not working, retired	45
Small business owner, artisan	38
Executive, higher education	38
Intermediate profession	31
Office worker	25
Manual worker	21
Professional situation	
Self-employed	52
Wage earner	27
Unemployed	23
Religion	
Regularly practicing Catholic	68
Occasionally practicing Catholic	50
Nonpracticing Catholic	33
No religion	13
Total	36.5

SOURCE: Postelection survey by SOFRES.

While farmers and people not working—including the retired, unemployed, or handicapped—voted strongly in favor of the incumbent majority in 1997, only 25 percent of clerical workers and 21 percent of factory workers did so. And the factory workers were more likely to vote for the National Front than for the moderate right. Even executives voted more to the left than to the right. While 52 percent of self-employed people voted for the right, only 27 percent of wage-earners and 23 percent of those unemployed voted the same way. Finally, while the right remains the majority among practicing Catholics, whose numbers are continually decreasing in France, only 33 percent of nonpracticing Catholics and 13 percent of those with no religion voted for the right. More than ever before, the sociological foundation of the right rests on the self-employed and on elderly people, as well as on practicing Catholics. Wedged between the left and the National Front, the right's position has been weakened among wage earners and young people. This also explains the defeat of a majority party whose inability to extend itself beyond its traditional framework presaged weakness for the future.

In conclusion, the defeat of the right is the product of a multiform crisis only made worse by the defeat itself. This crisis is first of all a crisis of leadership. After banishing Juppé, Séguin took control of the direction of the RPR, against the wishes of the president of the republic. From that point on, the relationship between these two men, both of whom hope to run in the next presidential election, can only be one of conflict. More broadly, the RPR henceforth will be divided strongly among followers of Chirac, Balladur, and Séguin. The UDF, for its part, does not have one uncontested leader. François Léotard had to abandon control of the Republican Party, renamed the Liberal Democrat Party, to Madelin, leaving the leadership of the UDF empty. As for the other large constituency of the UDF, the Democratic Force, its leader, François Bayrou, plans to work on his own behalf. Discredited by his defeat and no longer in control of the RPR, Chirac has been a weakened influence, and he is not likely to emerge as the uncontested leader of the right any time in the near future.

The crisis in question also concerns organization. The moderate right was not capable of reunifying itself into a single, large, conservative party, which left it wide open to heated competition among its constituent organizations. If the RPR is divided, the UDF has a weak consistency and unity. The right has no mechanism for allowing its factions to choose a mutually agreed-upon candidate for the first round of the presidential election; this factor has cost it victory in the past, in 1981 and 1988.

This crisis is also strategic. The National Front is menacing, and the moderate right has become preoccupied by the rise of a party that could lure away that portion of its popular electorate attracted by the racist and nationalistic discourse of the extreme right. While some within the center right are pleading for a dialogue with the National Front, the principal leaders of the right refuse such a reconciliation, and they follow their own convictions and those of the majority of their electorate; this may lead toward political schism in the long run. Most certainly, for the time being, Le Pen's outrageously provocative racist discourse makes such a coming together impossible. If the National Front changed its tactics, however, the unity of the moderate right could be challenged.

Finally, the crisis is ideological. Between the Gaullist, Christian-Democrat, and liberal traditions that make up the right, no one is capable of presenting a single clear political line of thought. Hesitating between liberalism and conservatism *à la française,* the right is split between choices that are contrary and equally dangerous. This is what led Jacques Chirac to uphold Juppé's middle-of-the-road line until the very end. This line of thought, however, was defeated in the last election, and so today a void exists in the right. We must also mention in connection with this the various disagreements concerning Europe.

Most certainly, the past two decades have shown that the French more often take action against administrations on the way out than they elect an opposition by majority vote. A Socialist government failure could return hope to the right, but it would still be necessary for the right to constitute a credible alternative at the time, if that should happen. This is not the case today, and it is not certain that this could even be the case in the near future, taking into account the multiform crisis that we have described. The right today is incontestably experiencing its most serious crisis since the beginning of the Fifth Republic. The unfortunate decision of Jacques Chirac to dissolve the National Assembly certainly played a major role in the defeat of the right, and the right's electoral campaign was disastrous. Chirac's decision cannot explain everything, however. The right was not in good shape, and perhaps, after all, we must believe Chirac's assertion, offered to justify his decision, that the right would have lost the election in 1998 anyway. This means, at the very least, that recovery for the right will take a very long time.

Chapter 6

The Stability of the French Party System: The Enduring Impact of the Two-Ballot Electoral Rules

Joseph A. Schlesinger and Mildred S. Schlesinger

The legislative elections of 1997 confirmed the remarkable stability of the French party system. Through three republics and numerous changes of labels, the four parties that monopolized the National Assembly after the 1997 elections—the Gaullist Rally for the Republic (RPR), the Union for French Democracy (UDF), the Socialists, and the Communists—have dominated French party politics. Their domination has been closely related to their mastery of the single-member district, two-ballot rules that have been used for most elective offices since the Third Republic. Of the thirty national legislative elections held since the constitutional establishment of the Third Republic in 1875, twenty-three have been held under these rules (Campbell 1965; Cole and Campbell 1989).

The party system has remained stable even as, over the course of the Fifth Republic, the four parties' political fortunes have fluctuated. During the first decade of the Fifth Republic, one dominant party emerged, the entourage that formed around that republic's founder and towering figure, General Charles de Gaulle. In control of Parliament and led by the newly popularly elected president, the Gaullists dominated French politics in a manner without precedent in the earlier republics.

With the departure of the General from French politics, the Gaullist party's dominance was challenged in the 1970s. That challenge came both from the Socialist Party and from the Gaullists' allies. The most serious challenge to Gaullist dominance came from the Socialist Party, reorganized under the leadership of the wily Fourth Republic politician, François Mitterrand. But the party was challenged also by its erstwhile docile ally, the Independent Republicans, under the leadership of an ambitious local political notable and national technocrat, Valéry Giscard d'Estaing. During the 1970s, the Socialist Party, by transforming the Communists into more reliable allies, increased its numbers appreciably in the National Assembly. Meanwhile, the Independent Republicans' Giscard captured the presidency from the Gaullists and united disparate center forces into an umbrella political organization, the UDF, thereby improving his party's standing in Parliament.

During the 1980s, the Socialists emerged at last as the governing alternative to the Gaullists. They controlled the presidency for fourteen years, electing Mitterrand to an unprecedented two terms. The party also held majorities in the National Assembly for ten of these fourteen years, thereby also controlling the office of prime minister, with and without the declared support of the Communist Party.

During the 1990s, a breathtaking change of power took place. In the legislative elections of 1993, the Socialist Party lost 200 seats in the National Assembly, suffering the worst defeat of any party in the history of the republic. Meanwhile, the Gaullist RPR emerged newly triumphant, electing more deputies than any other party (244), while its ally, the UDF, elected 212 deputies. This gave the Gaullist prime minister, Edouard Balladur, control of the largest Assembly majority in the republic's history. It allowed him to share power with a weakened and dying Socialist president for two years, until the RPR recaptured the presidency in 1995. Yet just four years after the Socialists' crushing defeat of 1993 and two years after their loss of the presidency, the electorate again reversed the party's political fortunes. In the 1997 legislative elections, called nine months early by the Gaullist president, Jacques Chirac, to strengthen his hand in taking unpopular decisions, the president lost his majority and the Socialists regained control of the government.

The Two-Ballot Electoral Rules

Despite this stunning alternation of power, the legislative elections of 1997 merely confirmed the staying power of France's four longtime political parties. This was due in large part to the Fifth Republic's reversion to the single-member-district, two-ballot election, following the short-lived Fourth Republic's flirtation with proportional representation. Only in 1986 was a version of proportional representation used again. Indeed, the Fifth Republic made two important changes in the Third Republic's rules that reinforced the advantage the two-ballot rules gave the four parties. In order to give winning candidates as large a popular mandate as possible, the number of candidates who could qualify for the second ballot was reduced. New candidates were no longer permitted to enter for the second ballot. Candidates qualified for the second ballot only if they received a certain percentage of votes on the first ballot: for the election of 1962, 5 percent of the valid votes cast (*suffrages exprimés*); for the elections of 1967, 1968, and 1973, 10 percent of the registered voters (*électeurs inscrits*); for the elections of 1978, 1981, 1988, 1993, and 1997, 12.5 percent of the registered voters. If only one candidate met the requirement, the next highest vote getter on the first ballot could contest the second ballot; if no candidate on the first ballot qualified, the top two vote getters ran. These restrictions reduced the second contest largely to two-person races—to triangular races at most—circumstances that were destined to favor the most experienced and best known political organizations.

The Impact of the Two-Ballot Rules on French Parties: Strategies and Appeals

Over the course of many years, each of the four main parties developed a distinctive strategy for winning within the two-ballot rules that contributed to its durability, despite reversals in electoral fortunes. Each party has cultivated one of four distinctive strategies (Schlesinger and Schlesinger 1990, 1995). One way of winning involves maximizing support on the first ballot. The RPR and its predecessors developed this strategy, which requires appealing to voters as their first choice. Since first choices are likely to be firmer than second or compromise choices, this appeal is broad and strong, speaking to the basic needs of voters for stability and security. This appeal to defense of the public interest or the general good is the obverse of a sharply defined ideological appeal, which may also attract first-choice votes, although it tends to restrict the wide support needed in order to peak on the first ballot.

No one was more successful in this broad appeal than the Gaullist party's leader and founder of the Fifth Republic, General Charles de Gaulle, during the 1960s. De Gaulle, after all, could literally claim that he and his supporters provided the bulwark against anarchy and disaster. In contrast, the version of the Gaullist appeal crafted by President Chirac for the legislative elections of 1997 proved far less successful. To ask the French electorate for its support in resolving the Algerian crisis or ending the street violence of 1968, both of which clearly threatened the nation's stability, was one thing. To ask the electorate to make vague sacrifices for the sake of a European currency that, by competing with the dollar, would eventually reduce record unemployment and bring prosperity to France, was a different matter, as the results of the 1997 elections demonstrated.

Yet another strategy for winning within the two-ballot rules involves maximizing support on the second ballot. The Socialist Party and its predecessors cultivated this strategy, which requires appealing to many voters as their second choice. Of course, given the need to reach the second ballot, the appeal must attract enough first-choice votes, perhaps including those of voters willing to vote on the first ballot for a second-choice candidate more likely to win. Designed to attract voters with other partisan preferences on both ballots, the appeal of the second-ballot strategy is specific and complex, targeting different groups of voters without antagonizing any.

During the 1970s and 1980s the Socialist Party refined this appeal under the leadership of François Mitterrand. Mitterrand had honed this approach during the Fourth Republic, negotiating a position in almost every government of every political stripe. In the Fifth Republic he used his skills to attract diverse groups of voters to the Socialist Party, newly reorganized under his leadership. Crafting the Common Program to secure Communist votes in the 1970s, in the 1980s he moved his party to the moderate program of *ouverture* (opening up), designed to attract UDF voters unhappy with their party's support of the RPR agenda (Schlesinger and Schlesinger 1998).

In the 1997 elections Mitterrand's successor, Lionel Jospin, performed a similar balancing act. In contrast to the Gaullist government, he addressed the electorate's most pressing concern, high unemployment, with specific measures, such as the creation of 750,000 jobs through incentives to the public and private sectors and reduction of the workweek, without repudiating the goal of a common European currency. While his political opponents and American and British observers derided his proposals, many French voters clearly saw them as the preferable alternatives to ambiguous sacrifice for abstract monetary goals that even the most sophisticated among them found difficult to grasp.

A third strategy for winning under the two-ballot rules involves doing well on both ballots. This strategy, cultivated by the UDF and its predecessors, requires appealing to voters as both a first and second choice. It is best achieved by a candidate's personal appeal of competence and trust. In the 1970s this appeal was perfected by the founder of the UDF, its first and only president of France, Valéry Giscard d'Estaing. Descended from a distinguished family of politicians, he built his elective career on the political base established by his maternal great-grandfather and his grandfather, using the appeal of trust in the local notable.

At the same time Giscard also gained a national reputation as the preeminent government expert in finance and the economy. Graduate of the prestigious *École nationale d'administration* (ENA), member of the highly selective civil service corps of *inspecteurs des finances*, he became minister of finance and the economy in 1962 at the age of thirty-six, a position he held in almost every government until his run for the presidency of France in 1974. If he appealed at the local level as a member of a respected and trusted family, in his successful run for the presidency his strongest selling point was the expertise he could employ in dealing with the troubled economy.

In the elections of 1997, even as the UDF participated with the RPR in the campaign, Giscard and his successor as president of the UDF, François Léotard, sought to distinguish themselves from the RPR. While members of the UDF had indeed participated in the government, both Giscard and Léotard implied it was the Gaullist prime minister, Alain Juppé, who had mismanaged its affairs. And after all it was the Gaullist president, Chirac, who, instead of dismissing his inept and unpopular prime minister, had taken the disastrous step of calling early elections. Both the prime minister and the president had then gone on to demonstrate further incompetence by badly managing the electoral campaign. In other words, if the electorate had rejected the governing majority, it was not because of the majority's policies but because an incompetent government, under Gaullist leadership, had lost the electorate's trust.

Finally, the two-ballot rules accommodate an electoral strategy that allows a limited number of victories by maximizing support on either ballot. This strategy, which has been employed by the Communist Party, rests on a limited appeal to voters as either a first or second choice, an appeal tailored to a restricted but concentrated number of voters. Embodied in a specific program addressing these voters' concerns, it is directed at low-income urban workers clustered in the suburbs of the large cities and at agricultural workers in a few rural enclaves.

Never has the Communist Party had a more skilled interpreter of this appeal than Robert Hue, the leader who conducted its 1997 electoral campaign. As the party's candidate in the presidential campaign of 1995, Hue skillfully contrasted the failed urban policies of the Gaullist government and the Socialist president with the serious efforts of Communist mayors, including himself, to deal with the pressing problems of unemployment and immigration. In the 1997 elections, even as he exploited improved relations with the Socialist Party, he distanced his party from the Socialists' commitment to the euro and their more nuanced stands on the thirty-five-hour week, the increase in the minimum wage, and the end to privatization.

The Need for Alliances among the Four Parties

While the two-ballot rules nurtured four parties that specialized in distinctive electoral strategies and appeals, they also encouraged those four parties to form electoral alliances. Under the two-ballot rules, electoral alliances are essential to the successful implementation of each party's strategy. Since the rules invite many parties to compete on the first ballot, and at the same time strictly limit access to the second ballot, no one party can take for granted enough electoral support for a first-ballot victory, access to the second ballot, or election on the second ballot. These can only be assured by concluding an electoral agreement with another party, most obviously one whose strategy and appeal are compatible. Hence, over the years, as the four parties cultivated distinctive strategies and appeals, they also forged distinct and overt alliances that worked to their mutual advantage. In the Fifth Republic, alliances have been forged between the RPR and the UDF on the one hand, and the Socialist Party and Communist Party on the other. One alliance derives from the compatibility of first-ballot and dual-ballot strategies and from generalized appeals to defend the public interest, competence, and trust. The other alliance derives from the compatibility of second-ballot and limited strategies and from diverse and targeted appeals. Each of these alliances has required the partners to agree on a common tactic in elections.

The RPR-UDF Alliance: The Single Candidate

For the RPR and the UDF, both of which seek to peak on the first ballot, the alliance of choice has been agreement on a single candidate before that ballot. Although this arrangement has worked more to the Gaullists' advantage, over the course of the Fifth Republic the benefits to both parties have equalized. Initially in a dominant position, the Gaullists had first sought to absorb, rather than to cooperate with, their ally. Then, faced with determined resistance, they had used the considerable superiority of their resources to impose upon the Independent Republicans the strategy of the single candidacy. As a party favoring the dual ballot, the Independent Republicans were ambivalent toward this tactic but accepted it, given their junior status (Charlot 1971; Charlot 1973, 139-40; Goguel 1983, 500-503).

In the legislative elections of 1978, however, the Independent Republicans, strengthened by their reincarnation as the UDF, came closest to abandoning the single-candidacy tactic. Even as tensions between the two allies reached their highest point, the UDF, bolstered by its newly confederated forces, as well as its control of the presidency, contested a record number of districts with the Gaullists, allowing the electorate to decide between them in contests that went to a second ballot. In only 130 constituencies of 474 in metropolitan France did the two allies agree on a single candidate (Charlot 1980, 81-87; Colliard 1979; Frears and Parodi 1979, 23-27, 32, 38-42). The result was an election that secured the UDF's distinctive partisan status by bringing it close to the Gaullists' strength in the National Assembly (see table 6.1).

Faced with the prospect of defeat in the subsequent two legislative elections, however, the UDF reverted, in most districts, to taking the single-candidacy approach in alliance with the Gaullists. In 1981 the RPR and UDF agreed on single candidates for 385 out of 474 constituencies. In 1988, when the number of constituencies in metropolitan France increased to 555, the two allies agreed on a single candidate in 536 districts (Charlot 1988, 62-69; *Le Monde* 1988, 36-37; Ysmal 1986, 177-78, 194-95). This practice of cooperation carried over to the victorious elections of 1993 and the disappointing elections of 1997. In 1993 the two parties agreed on a single candidate for 495 constituencies, and in 1997, for 545 of 555 constituencies. Within the alliance, while the RPR retained somewhat greater power, the relative power distribution between the two allies remained stable and moderate.

The Socialist-Communist Alliance: The Trial Run

For the Socialist and Communist Parties, both of which rely heavily on rallying second-ballot support, the alliance of choice has been the trial run. The trial run allows both parties to run candidates on the first ballot, while projecting that the party whose candidate runs behind will withdraw for the second ballot.[1] This has been a much easier alliance to implement than that of the UDF and RPR. While prior agreements and promises of mutual assistance may facilitate this alliance, they are not essential. The implementation of the alliance ultimately rests with the voters. Resolving the difficult problem of whose candidate will benefit from the alliance is turned over to the electorate. Indeed, the requirement for access to the second ballot can render the problem moot.

The Socialists and Communists have implemented the trial run more or less enthusiastically throughout the course of the Fifth Republic. It is true that during the 1970s, as it became clearer that the alliance was working to the Socialists' advantage, the Communists became increasingly uncomfortable with the arrangement. During the election of 1978 they held aloof from any formal agreement for the first time since 1962, until the eve of the second ballot (Boy and Dupoirier 1986; Frears and Parodi 1979, 18-23, 42-44, 73-75, 85-97; Parodi 1978). In the two subsequent campaigns provoked by the election and reelection of the Socialist president, however, the Communists had no choice but to accept without

TABLE 6.1. THE FOUR STABLE PARTIES IN THE FRENCH FIFTH REPUBLIC: SEATS IN THE NATIONAL ASSEMBLY AFTER EACH DUAL BALLOT ELECTION

	Gaullist era						*Emergent competition*				*Socialist era*				*Alternation*			
	1962		*1967*		*1968*		*1973*		*1978*		*1981*		*1988*		*1993*		*1997*	
Party	*%*	*Number*	*%*	*Number*	*%*	*Number*	*%*	*Number*	*%*	*Number*	*%*	*Number*	*%*	*Number*	*%*	*Number*	*%*	*Number*
Communist	8.2	40	14.5	71	6.8	33	15.0	73	17.6	86	8.8	43	4.7	27	3.8	22	5.9	34
Socialist	13.1	64	23.8	116	11.7	57	20.5	100	21.1	103	53.9	263	44.9	258	9.0	52	41.9	242
Subtotal	21.3		38.3		18.5		35.5		38.7		62.7		49.6		12.8		47.8	
Gaullist[a]	44.3	216	36.9	180	55.3	270	33.0	161	29.1	142	16.2	79	22.1	127	42.3	244	23.2	134
UDF[b]	16.8	82	15.8	77	17.8	87	22.7	111	21.9	107	10.5	51	20.0	115	36.7	212	18.5	107
Subtotal	61.1		52.7		73.1		55.7		51.0		26.6		42.1		79.0		41.8	
Four-party total	82.4		91.0		91.6		91.2		89.8		89.3		91.7		91.9		89.6	
Seats in legislature		488		488		488		488		488		488		575		577		577

SOURCES: Electoral data and party membership, 1962–97: Ministère de l'Intérieur, *Les Élections législatives de 1962, 1967, 1968, 1973, 1978, 1981, 1988, 1993* (Paris: Imprimerie Nationale); *Le Monde, Les Élections législatives, 25 mai–1er juin 1997* (Paris: *Le Monde, Dossiers et documents*).

NOTE: Number = number of seats. The number of seats for each party includes only the deputies who joined that party at the beginning of the legislature. Thus we have not included those with a limited commitment, i.e., those who were allied (*apparentés*) with the party. There also were a few deputies in each legislature who had no party affiliation (*non-inscrits*).

a. Throughout the Fifth Republic the Gaullists have changed their labels. Since 1976 they have called themselves "Rassemblement pour la république."

b. The UDF (Union pour la démocratie française) was not formed until 1978. The numbers in the table for earlier legislatures are for the parties whose members ultimately joined the UDF. In the 1988 legislature these also included the members of the Union du centre, a party whose members had come from the UDF and were to return to it in 1993.

objection the trial run. In these elections the alliance worked to the overwhelming advantage of the Socialists. But it also helped to salvage the Communist Party in the National Assembly. As the elections of 1993 and 1997 confirmed, in times of political adversity and political good fortune, the arrangement worked to the parties' mutual advantage. This was true whether relations between them were cool as in 1993 or, as in 1997, at their most affable since the early 1970s.

The Electoral Results of 1997: The Stability of Partisan Strategies, Appeals, and Alliances

Given the dramatic and unanticipated results of the 1997 elections, any analysis of their effect on the party system must emphasize above all that nothing had changed. The elections left the same four parties dominant. True, the French electorate, having in 1993 handed the Socialist Party the most humiliating defeat in its history, had only four years later given control of the government back to the party. True, the Communist Party, having watched its delegation in the National Assembly steadily decline after 1978, increased its ranks by more than 50 percent. True, the RPR and UDF, having won, in 1993, the largest majority in the National Assembly since the *Bloc national* of 1919, now found themselves in opposition and their Gaullist president reduced to sharing power with a Socialist prime minister for five long years. But the elections had merely altered the relative standings of the four parties, as competitive elections are wont to do. As table 6.1 shows, the 1997 elections left the same four parties in control of the National Assembly; while the parties' individual fortunes fluctuated considerably over time, the percentage of seats they controlled together fluctuated within a narrow range, from a low of 82.4 percent in 1962 to a high of 91.9 percent in 1993, the percentage dropping to 89.6 in 1997.

The four parties' domination after the 1997 elections reflected a continuation of the distinctive electoral strategies and alliances that had underwritten their viability over the course of the Fifth Republic. This was as true of the RPR and the UDF, which sustained serious losses, as of the Socialist and Communist Parties, which made impressive gains. Tables 6.2 and 6.3 (page 141) reveal clearly that the RPR and the UDF won by maximizing their support on the first ballot, thanks to the nature of their appeals and their implementation of the single candidacy. As table 6.2 shows, in 1981, the banner year for first-ballot victories, the UDF took 74.5 percent of its victories on the first ballot, followed by the RPR with 58.3 percent. While this was the election that brought the Socialists to power, resistance to the Socialists came from RPR and UDF candidates with strong first-ballot appeal and good relations with their ally.

In the 1990s, due to the performance of the National Front (FN), which we discuss later, the number of first-ballot victories declined. Yet in both elections the RPR and UDF had a monopoly on these victories. In the victory of 1993, the two parties had an almost equal percentage of first-ballot victories, while the Socialists and Communists won no seats on the first ballot. In the defeat of 1997, an election that saw a record low number of first-ballot victories (twelve), ten of those were won by RPR and UDF candidates; two seats were taken by candidates unaffiliated with any of the four parties.

Confirmation of the electoral strategies of the RPR and the UDF, and of the success of their alliance, is also demonstrated in table 6.3 on page 141, which displays, by party, the average electoral margin on the first ballot of candidates who won on the second ballot. In almost every election since 1962, UDF and RPR candidates compiled the highest margins on the first ballot, although those of the RPR's candidates were always higher. In 1978 the Communists had a slightly higher margin than the UDF; in 1988 the Communists' margin exceeded that of both RPR and UDF candidates. But in an election where the party had suffered its worst defeat since 1932, only the candidates in the party's most secure strongholds survived. In the RPR-UDF victory of 1993 and their defeat of 1997, the margins of both parties' candidates approached each other and clearly exceeded those of both the Communists and the Socialists.

At the same time, the electoral results of 1997 confirmed the difference between the two parties' strategies that had helped the UDF survive as a distinct organization—the ability of its candidates to attract broader support on the second ballot. In examining the relationship between the Gaullists and the UDF's predecessor, the Independent Republicans, in the 1960s and early 1970s, electoral studies had highlighted the similarities in their electoral and geographical support, implying that the smaller party had a weak base for continued viability, and predicting that the UDF would be absorbed by its more powerful ally.[2] When that party not only failed to be absorbed, but actually grew, electoral studies began to examine its ability, like the Socialists', to attract votes on the second ballot beyond its expected base of support (Charlot 1980; Frears and Parodi 1979, 83-97; Jaffré 1980; Laurens 1988; Parodi 1978, 26, 29). Yet table 6.4 (page 142) reveals that this important difference from the Gaullists was observable not just in the 1990s, but early on in the Fifth Republic.

In the same way that the electoral results of 1997 revealed the distinctive strategies as well as the alliance of the RPR and UDF, they demonstrated the Socialists' particular style. The 1997 results confirmed, as tables 6.2 and 6.3 have shown, the poor record of Socialist candidates on the first ballot. Even the Communist Party did better on this score, although in neither the defeat of 1993 nor the victory of 1997 did either party elect a deputy on the first ballot. Still, in 1997 and 1993, as in all the previous elections, Communist candidates who won on the second ballot always did better on the first ballot than did the Socialists.

As table 6.4 shows, it was on the second ballot that Socialist candidates shone. Until the election of 1981 they significantly outperformed every party in rallying support for the second ballot. Then, in the elections of the 1980s and 1990s, as the Communist Party was forced to retreat to its strongholds, it outperformed the Socialists in this respect. Still, the Socialist Party continued to demonstrate that maximizing support on the second ballot distinguished it from the RPR and the UDF. It also showed how effectively it used the trial run with its Communist ally.

The electoral results of 1997 confirmed the Communist Party's standing as a stable niche party within the party system. Tables 6.3 and 6.4 show that in 1997, from its limited but concentrated base, the party's successful candidates accumulated a higher average margin of support than did those of the Socialist Party on the first ballot, and a higher average margin of support than did the Socialists, the RPR, and the UDF on the second ballot. Thanks also to the successful use of the trial run, the Communist Party was able to translate this performance into a reversal in the steady decline in its representation after the elections of 1978 (see table 6.1, page 137). But as tables 6.2–6.4 show, the party's performance in 1997 was also a continuation of the pattern that allowed it to remain one of France's four main parties.

The Four Parties' Personnel Continuity

In 1997 the four parties' staying power was reflected not only in the continuity of their electoral strategies and appeals, but also in that of their elected personnel. Despite the dramatic reversal of political fortunes that the elections of 1997 had brought about, the Socialist and Communist successes were due neither to the parties' presentation of new candidates, nor to RPR-UDF failures leading to the electorate's wholesale rejection of the old. All four parties' successes were won largely with personnel they had already presented to the electorate. In 1997 the Socialist Party reversed its fortunes with 51 incumbents, 69 former deputies, 25 candidates who had been unsuccessful in 1993, and 13 *suppléants* (stand-ins) who in 1993 had run with Socialist candidates.[3] Thus 65 percent of the Socialists victorious in 1997 had been presented to the electorate during the disastrous elections of 1993. Among the remaining successful Socialists, almost all had previously been elected to local offices in their districts.

TABLE 6.2. NATIONAL ASSEMBLY SEATS WON ON THE FIRST BALLOT, BY PARTY

	Gaullist era						*Emergent competition*				*Socialist era*				*Alternation*			
	1962		*1967*		*1968*		*1973*		*1978*		*1981*		*1988*		*1993*		*1997*	
Party	*%*	*Number*	*%*	*Number*	*%*	*Number*	*%*	*Number*	*%*	*Number*	*%*	*Number*	*%*	*Number*	*%*	*Number*	*%*	*Number*
Communist	22.5	40	11.3	71	18.2	33	11.0	73	4.7	86	16.3	43	3.7	27	0.0	22	0.0	34
Socialist	3.1	64	0.9	116	0.0	57	1.0	100	0.0	103	17.5	263	14.0	258	0.0	52	0.0	242
Gaullist	19.9	216	23.3	180	40.4	270	13.0	161	21.2	142	58.3	79	29.9	127	17.2	244	5.2	134
UDF	42.7	82	27.3	77	37.9	87	18.0	111	18.7	107	74.5	51	29.6	115	17.0	212	2.8	107

SOURCES: See table 6.1 (page 137).

TABLE 6.3. AVERAGE ELECTORAL MARGINS OF SECOND-BALLOT WINNERS ON THE FIRST BALLOT

	Gaullist era						*Emergent competition*				*Socialist era*				*Alternation*			
	1962		*1967*		*1968*		*1973*		*1978*		*1981*		*1988*		*1993*		*1997*	
Party	*%*	*Deputies*	*%*	*Deputies*	*%*	*Deputies*	*%*	*Deputies*	*%*	*Deputies*	*%*	*Deputies*	*%*	*Deputies*	*%*	*Deputies*	*%*	*Deputies*
Communist	5.6	31	4.5	63	5.1	27	8.4	65	9.1	82	4.7	36	11.5	26	3.9	22	5.3	34
Socialist	0.8	62	0.7	115	-1.2	57	1.6	99	4.5	103	3.1	217	7.6	222	-0.4	52	3.8	242
Gaullist	13.2	173	15.5	138	14.9	161	13.4	140	12.2	112	11.5	33	10.2	89	15.3	202	10.5	129
UDF	3.5	47	9.3	56	10.6	54	9.1	91	8.6	87	9.0	13	7.7	81	14.2	176	9.7	104

SOURCES: See table 6.1.

NOTE: Deputies = the number of second-ballot winners for the party.

NOTE: The electoral margin is the difference in percentage of the total vote received by the winning candidate and the candidate receiving the next highest number of votes.

TABLE 6.4. DIFFERENCES IN AVERAGE ELECTORAL MARGINS BETWEEN THE TWO BALLOTS

	Gaullist era						*Emergent competition*				*Socialist era*				*Alternation*			
	1962		*1967*		*1968*		*1973*		*1978*		*1981*		*1988*		*1993*		*1997*	
Parties	*%*	*Deputies*	*%*	*Deputies*	*%*	*Deputies*	*%*	*Deputies*	*%*	*Deputies*	*%*	*Deputies*	*%*	*Deputies*	*%*	*Deputies*	*%*	*Deputies*
Communist	0.3	31	5.9	63	0.4	27	0.9	65	3.0	82	18.9	36	29.5	26	8.0	22	19.3	34
Socialist	16.0	62	16.8	115	10.5	57	11.1	99	7.0	103	13.2	217	5.7	222	9.5	52	10.8	242
Gaullist	2.3	173	-5.7	138	-2.1	161	-3.7	140	-0.2	112	-3.8	33	-1.3	89	1.5	202	1.0	127
UDF	5.3	47	1.6	56	5.0	54	0.6	91	4.5	87	-3.2	13	0.3	81	4.6	176	2.8	104

SOURCES: See table 6.1 on page page 137.

NOTE: Deputies = the number of second-ballot winners for the party.

NOTE: The electoral margin is the difference between the winning candidate's percentage of the total vote and the second-place candidate's percentage of the total vote. A negative difference between the two electoral margins indicates that, on the second ballot, the winner lost votes in relation to his or her nearest competitor.

In 1997 the Communists also reversed the decline in their political fortunes with known candidates. Of the 34 Communists elected in 1997, 15 were incumbents, 3 were former deputies, 3 were candidates who had been unsuccessful in the elections of 1993, and 3 had run as *suppléants* in the elections. Thus 71 percent of the Communists victorious in 1997 had participated in the elections of 1993. Moreover, of the remaining Communists, 8 were well-known local officeholders in their districts: 6 were both mayors and representatives to the departmental councils, including the party's first secretary, Robert Hue; one was a mayor; and one was a departmental councilor.[4] Also elected to the National Assembly in 1997 was a recently elected senator.

In 1997 most of the RPR and UDF candidates who survived their parties' electoral defeat had been elected to the National Assembly in 1993. Of the 107 UDF candidates elected to the National Assembly in 1997, 96 had been elected deputies in 1993. Of the remaining 11, three had run as *suppléants* in 1993; all but one held local office in their districts. Of the 134 RPR candidates elected to the National Assembly in 1997, 123 had been elected to the National Assembly in 1993. Of the 11 newly elected deputies, three had been *suppléants*, and one had been a candidate in 1993; all held local office in their districts. Thus the 1997 elections, despite their dramatic effect, did not result in the widespread renewal of the parties' elective personnel, just as they had not resulted in shifting the parties' domination of the National Assembly, nor in the alteration of their electoral strategies and alliances.

The Two-Ballot Rules and New Parties

The four main parties have dominated French politics because they have mastered the two-ballot rules, not because the rules exclude other parties. As table 6.1 (page 137) shows, over the course of the republic about 10 percent of each legislature has consisted of deputies unaffiliated with the four main parties. We have already pointed out that the two-ballot rules allow many candidates to compete on the first ballot. Indeed, since public financing of political campaigns is readily available to minor parties, the attraction for these parties to run on the first ballot is great, for it gives them the opportunity to test their appeal. Thus the newspaper *Le Monde* listed forty partisan labels that appeared on the first ballot in the 1997 elections (*Le Monde* 1997, 40).

The principal disadvantage these parties face in breaking the hold of the four main parties on French politics is their difficulty in gaining entry to the alliances that have sustained those parties. These alliances have been essential, not only to success in the legislative elections, but also to success in the elections, held under the same rules, for mayors and representatives to departmental councils. As we have seen, these offices can be important stepping stones to the office of deputy. Candidates and parties unable to operate within one of the two alliances have had little chance of winning appreciable numbers of offices at either the local or national level.

New parties have been forced to accept limited successes. They have needed to rely for these either on dissension between alliance partners or on the willingness of the four parties to grant them limited access to their alliances. This has been far more likely on the part of the Socialists and Communists, who practice the trial run. A single candidate has understandably had more difficulty breaking into the RPR-UDF arrangement before the first ballot. Another alternative for those in lesser parties who wish to pursue elective office careers has been to migrate to one of the four main parties.

The National Front is the most conspicuous of the parties that have tried to alter the party system. An analysis of its electoral performance in 1997 reveals the problems these parties face. There are three ways to evaluate any party's electoral performance within the two-ballot rules: its success in winning elections, its success in competing for offices on the second ballot, and its success in attracting electoral support on both ballots.

The National Front's Success in Winning Office

In analyzing the stability of the French party system, confirmed by the elections of 1997, we have focused on the four main parties' success in electing deputies to the National Assembly. The reason is simple: the principal purpose of parties in democracies is to win elections. Judged by this standard, the National Front's performance has been poor. After electing thirty-five deputies in 1986, the one election held under proportional rules, the Front elected one deputy in 1988, no deputies in 1993, and one deputy in 1997. Yet even among the Front's few successful candidates, changing parties has seemed the best course for furthering their officeholding careers. Thus Yann Piat, the one National Front incumbent reelected in 1988, left the party during the course of the legislature to join the UDF; she went on to win reelection in 1993 as a UDF candidate. Jean-Jacques Peyrat, another FN deputy elected in 1986, lost his bid to return to the National Assembly in 1993, but in 1997 he succeeded as the RPR's candidate, defeating the Front's candidate on the second ballot by 71 percent of the vote.

One important reason for the Front's failings in the legislative elections has been its inability to elect the local officials who make up the majority of successful candidates for the office of deputy. In contrast, all four main parties have been able to draw on large pools of mayors and representatives to the departmental councils. Also elected under two-ballot rules, these local officials have made up the principal personnel that the four parties have relied on, as we have seen, to win in the single-member districts of the National Assembly.

In contrast, the Front's elective record at the local level has been poor. Indeed, the Front's election of three mayors in the municipal elections of 1995 and of one mayor in a subsequent by-election merely called attention to its shortcomings in this respect. The Front's four mayoralties must be viewed against the overwhelming number of those controlled by the four main parties among the more than 36,000 mayors chosen in France (Darley and de Fleurian 1992). Thus the Front's four successes stand in stark contrast even to those of the Communist Party, which after the municipal elections of 1995 controlled forty-one mayoralties, only in cities with more than 30,000 inhabitants (*Le Monde* 1995a, 6). The Front's record in electing representatives to the departmental councils has been even more dismal. After the last departmental elections in 1994, the Front held a mere 4 seats and the Communist Party 236, which were concentrated enough in two departments to give it control of their presidencies (*Le Monde* 1994, 27-46).

The Front's weakness at the local level has troubled even some of those in that party's ranks. The Front's second-in-command, Bruno Mégret, explained Le Pen's decision not to run in the elections of 1997 as the result of his never having developed "a strategy of local implantation."[5] Mégret himself felt confident that he would be elected to the National Assembly, having taken control of the mayoralty of Vitrolles, a town of 35,000 in southeast France. His confidence was reinforced because his *suppléant* was another FN mayor in the district. Much to Mégret's dismay, not only did he lose the election, but the seventy-year-old Socialist incumbent, Henri D'Attilio, another long-time mayor and departmental councilor in the district, whom Mégret had almost defeated in 1993, won handily, beating Mégret even in the town of Vitrolles. The only FN candidate to win in 1997 was the mayor of Toulon, the principal city in the area.

The Front owes its poor record in winning elective office to its inability to break into either of the two alliances that have dominated under the two-ballot rules. It has become increasingly isolated from the two parties for which its supporters have shown the greatest affinity, the RPR and the UDF—hence the strong negative reaction of Front activists to the remark of their leader, Jean-Marie Le

Pen, that he preferred a Socialist victory in the 1997 election. Yet the possibility that the RPR and UDF leadership will move toward any accommodation with Le Pen's Front has grown increasingly unlikely, largely because the Front's increasingly strident racism and anti-Semitism has antagonized parts of their electorate.

Leaving aside the probability that cooperation with the Front would cost more votes than it would gain, the RPR-UDF formula for winning has made it difficult for them to encompass any new party. In order to maximize their votes on the first ballot, these two parties have created an alliance that requires agreement on a single candidate before the first ballot. This agreement has not always been easy to implement among party aspirants. To include the Front in this arrangement would require a level of forbearance among RPR and UDF office seekers that as yet has not been evident. Candidates of parties with proven records of winning office are unlikely to defer to those of a party that has had few successes. Ultimately, under the single-member district, two-ballot rules, the Front has gained nothing that would help it bargain with the RPR-UDF alliance.

Despite Le Pen's blustering after the 1997 elections that the Front had determined the electoral outcome, the leaders of the RPR and the UDF knew this was not the case. As this chapter demonstrates, they knew they no more owed their defeat of 1997 to the Front than they owed to it the victory of 1993. Indeed, being on the blacklist that Le Pen substituted for blanket condemnation was as likely to help prominent members of the outgoing majority as it was to harm them. Of the eleven most prominent RPR and UDF candidates on Le Pen's blacklist, eight, including the Gaullist Prime Minister Juppé, won election. Among the three on the list who were defeated was Gérard Longuet, who had earlier resigned as minister because of allegations of corruption.

In the wake of defeat, both RPR and UDF activists wondered whether the time had not come for their parties to come to an agreement with the Front. They cited as their model the Socialist Party's agreement with the Communist Party, concluded under Mitterrand in the early 1970s. But the leaders of the RPR and the UDF, if not all the rank and file, knew that such a comparison was invalid. Mitterrand had, with the Common Program, merely made more conclusive an electoral arrangement that dated back to 1936. In any event the Communist Party—one of the four main parties, unlike the Front—had bargaining power within the two-ballot rules. The leaders of the UDF and the RPR could certainly agree that everything should be done to attract the Front's voters, short of antagonizing their own electorate. But they saw little electoral advantage in coming to terms with the Front that Le Pen embodied.

The National Front's Success in Competing on the Second Ballot

Another way to assess the Front's performance in the elections of 1997 is to note the number of districts it was able to contest on the second ballot against candidates of one of the four main parties. A sign of the Socialists' weakness in 1993 was the 100 districts in which the Front candidate was either the principal opponent or part of a triangular race on the second ballot. In 1997 the Front accomplished the same feat in 133 districts. There was, however, an important distinction: although the Front was able to vie for more districts, the number in which it was the principal opponent declined from 86 in 1993 to 56 in 1997, a far less impressive accomplishment. Its remaining 76 contests were triangular races, where it always ran third.

Of even more interest is the effect that the presence of FN candidates on the second ballot had on the electoral performance of the four main parties' candidates. As in 1993, the Front's presence in 1997 swelled the electoral margin of the victors, no matter what the party. If anything, the effect in 1997 was even more dramatic. Tables 6.5 and 6.6 (page 148) illustrate this effect. As table 6.5 demonstrates, all four parties' winning candidates did best when their opponents were FN candidates. They did most poorly in 1993 against Socialist opponents, and against Communist candidates in 1997.

TABLE 6.5. WINNING CANDIDATES' SHIFT IN ELECTORAL MARGINS AGAINST OPPONENTS BETWEEN BALLOTS IN THE 1993 AND 1997 LEGISLATIVE ELECTIONS

	1993		*1997*	
Closest opponent on second ballot	*Margin*	*Number*	*Margin*	*Number*
National Front	10.93	86	21.33	55
Gaullist	7.37	48	7.62	138
UDF	6.21	54	7.83	129
Communist	-1.17	21	-5.05	3
Socialist	-1.87	236	-1.33	171

SOURCES: See table 6.1 on page 137.

NOTE: Number = number of winning candidates.

NOTE: The electoral margin is the difference between the winning candidate's percentage of the total vote and the second-place candidate's percentage of the total vote. A negative difference between the two electoral margins indicates that, on the second ballot, the winner lost votes in relation to his or her nearest competitor.

TABLE 6.6. AVERAGE SHIFT IN ELECTORAL MARGINS BETWEEN FIRST AND SECOND BALLOTS, WITH AND WITHOUT THE NATIONAL FRONT ON THE SECOND BALLOT

	1993				*1997*			
	With the National Front		*Without the National Front*		*With the National Front*		*Without the National Front*	
	Margin	*Number*	*Margin*	*Number*	*Margin*	*Number*	*Margin*	*Number*
Gaullist	7.83	45	-0.39	158	8.98	30	-1.46	100
UDF	11.12	45	2.63	131	11.99	28	-1.49	76
Socialist	7.79	5	9.63	47	9.75	45	7.42	190
Communist	12.84	4	6.89	18	15.24	17	11.58	13

SOURCES: See table 6.1 on page 137.

NOTE: Number = number of deputies.

NOTE: The electoral margin is the difference between the winning candidate's percentage of the total vote and the second-place candidate's percentage of the total vote. A negative difference between the two electoral margins indicates that, on the second ballot, the winner lost votes in relation to his or her nearest competitor.

Table 6.6 shows the effect of the Front's presence on the four main parties' performance from one ballot to another. In 1997 all four parties improved their margins of support between the two ballots most impressively when the Front was in the contest, even more so than in 1993. Interestingly enough, Communist candidates performed best against the Front, although it was the Communist electorate that was often singled out as most susceptible to the Front's appeal. But even the RPR, whose margin of support between ballots had declined in previous elections, improved its margin in 1993 and 1997 against FN candidates. Without the Front in the contest, the RPR margin reverted to its usual level.

The National Front's Success in Attracting Votes on Both Ballots

Finally, the Front's performance in the legislative elections of 1997 can be evaluated in terms of its electoral support. This is, however, the least reliable way of weighing relative partisan strength. Since these are two-ballot elections, electoral support on both ballots should be evaluated. The existence of two ballots, one on which many parties can compete and a second that strictly limits the number of competitors, turns voters as well as parties into strategic players. This means that each election will be held under different circumstances. For one thing, the electorate will not be the same: new voters will participate in the second ballot, while old voters will drop out. Moreover, the logic of the two-ballot election, as we have seen, leads parties with serious aspirations for winning to engage in alliance practices that limit their participation on both ballots.

Consequently, reading first-ballot votes alone as the sign of a party's relative electoral support is deceptive; to do so means that the support of voters who choose to participate only in the second and decisive round of the elections will not be counted. It also means that the support of parties who agree on a single candidate before the first ballot, in order to win as many seats as possible, cannot be accurately assessed.

During the 1980s and 1990s the RPR and UDF agreed on a single candidate before the first ballot in the majority of electoral districts. As discussed, in 1997 they reached agreement in almost all districts, which was a record number. In 1997 the RPR ran in 288 districts in metropolitan France, polling 16.6 percent of the vote on the first ballot. The UDF ran in 265 districts, polling 14.9 percent of the vote on the first ballot.

In contrast, the National Front, which was a weak officeholding party unable to conclude any alliances, took advantage of the first ballot to run candidates in all 555 districts in metropolitan France. While this tactic ruled out almost any chance of winning, it did allow the Front to accumulate 15.2 percent of the vote. Yet given these circumstances, it would be presumptuous to draw conclusions about its electoral support compared to that of the UDF and RPR. Indeed, its tactic of placing candidates in as many districts as possible on the first ballot in order to accumulate votes was a sign of electoral weakness, not strength, and of its inability not only to conclude the necessary electoral agreements with other parties but to attract their voters' support. In its early years, the Communist Party had used the same tactic, until it was able to end its political isolation by joining Radicals and Socialists in the Popular Front of 1936 (Schlesinger 1978).

The first-ballot vote can be a deceptive means of assessing the relative support of the Socialists and Communists, whose alliance involves the trial run. Thus in 1997 the Socialist Party polled 24.6 percent of the vote, running in 482 of the 555 districts. In the remaining districts the Socialist Party accommodated its smaller allies, the Radical Socialists and the Greens, as well as the Citizens' Movement, a breakaway group from the Socialist Party. Benefiting from this arrangement, which also included the Communists, these smaller parties, unlike the Front, together elected thirty-five deputies, enough to form a separate group in the National Assembly.

It is true that in the election of 1997 the Communist Party had candidates in 538 of the 555 districts and polled only 9.9 percent of the vote. But here we should take into account the Communist voters' long experience as strategic voters. Not only have they been willing to honor the trial run for the second ballot, but they also have been prepared to vote on the first ballot for a second-choice candidate with a realistic chance of winning on the second ballot. This was clearly the case in the presidential election of 1995, and it helped to account for the Socialist Jospin's surprise first-place showing on the first ballot.

Nevertheless, since the second ballot decides the outcome of the elections, as the electorate well knows, it could be argued plausibly that the distribution of electoral support on the second ballot is an equal, if not better, gauge of relative partisan electoral support. This is especially true in an election such as that of 1997, in which the level of abstention on the second ballot in metropolitan France declined by 3.2 percent, indicating the electorate's increased mobilization for the second ballot. As tables 6.5 and 6.6 (page 147) indicate, the mobilization of the electorate for the second ballot worked to the benefit of the four main parties.

Of course the second ballot was affected even more by the implementation of the four parties' alliances. Enjoying the advantages of the trial run, the Socialist Party, running in 414 districts, saw its second-ballot support increase the most, to 37.1 percent. But in the decisive round, with limited competition, the RPR and the UDF also substantially increased their support. Running in 259 districts on the second ballot, the RPR saw its electoral support rise to 23.6 percent of the vote; the UDF, running in 231 districts, saw its support rise to 21.9 percent.

Meanwhile, the Front's support declined in 1993, not only in the first ballot, but in its second-ballot support. In 1993 the Front had polled 12.7 percent of the vote on the first ballot; running in 100 districts on the second ballot, the Front saw its support decline by 6.9 percent, to 5.8 percent of the vote. In 1997 the Front's support on the first ballot rose to 15.2 percent; but on the second ballot, running in 133 districts, the Front saw its support decline by 9.5 percent, to 5.7 percent. On the first ballot, the Front still outpolled the Communist Party, which received 3.6 percent of the vote on the second ballot. But on the second ballot, the Communist Party, having respected the trial run, ran in only 37 districts, all but 3 of which the party won. Clearly on the second ballot the Front lost support among its initial electorate, while the support it could count on from voters from parties whose candidates had dropped out was negligible.

The Endurance of the Four Main Parties

Our analysis of the 1997 elections confirms the stability of the French party system, whatever the drama occasioned by the Socialists' rapid and unexpected return to power. The four major parties in evidence since the start of the Fifth Republic remain in control of elective office and therefore of the republic as well. Indeed, all four parties can trace their origins to the Third Republic when, with the adoption of universal manhood suffrage and the two-ballot rules for most elections, modern French political parties emerged (Schlesinger and Schlesinger 1990, 1094-96).

The endurance of the four main parties owes much, as we have pointed out, to that of the two-ballot system. This has been true despite the French penchant for experimenting with both political institutions and electoral rules. The French politicians who devised the two-ballot rules for French elections can view their efforts in the same way as the wallpaperer who in 1956 drove around the streets of Paris with a sign on his truck reading, "Republics may come and go, but our work endures."

The appearance of political parties such as the National Front must also be kept in historical perspective. As other political observers have already pointed out, of course, the presence of French political organizations preaching xenophobic and anti-Semitic messages and prone to strong-arm tactics is by no means new. Indeed, the Front can trace its lineage to such organizations in the Third and Fourth Republics in the career of Le Pen. Le Pen embarked on his political career under the tutelage of Pierre Poujade, whose extremist, antiestablishment *Union et fraternité française* burst upon the political scene in 1956, for the last elections of the Fourth Republic. Taking advantage of the Algerian crisis and the proportional representation rules used during the republic's brief life, Poujade's party elected forty-one deputies to the National Assembly, including Le Pen. Poujade himself, the son of a member of the *Action française*, an antirepublican league founded before World War I, had belonged to the youth movement of Jacques Doriot's fascist party in the 1930s.

Placing the Front in historical perspective also means considering the fate of its predecessors. During the serious economic and diplomatic crises of the 1930s, the majority of the French electorate turned not to Doriot, but to the Popular Front, the alliance of Radicals, Socialists, and Communists who, under the two-ballot rules, came to power in 1936. To resolve the crises of the Fourth Republic, the majority of elected representatives turned in 1958 not to Pierre Poujade, but to Charles de Gaulle. Instituting the Fifth Republic, de Gaulle and his advisers immediately abandoned proportional representation and returned to the single-member district, two-ballot rules for electing deputies to the National Assembly. Under the two-ballot rules, in the economic crisis of the 1990s, the vast majority of the French electorate turned not to the National Front but in 1993 to the RPR-

UDF alliance, and in 1997 to the Socialist Party and its allies, including the Communists. If anything, as we have seen, the very presence of FN candidates on the second ballot was enough to swell their opponents' electoral support, whatever their party. This is not to deny that the Front enjoys support among French voters. It is merely to point out that the support enjoyed by the four main parties is vastly greater. In 1997 the French electorate, as it had over the course of three republics, continued to sustain the same party system.

Chapter 7

Cleavage Voting and Issue Voting in France

Daniel Boy and Nonna Mayer

European political parties are constructed on the basis of religious and professional cleavages, with the leftist parties taking up the cause of the rights of workers, and the parties on the right representing the interests of the middle and upper classes. France is no exception to this rule. The pioneering work of Michelat and Simon (1977) has brought to light two "heavy" variables of electoral sociology: social class and religion. This "sociological" model, which relates voting to identification with a group (professional, residential, or denominational) and which is close in many aspects to the explanatory model put forth by the Columbia School in *The People's Choice* (Lazarsfeld 1944), is today being questioned. The global influence of religion, in politics as in the whole of social life, is in decline as it is measured by declared religious affiliation, belief in God and in fundamental dogmas, regular church attendance, and worship practices (baptisms, marriages, funerals), or even the recognized place of religion in daily life (Lambert 1995; Poulat 1994). This phenomenon is particularly marked in young people, as each new generation manifests a greater detachment from religion than its predecessor (Lambert and Michelat 1992). At the same time, one observes a decline in class voting, which may be ascribed to France's passage from an industrial society to a "postindustrial" society (Clark, Lipset, and Rempel 1993; Dogan 1996). Improved schooling (particularly in higher education), the media, and the rise of "postmaterialist" values (Inglehart 1990; Dalton, Flanagan, and Beck 1984) favor the political emancipation of the people and the emergence of a new category of voters, who are "individualistic" and "rational" (Lavau 1986; Habert and Lancelot 1996). Better informed and more politicized, they are less dependent on political parties and more able to decide among specific issues at stake and opposing candidates. Eventually this "issue voting" or "value voting" will replace the "cleavage voting" based on religious or socioprofessional factors (Franklin et al. 1992).

Other authors foresee instead the birth of new cleavages due to education, modes of consumption or lifestyle, or sector of activity. Some researchers insist, for example, on a major opposition between public and private workers, and even between consumers of public goods (social lodging, public transportation, and public medicine) and private goods (individual cars, individual housing, and private health care), the former voting more with the left and the latter more with the right (Dunleavy and Husbands 1985). Still others insist there is a growing specificity of the education and sociocultural sectors and, even more, of those professions linked to the production of immaterial and collective services (Kriesi 1989; Parkin 1968).

Old Cleavages

In order to verify the usefulness of these hypotheses, we have made use of the indicators that were the most predictive in our 1978 and 1988 electoral investigations of the voting behavior of the French—religious practice and socioprofessional category—and related them to voting in the legislative elections of 1997. With the growing polarization of the National Front electorate preventing its assimilation with the moderate right, we distinguished, as we did in 1988, among voting trends for the left (including Ecologist Party candidates), the right, and the National Front candidates.[1]

Religion

Although Catholicism remains the primary religion of France, the proportion of French people who declare themselves to be Catholic is diminishing, from 82 percent of French people of voting age in 1978 to 73 percent in 1997. Among the Catholics, the decline in church attendance has been confirmed. Regular practitioners, who go to mass at least once or twice per month, have fallen from 21 percent of the registered electorate in 1978 to 16 percent in 1997. As to those who still go to mass every Sunday, they make up only 10 percent, compared with 16 percent in 1978.[2] In all, nonpracticing Catholics represent 41 percent of first-round voters, with those who practice (even not regularly) making up a third, and those who belong to another religion or who do not declare any religious affiliation making up a little more than a fourth. There are just as many indications of the declining influence of Catholicism, confirmed by recent polls that show a growing autonomy for Catholics, even for those who observe regularly, concerning the official position of the Church, notably in the domain of sexual morality (Michel and Luneau 1995).[3]

One could still observe in 1997, however, a strong relationship between electoral choice and the frequency of religious practice. The vote for the right-wing UDF-RPR in the first round ranged from 14 percent among voters who declared themselves to be without religion to 70 percent among regularly practicing Catholics who attend mass at least once per month; inversely, the vote for the left ranged from 69 percent to 23 percent (see figure 7.1).

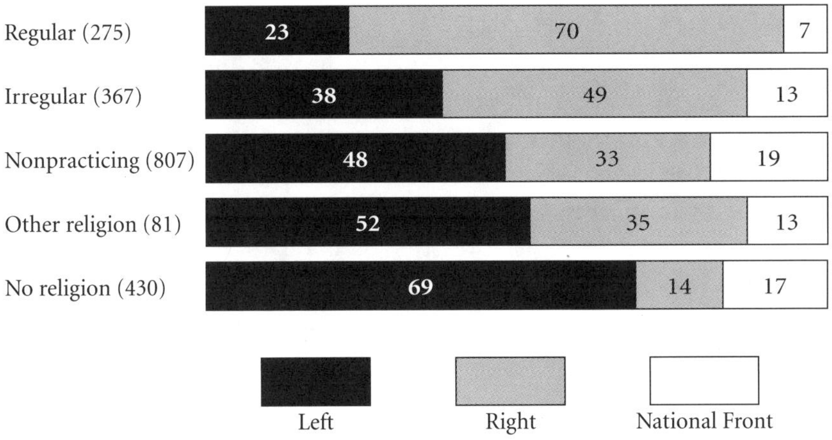

FIGURE 7.1 VOTE BY CATHOLIC RELIGIOUS PRACTICE, 1997

SOURCE: See note 1, page 263.

These differences of 56 and 46 percentage points, respectively, are weaker than those found in 1978, when they remained considerable, reaching 68 percentage points. If one adopts a finer classification for the variables of practice, the electoral influence of religion appears still more clearly, with the level of the vote for the right in the Catholic community ranging from 73 percent among those who attend church every Sunday to 33 percent among those who never set foot in church. The religious cleavages thus have maintained their importance, as attested by the liveliness of current debates—such as those over private school, or more recently those concerning the commemoration of the baptism of Clovis (496 A.D.), the first king of France converted to Catholicism. If religious divisions have subsided slightly since the 1970s, it is because the FN is progressively penetrating categories of the electorate that until recently had aligned with the left. Compared to the UDF or the RPR, Le Pen's party made its worst impression with practicing

Catholics, in spite of efforts aimed at Catholics and despite a strong traditionalistic Catholic presence among his potential followers (Camus 1996, 231-52). The fact that the bishops of France have several times firmly taken positions against the FN and pointed out how its message contradicts that of the Gospels undoubtedly has worked toward turning the most religious away from extremist temptation. As for the universalistic and egalitarian values of the left, they can only block penetration by the FN of the minority group of committed atheists (3 percent of the sample), who claim never to go to church even for ceremonies, and among whom the level of voting for the FN is at 11 percent. It is over nonpracticing Catholics belonging to neither of these two extremes that Le Pen's party has the most influence, reaching 19 percent of those who no longer go to church except for ceremonies.

This electoral cleavage might reflect the effect of other variables linked to religious behaviors: demographic (age or sex), economic (income or property), or sociocultural (profession, level of education, religion). It is known that Catholic observance is more frequent among women, among elderly persons, and, in rural areas, particularly among farmers. Nevertheless, in rural as well as in urban communities, and among women and men equally, no matter what their ages, the frequency of voters' religious practice is positively related to the probability of their voting for the moderate right.

Social Class

If one defines social class according to the relationship of individuals to the means of production and exchange, the socioprofessional nomenclature of the National Institute of Statistics and Economic Studies (INSEE) gives an approximate indicator that allows us to distinguish between the self-employed, who own their own businesses, and wage earners, employed persons who work for a boss, including differences between blue-collar and white-collar workers. The persons questioned were classified according to their profession at the time of the poll, and those who had stopped working—whether they were unemployed, retired, or women who had worked earlier in life—were reclassified according to their last profession, in order to create the largest database of workers.[4]

In the legislative elections of 1978, 70 percent of manual workers voted for the left. They were the socioprofessional group by far the farthest to the left, outdistancing nonmanual workers by 16 points. By 1997 there were no longer differences between manual and nonmanual (clerical) workers (see figure 7.2). In both groups, the left just barely captured the majority. The global difference between left voting of the self-employed and salaried workers has also declined, dropping

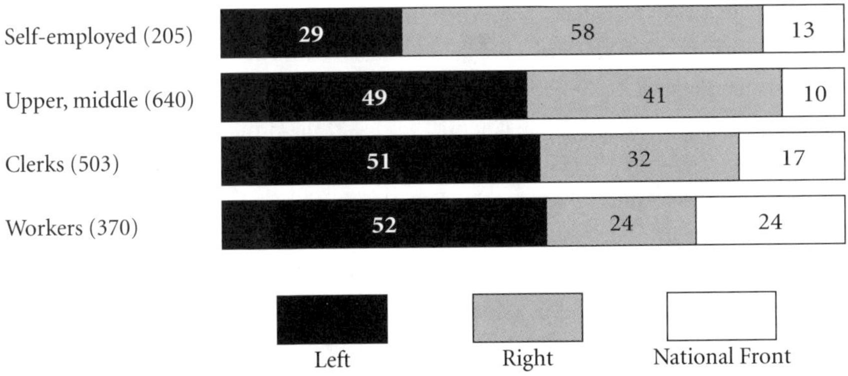

FIGURE 7.2 VOTE BY OCCUPATIONAL CLASS, 1997

SOURCE: See note 1, page 263.

from 42 to 23 percent. Twenty years ago, the more an individual was integrated into the working-class world, the better his or her chances were of voting for the left. Between those who had not a single worker "attribute" and those who had three, there was a 40-percentage-point difference. Paradoxically, in 1997 it was among the workers who were the most integrated into this group (where the left formerly found its best support) that Le Pen had the most success, with figures in the first legislative round ranging from 13 percent among those having no worker attributes to 33 percent among those who had three (see figure 7.3).

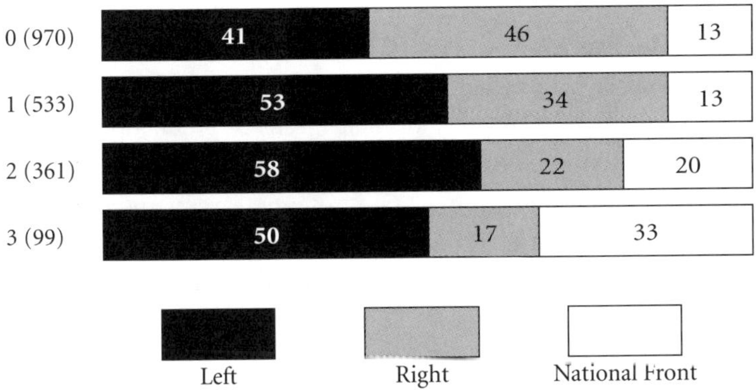

FIGURE 7.3 VOTE BY NUMBER OF WORKING-CLASS ATTRIBUTES (PERCENTAGE OF VALID VOTES)

SOURCE: See note 1, page 263.

This paradox translates into the disarray of a working class particularly touched by industrial restructurings and crisis. From the 1982 census to that of 1990, its proportion in the active population dropped from 38 percent to 31 percent (Cezard and Dussert 1993; Chenu 1993) and the proportion of unemployed workers has risen from 9.6 percent to 14.2 percent. The most affected categories of workers are those among whom the French Communist Party used to find its privileged support: the trained workers, working in big businesses, in sectors such as the automobile industry, arms, naval shipyards, mines, and metallurgy.[5] Such "worker fortresses" are gradually disappearing, and the very definition of manual work is in the process of changing. Today two workers out of five work in the third sector, as chauffeurs, packers, or storekeepers, or in specialized services, such as temporary work or cleaning. These work situations are characterized by isolation and increasing precariousness, and the boundaries between clerical worker and manual worker have become fuzzy, without any traditions of union battles and collective action; thus workers are much more receptive to the discourse of Le Pen. One can observe the same phenomenon, although less rigorous, among sales and clerical workers, a category which is primarily female and where unemployment, just as among manual workers, affects one worker in seven. The National Front is progressing among the most disadvantaged wage earners, thanks to the deceptions that arose when the left came to power (Mayer 1996).

At the same time, the left stood its ground among the non-manual-labor wage-earning class, conquered by the Socialist left in the 1970s (Grunberg and Schweisguth 1981; 1983). Its 1997 votes are comparable to those that it received in 1978, with the National Front clearly receiving less support—10 percent versus 15 percent, on average (see figure 7.2, page 157).

As for the self-employed, whether mechanics or grocers, farmers, heads of business, or doctors, they are the owners of their means of production and are attached to free enterprise and individual initiative. They feel threatened by a left that seems to them to be too attentive to the rights of wage earners and too favorable toward regulatory intervention by the state in social and economic life. Their roots in the right are not new, as they may be observed during the entire Fifth Republic (Mayer 1986). These roots became more pronounced in the 1980s, thanks to the electoral dynamic initiated by the union of the Socialist and Communist left, which was solidified by the signing of a Common Program in 1972. The self-employed became worried about a potential victory by the "sociocommunists." This phenomenon also reflects recent transformations in employment circumstances. Between the 1982 census and that of 1990, the number of small family businesses and artisan shops—encompassing those most likely to vote for the left—dropped. With the decline of traditional trades (grocer, textile and leather worker, construction worker) came the rapid expansion of business in the city center (Peron 1993), with workers providing services and artisans art. These new businesspeople and artisans are of a higher social and cultural class, in the image of their clientele, and they tend toward a bourgeois outlook, which explains their move toward the right. The same is true of farmers (particularly young farmers) when the average size of their business ventures increases (Barthez 1996).

At the point where these social evolutions intersect, the electorate splits into two opposing camps: the self-employed, who are mostly influenced by the right, and the wage earners, who vote most often for the left. The more an individual is integrated into one of these two worlds, the more he or she is likely to belong to either the right or the left. To verify this, we have constructed an integration indicator for self-employed people and wage earners, based on the model perfected by Michelat and Simon (1977) in order to pinpoint a person's attachment to the working class. This measure takes into account the professional status of the individual at the time of the investigation, the professional status of that person's father at the time the individual left school or the university, and the professional status of the individual's future spouse. From this data we can obtain an indicator varying from 0 to 3, depending on the number of connections an individual has with the milieu of the self-employed or wage earner. This leads to a considerable increase in nonsalaried employees' importance in French society, because 38 percent of the study population had at least one connection with the self-employed milieu, whereas in the 1990 census the self-employed represented only 13 percent of the work force. Of those we studied, the propensity to vote for the right, or at least the moderate right, in the first round of legislative elections in 1997 rose steadily along with the number of their self-employed connections or "attributes," rising from 29 percent of those with none, to 72 percent of those with three (see figure 7.4 on page 160), while the level of voting for the left dropped from 53 to 22 percent. The vote for the National Front evolved in exactly the same way as did that for the left, being weakest among those individuals who are most integrated into the world of the self-employed and who vote in huge numbers for candidates of the moderate right. Inversely, only 8 percent of voters have no tie to the world of salaried employees; the frequency of the vote for the left rises from a third among this group to 56 percent among those with three wage-earner attributes. Even in this case, the National Front vote rises according to the number of ties people have with the salaried worker class (see figure 7.5 on page 160).

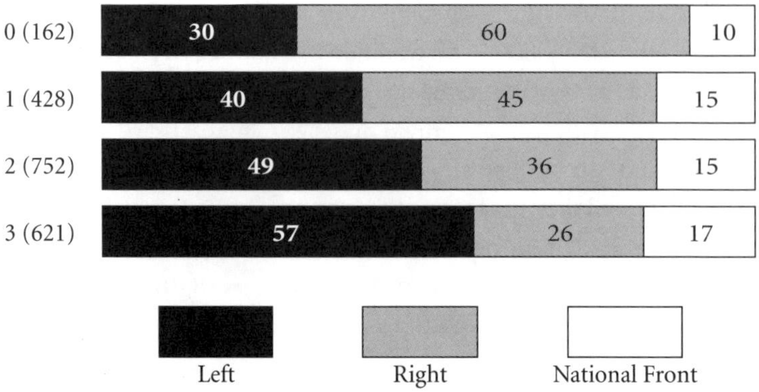

FIGURE 7.4 VOTE BY NUMBER OF SALARIED ATTRIBUTES (PERCENTAGE OF VALID VOTES)

SOURCE: See note 1, page 263.

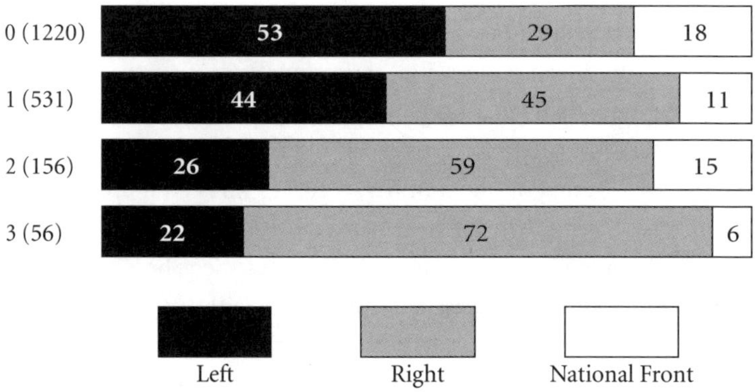

FIGURE 7.5 VOTE BY NUMBER OF SELF-EMPLOYED ATTRIBUTES (PERCENTAGE OF VALID VOTES)

SOURCE: See note 1, page 263.

The cleavage between the self-employed and wage earners might reflect the effect of other variables linked to political behavior: demographics (age or sex), economics (income or property), or sociocultural factors (profession, level of education, or religion). The households of the self-employed have an average income level four times greater than that of the households of wage earners, and they own real estate and property worth eight times more.[6] The self-employed often live in rural communities, are older, and are more likely to be practicing Catholics. The relatively high scores on these variables that exist for the self-employed group might increase their probability of voting for the right. However, after controlling on these other variables, the self-employed still tend more to the right than do wage earners; that is, regardless of any correlations of sex, age, income, net worth, religious practice, level of education, and residence in a rural or urban community.

The main class cleavages brought to light by our 1978, 1988, and 1995 studies have not disappeared, but rather have shifted because of the effects of social and political change. The principal differences exist no longer between manual workers and clerical workers, but between the self-employed and wage earners, with a resurgence of the left among salaried upper and middle classes compensating for its decline within the working class. These results agree with those of other studies carried out in Great Britain (Heath, Jowell, and Curtice 1985; Heath et al. 1991; Cautrès and Heath 1996) and in the United States (Hout, Brooks, and Manza 1995). The authors of these studies criticized both the rudimentary nature of socioprofessional classifications (manual worker/nonmanual worker, working class/nonworking class) used by those who concluded that "class voting" was disappearing, and the statistical instruments (particularly the Alford index) used to measure the association between voting and class. They concluded, on the basis of more detailed classifications and sophisticated methodology, such as the use of loglinear models, that the relationship between voting and class fluctuates. In the long run, realignments and nonalignments are balanced out as soon as one accepts that there is no unique and invariant model of "class voting." Then, the working class vote for the left, and the salaried upper- and middle-class vote for the left, are both examples of class "realignments."

New Cleavages

An analysis of global class cleavages is incomplete, however, without a more detailed analysis of individuals' professional situations. Such an analysis should take into account the nature of the work and the levels of education and of training that it requires, as well as the socioprofessional sector within which the work falls. Such an analysis would seek potential "new" transversal cleavages that are specific to the transition toward postindustrial society.

The world of the self-employed seems relatively homogeneous, solidly rooted in the right, and this impression of political homogeneity undoubtedly reflects the group's social homogeneity. The rate at which the milieu of the self-employed reproduces itself (autoreproduction) remains high, with parents passing down to their children, if not their businesses or their land, at least the aspiration to work on one's own and to be "one's own boss." The work of the self-employed remains largely family work, involving spouses and children. Homes and workplaces are often interconnected, and the separation between work activity and leisure generally is less distinct for this group than it is for the wage-earning class, with many self-employed individuals continuing their trades after retiring. All these factors contribute to the ideological and political unity of the self-employed.

TABLE 7.1. VOTE IN 1997 BY OCCUPATION (IN PERCENTAGES)

	Left	*Right*	*National Front*	*N*
Self-employed				
Farmers	27	71	2	79
Craftsmen	36	34	31	51
Shopkeepers, industrialists	27	60	12	75
Professionals	35	56	9	34
Upper and middle classes				
Upper management	38	49	13	158
Teachers, professors	67	32	2	96
Medical and social workers	57	41	2	67
Middle management	39	40	21	135
Foremen	46	48	6	74
Technicians	66	22	12	74
Clerical workers				
Sales assistants	66	27	9	88
Office clerks	51	32	17	322
Service sector[a]	62	31	7	48
Working class				
Skilled workers	54	22	23	224
Unskilled workers	48	26	26	123
Total sample	48	37	15	1963

SOURCE: See note 1, page 263.

NOTE: Occupation = present occupation of respondent or former occupation (if unemployed or retired).

a. For example, personnel employed as waiters, beauticians, housekeepers, or janitors.

Two groups, however, offer notable exceptions. Farmers exhibit a marked reticence toward the National Front, which receives only 2 percent of their votes (see table 7.1). As a group, they are characterized by several factors that prevent the infiltration of FN ideas: strong religious practice, a privileged relationship with the Gaullist movement, an active union framework, and strong social cohesion (Mayer 1995). Artisans, on the contrary, are the only category of self-employed among whom the FN is gaining electoral ground. Their behavior is similar to that of the working class, to whose milieu they are professionally and socially very close. Like the working class, artisans perform manual labor in making or transforming the products they sell. Of all the self-employed, they have the greatest number of family connections with workers (i.e., the greatest proportion of worker attributes).

Public People, Private People

The world of the wage earners, on the other hand, is more diverse. A leading factor differentiating members of the wage-earning class is whether they work in the public or private sector (Boy and Mayer 1997a). In the context of the economic crisis that France currently is going through, with more than 13 percent unemployed, the scope of state intervention is a recurrent theme of political conflict, as is the legitimacy of the protected public sector, which largely is shielded from the constraints of the market. An individual's personal position with respect to this conflict thus has a particular importance. One might expect that public-sector workers tend to support the leftist political forces that most readily affirm that sector's existence, oppose talk of privatization, and defend the principle of state intervention in the economy in the name of regulating market mechanisms.

The political differences go in the expected direction (see table 7.2 on page 164). Whatever the professional group may be, belonging to either the public or private sector differentiates political behavior. While these differences are very modest in the case of workers (50 percent versus 56 percent who vote for the left), they are more visible among managers and professionals, because among those in the private sector, 41 percent claim to vote for the left, versus 63 percent of those in the public sector who make the same claim. It is true that educators represent an important fraction of this group in the public sector. In fact, their distinctive leftist political orientation came about at the end of the nineteenth century, in the battles for republican secular schools. A deeper analysis shows, however, that even when we put the case of educators to the side and consider only executives, those in the public sector have a political orientation distant from that of their counterparts in the private sector (57 percent of them vote for the left versus 34 percent, respectively). Thus it is neither the "teaching function," nor the political traditions of that milieu, nor the absence of a constraining framework that determines a more marked vote for the left, but rather the fact of working in the public sector.

TABLE 7.2. VOTE IN 1997 BY OCCUPATION AND TYPE OF EMPLOYMENT (IN PERCENTAGES)

	Left	*Right*	*National Front*	*N*
Upper and middle classes				
Private-sector	41	46	14	331
Public-sector	63	31	6	268
Clerical workers				
Private-sector	53	36	11	250
Public-sector	50	27	23	24
Working class				
Private-sector	50	25	25	291
Public-sector	56	22	22	78

SOURCE: See note 1, page 263.

NOTE: Occupation = present occupation of respondent or former occupation (if unemployed or retired).

This cleavage is not recent. Already in the legislative elections of 1973, one could note a difference of 10 percentage points in the level of voting for the left, depending on whether wage earners worked in the private or public sector;[7] but for a long while this cleavage has incited less interest than cleavages between manual workers and nonmanual workers, or between the self-employed and wage earners, because its scope was much smaller.[8] It was only in 1978 that the question of type of employment was asked in a systematic manner in electoral polls. Since that time, the economic crisis and the rise of unemployment—which brutally touches wage earners of the private sector and makes public-sector wage earners seem like privileged individuals who are assured job security and a better retirement—clearly contributed to the persistence of this cleavage during Mitterrand's two seven-year terms of office (Boy and Mayer 1997a). The simple fact of being a public or private wage earner made a 10-percentage point difference in voting for the left during the first round of legislative elections in 1997 (see figure 7.6).

As with the cleavage between the self-employed and wage earners, that between the private and public sectors divides not only the workers but their families as well. Beyond the concept of a professional group is an entire social milieu rooted in the left, which is linked to the notions of public service and the collective

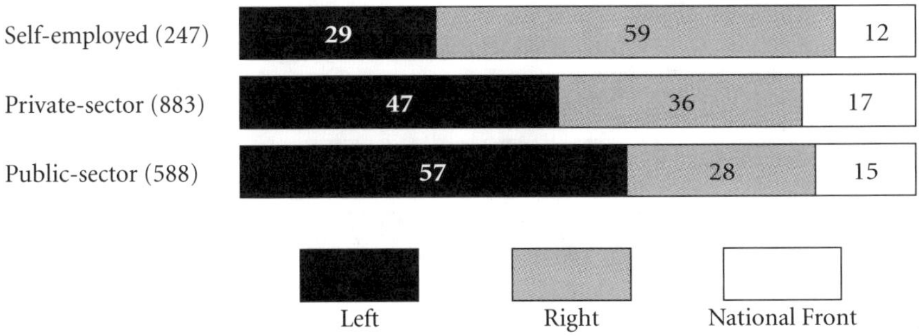

FIGURE 7.6 VOTE BY TYPE OF EMPLOYMENT (PERCENTAGE OF VALID VOTES)

SOURCE: See note 1, page 263.

interest.[9] The public milieu is also a relatively homogeneous one, in which the appeal of public service seems to be passed down from one generation to another, influencing even the choice of a spouse: public-sector wage earners questioned in the 1995 study were twice as often children of wage earners in the public sector than of workers in the private sector, and when they were married, their spouses nearly twice as often worked in the public sector.[10] In all, if one takes into account these social ties, the public sector has an electoral influence that goes far beyond its numerical impact among the employed. In fact, nearly half of the voting-age population has at least one link with the public sector, if we include spouses and children. Just as integration into the world of manual workers or that of the self-employed rises with the number of manual-worker or self-employed attributes—and consequently, so does the probability of voting either for the left or for the right—the frequency of votes for the left goes up steadily with the number of ties to the public sector (see figure 7.7), ranging from 42 percent among those who have no ties to 73 percent among those who have three.

The Socioprofessional Category

A second cleavage of the wage-earning class places production wage earners (employed staff members and workers) opposite "mid-level wage earners," who have been attracted in growing numbers to the left and especially to the Socialist Party after its reconstruction at the time of the Congress of Epinay in 1971 (Grunberg and Schweisguth 1981; 1983). The mid-level wage-earner category includes the majority of non-factory-worker wage earners, executives and intermediary professionals, technicians, engineers, educators, medical and social workers, and so on. With the expansion of the public sector and its services, the number of its

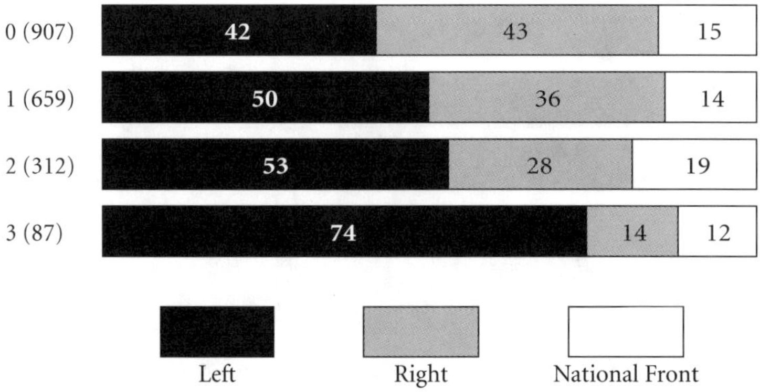

FIGURE 7.7 VOTE BY NUMBER OF PUBLIC-SECTOR ATTRIBUTES (PERCENTAGE OF VALID VOTES)

SOURCE: See note 1, page 263.

employees more than doubled between the 1954 census and the 1975 census, achieving an influence today comparable to that of manual workers. It was among this social group that the left's influence progressed the most between the legislative elections of 1967 and 1978. Workers in this category were inclined to the left because of their situation as wage earners, their working-class social backgrounds, and their employment either in the public sector or in large corporations, where the traditions of union struggle and of collective action have been particularly steadfast. As educated urban young people detached from religious practices, they also were particularly sensitive to the hedonistic, individualistic, and permissive values that developed in the 1960s, the years of "cultural liberalism" (Grunberg and Schweisguth 1981; 1977; 1983), which was the French version of the "postmaterialism" analyzed by Ronald Inglehart (1990).[11] Their very adhesion to these values has made them more receptive to the participatory management (*autogestion*) tone of Socialist discourse than to either the strict workers' orientation (*l'ouvriérisme*) of the PCF or the conservatism of the parties of the right. This phenomenon was also found in 1997, and it was particularly noticeable among educators, half of whom tended to vote in favor of Socialist or Ecologist candidates (versus a third of the general electorate who voted for these candidates).

The various models of interpretation evoked by this political specificity of the intellectual wage-earner professions are not contradictory. We have stressed how permeable these professions' social levels can be concerning the values of "cultural liberalism." Thus it follows logically that in their political choices, members of these professions favor the parties that defend these values. That is true for the

Socialist left, but it is most especially true for the Ecologists, whose cultural radicalism has never gone unnoticed. Another factor favoring orientation toward the left is more frequent inclusion in the public sector. This tends to be true for educators (67 percent of teachers and administrators vote for the left) but is also the case for nearly two-thirds of the health and social work professionals (57 percent vote for the left). Many scholars have also argued that the nature of the work in the education, social work, or health professions implies a large number of social relationships, which would incline workers to adopt values based on reciprocity and egalitarianism, as Herbert Kitschelt suggests (1995, 5). This cleavage holds true for many people in these professions who also are well educated—for example, 78 percent of executives and 57 percent of intermediate professionals have their French high school diplomas (*le Bac*), versus only 17 percent of sales and clerical workers and 3 percent of manual workers, according to the 1990 census—and whose work is more "intellectual" and further from the production sector. A higher level of education affects the particular demands a voter will make on the political system: a rise in cognitive capacity goes hand-in-hand with demands for improvement of the democratic process. The parties of the left and, even more so, the ecologist movements have become the most fervent defenders of democratic mechanisms. It has become a common practice to note that these professions, unlike the liberal professions, also define themselves by a contradiction between their high level of education and their relatively low social remuneration; this generates a certain frustration whose political outcome is a vote for the parties that contest the established order.

Inversely, these are the very professions that are most hesitant to vote for the candidates of parties such as the National Front, whose political discourse is simplified and anti-intellectual. The FN's results appear to be inversely related to the voters' level of education, since that party receives 10 percent of the vote among those with no high school diploma, which is double that of those with a diploma or a college education.

Hierarchy of Cleavages

A logistic regression allows us to show which variables of all those we have mentioned appear the most predictive, other things being equal, of electoral behavior in 1997. Our three dependent variables are the vote for the left (Ecologists included), the vote for the moderate right, and the vote for the National Front. Our five explanatory variables are professional status, religious practice, education level, age, and sex. These are ordinal variables, and they include the professional status—the self-employed, private-sector wage earners, and public-sector wage earners—along three dimensions. The first of these dimensions is the degree of control over the means of production and of exchange: unlike wage earners, the self-employed are "their own bosses." The second is submission to the rules of the market, which are much more restrictive for the self-employed and private-sector wage earners than for government employees. The third taps the degree of economic security that, in a recession, is greatest in the public sector.

All of the five variables come into play, but each one differently, depending on which vote is being considered (see table 7.3). Religion and professional status are the only two variables that significantly affect the vote for the left. If voters are detached from the Catholic religion and are wage earners (especially public-sector wage earners), this clearly raises the probability of their voting for Socialist, Communist, or Ecologist candidates, or for others from the extreme left. This same two-variable combination also is the main predictive factor of the vote for the moderate right. Integration into the Catholic community, as well as either business ownership or exploitation, are the main determinants of the vote for the UDF, the RPR, or the Villierist right. Two other factors also influence this vote, but in a less pronounced manner: age and level of education. The vote for the moderate right rises significantly among the oldest and most educated voters. The vote for the National Front is different from all the others. Sex and level of education are its best predictors, followed by age and religious practice. In 1988 the NF electorate had no strong social specificity, but today it has a clearly populist character. It is an electorate of socially and culturally disadvantaged, mostly young, males, who are detached from religion and who differentiate themselves to the same degree both from the moderate right and from the Socialist and Communist left.

Issue Voting

The 1997 survey incorporated a series of questions on the principal issues at stake in this election, in particular, social and economic politics, immigration, and European unification. From these questions we have formulated five synthetic measurements of these attitudes.[12]

The first scale (grouped under the heading "economic liberalism") measures positive or negative images of the notions of "profit," "privatization," and "public service." In addition, we elicited opinions about the social measures contained in the left's agenda: higher minimum wages, creation of public jobs, and reduction of the legal workweek to thirty-five hours. The second scale, using questions on the European Union's image and effects, measures "anti-Europeanism": feelings

TABLE 7.3. CLEAVAGES MODEL OF THE 1997 VOTE (LOGISTIC REGRESSION)

	Beta (β)	*Standard error*	*Significance level*
A. *Left vote*			
Type of employment	0.5665	.0788	.0000
Religious practice	-0.4730	.0434	.0000
Educational level	-0.0836	.0405	.0389
Age	-0.1627	.0663	.0142
Sex	0.0620	.1028	.5462
Constant	-1.9790	.3762	.0000
B. *Right vote*			
Type of employment	-0.6468	.0836	.0000
Religious practice	0.6127	.0484	.0000
Educational level	0.1901	.0431	.0000
Age	0.2937	.0714	.0000
Sex	0.1175	.1093	.2823
Constant	1.1903	.3987	.0028
C. *National Front vote*			
Type of employment	0.0566	.1252	.6515
Religious practice	-0.1748	.0664	.0085
Educational level	-0.2462	.0726	.0007
Age	-0.2523	.1055	.0168
Sex	-0.4650	.1673	.0054
Constant	-0.9830	.5899	.0957

SOURCE: See appendix., p. 156-7.

NOTES: Dependent variables coded 0/1: vote in the first round of the 1997 legislative elections for the left (extreme-left, Socialist, Communist, and Ecologist candidates), the right (UDF/RPR and Independent Right candidates), and the National Front candidates.

Independent ordinal variables: types of employment (self-employed, wage earners in the private sector, wage earners in the public sector), religious practice (no religion, religion other than Catholic, nonpracticing Catholic, irregularly practicing Catholic, regularly practicing Catholic), educational level (primary school degree, vocational school degree, high school, high school plus two years in university, university degree), age (18–24 years old, 25–39, 40–64, 65 and older), and sex.

that France has not benefited from its participation in the European Union, the tendency to approve of the EU's dissolution, and opposition to the single European currency. The third is a scale of "ethnocentrism," that is to say, the valorization of the group that one belongs to ("in-group") and the rejection of others ("out-groups").[13] This scale was constructed from several questions addressing national feelings, and the image of minorities living in France and their rights. The scale of "political distrust" was created by measuring people's degree of skepticism about the political and partisan system: this theme was present during the campaign as well.[14] Lastly, two questions concerning discipline at school and reestablishment of the death penalty created an indicator of "authoritarianism."

A series of logistic regressions, considering the votes for the left, the right, and the FN as dependent variables, and the five scales as ordinal explanatory variables, allowed us to measure their respective influence on the electoral choices in 1997 (see table 7.4).

Our results bring into focus the economic and social issues at stake. The elections of 1997 reactivated the cleavages among classical values in French politics. These themes mobilized voters all the more because the left coalition led a campaign against the unkept promises of the president. The "social fracture" that Jacques Chirac had promised to reduce, and that his government then seemed to have lost sight of, springs up as a dominant theme in the 1997 elections and contributes to orienting the political field along traditional power lines: on one hand, the desire to see the state intervene to provide relief for the deficiencies of the market, and on the other hand, the glorification of free enterprise, which is supposed to jumpstart the economy.

Besides the effect of economic liberalism, there also is a statistically significant negative relationship between the vote for the left and authoritarian and ethnocentric attitudes. The coefficients of association are clearly less high, however, than that of economic liberalism. In reality, it is not attitudes about immigrants or law and order, but rather economic and social considerations, that have determined the choice for the left at this time. In contrast, it is striking to note that attitudes concerning Europe or political distrust are practically not taken into account at all among the voters for the left. The opposite is true among voters for the moderate right, whose vote is linked significantly to a positive attitude toward both the European Union and political class and parties. Even in this case, however, these considerations weighed less heavily on their vote than those concerning the extent of state intervention, measured by the scale of economic and social liberalism. As for voters' perception of the Other and their authoritarian attitudes, these had practically no influence at all on their choices here.

Those who voted for the National Front differed from all others in that the five dimensions weighed nearly equally on their vote. The relationship to the Other, to immigrants, and to foreigners—to judge by the strength of the coefficient associated with ethnocentrism—is certainly a factor, but not a dominant

TABLE 7.4. ISSUES MODEL OF THE 1997 VOTE (LOGISTIC REGRESSION)

	Beta (β)	Standard error	Significance level
A. *Left vote*			
Anti-Europeanism	0.0963	.0928	.2992
Ethnocentrism	-0.4731	.0802	.0000
Economic liberalism	-1.4300	.0789	.0000
Authoritarianism	-0.3921	.0958	.0000
Political distrust	0.1694	.0655	.0097
Constant	4.9816	.3149	.0000
B. *Right vote*			
Anti-Europeanism	-0.3342	.0906	.0003
Ethnocentrism	0.2353	.0791	.0029
Economic liberalism	1.2160	.0735	.0000
Authoritarianism	0.2207	.0952	.0204
Political distrust	-0.4194	.0652	.0000
Constant	-3.0926	.2773	.0000
C. *National Front vote*			
Anti-Europeanism	0.5234	.1361	.0001
Ethnocentrism	0.6452	.1266	.0000
Economic liberalism	0.5616	.1041	.0000
Authoritarianism	0.5244	.1507	.0005
Political distrust	0.6193	.0989	.0000
Constant	-9.4973	.6595	.0000

SOURCE: See appendix (p. 156-7) and note 1, page 263.

NOTES: Dependent variables coded 0/1: vote in the first round of the 1997 legislative elections for the left (extreme-left, Socialist, Communist, and Ecologist candidates), the right (UDF/RPR and Independent Right candidates), and the National Front candidates.

Independent ordinal variables: scales of ethnocentrism, authoritarianism, and economic liberalism (recoded into four positions); anti-Europeanism (recoded into three positions); and political distrust (recoded into three positions).

one (see table 7.4C). It is followed closely by rejection of the system, and a distrust of parties and politics, whether left or right. The other variables—economic liberalism, authoritarianism, anti-Europeanism—come right behind in terms of their impact. All of these variables had a significant influence on votes for the National Front. Thus it is necessary to consider the importance of ethnocentrism in electoral matters as relative. Even when this dimension was very much present in the political debates of 1997, it was not the determining factor in the choice between left and right. Even the choice of National Front voters, who are by far the most ethnocentric, did not amount to a "racist" or "xenophobic" vote for or against the Other. Their vote for the National Front grew out of a complex combination of motivations wherein defiance with respect to the political and partisan system weighs almost as heavily as "national preference."

Finally, if one determines the proportional influence of cleavage variables (heavy variables) and value variables (at-stake variables) by comparing them in a logistic regression analysis based on the 1997 votes, the results clearly show which values weigh most heavily. In the vote for the left, economic liberalism appears to be the most predictive factor: the more one favors state intervention in the economy, the more likely one is to vote for the left. In second place comes the rejection of ethnocentrism, but neither professional status nor religion have any significant statistical influence. As for the vote for the right, it is, conversely, attachment to economic liberalism that determines this choice, followed by trust in the political system. A voter's degree of fidelity to Catholic religious practice, however, remains a considerable predictive factor compared to that of value variables: the more observant one is, the more one votes for the right. Lastly, the vote for the National Front may be explained, above all, by the voter's degree of ethnocentrism combined with opposition to the political system. Sex continues to be a more or less equivalent predictive factor, however: from one election to the next, there is a more marked tendency among men (particularly young men) to support Le Pen's party. Moving beyond issues such as the rejection of immigrants and the resentment of the political elite, a vote for the National Front also obviously plays on the evolving relationship between the sexes that began in the 1960s, and on the voter's acceptance or refusal of women's rights.

The electoral behavior of the French in 1997 thus may be explained according to individuals' ideological preferences and their social and religious membership or adherence. Class cleavages have not disappeared, but they have changed. The opposition between the self-employed and wage earners—and among the latter, the opposition between those in the public and private sectors—has assumed the same importance as the cleavage formerly existing between manual workers and nonmanual workers, because the National Front has attracted growing support in the ever-changing working-class milieu. Religion remains a powerful explanatory factor, especially in the vote for the moderate right. Lastly, however, the values systems of voters, according to the specific factors at stake in the election, determined their decisions.

Appendix: Description of Scales, Scores, and Coefficients

TABLE 7.5. SCORES AND COEFFICIENTS

Scales	*Average score*	*Standard error*	*Range*	*Standard alpha*
Ethnocentrism	5.8	3.6	0-14	0.72
Economic liberalism	12.4	4.8	0-28	0.75
Anti-Europeanism	2.5	1.8	0-6	0.72
Political distrust	7.6	2.5	0-13	0.63

Ethnocentrism Scale

The scale is built by scoring responses to the following statements: "Some races are less talented than others." "There are too many immigrants in France." "Now one no longer feels at ease as before." — "Agree completely," score = 3; "agree somewhat," score = 2; "disagree somewhat," score = 1; "disagree completely," score = 0.

"The North Africans (Magrébins) who live in France will one day be French like everyone else." — Same "agree-disagree" scale as above, but scoring is reversed so item attitudes run in the same direction.

"Yourself, you feel only French," score = 2; "more French than European," score = 1; "more European than French" or other response, score = 0.

Economic and Social Liberalism Scale

This scale is built from ratings of words. For words evoking a response of "very positive," score = 3; "somewhat positive," score = 2; "somewhat negative," score = 1; "very negative," score = 0.

The words were "profit," " private school," " privatization," "public service."

Respondents were also asked for personal responses to the following actions: "reducing the number of civil servants," "lessening social charges on business," "raising the minimum wage by 1,000 francs," "creating 350,000 public jobs," "reducing the workweek to 35 hours without reducing pay." — "Completely for," score = 3; "somewhat for," score = 2; "somewhat against," score = 1; "completely against," score = 0.

To make attitudes run in a consistent direction, scores were reversed when necessary. The following item was also included: "I think that priority must be given in the coming years to the competitiveness of the French economy," score = 1; or " . . . to the improvement of salaries," score = 0.

Anti-Europeanism Scale

This scale was built by scoring reponses to the following questions: "Are you completely for," score = 0; "somewhat for," score = 1; "somewhat against," score = 2; or "completely against," score = 3; "the fact that the European Union will have a single currency, which means that the franc will be replaced by the euro?"

"All things considered, do you think that France has benefited," score = 0; or "not benefited," score = 1; "from its membership in the European Union?"

"If it were to be announced tomorrow that the European Union was to be abandoned, would you feel regret," score = 0; "indifference," score = 1; or "relief?" score = 2.

Political Distrust Scale

This scale is built by scoring responses on the following items: "In your opinion, on the whole do politicians worry about what people like you think a lot," score = 0; "some," score = 1; "little," score = 2; or "not at all?" score = 3.

"Would you say that you are usually very close," score = 0; "somewhat close," score = 1; "hardly close," score = 2; or "not at all close," score = 3; "to one political party in particular?"

"For you, does the word 'state' evoke something very positive," score = 0; "somewhat positive," score = 1; "somewhat negative," score = 2; "very negative?" score = 3.

"Do you believe that currently democracy in France functions very well," score = 0; "somewhat well," score = 1; "somewhat poorly," score = 2; "very poorly?" score = 3.

"Which one of these three sentences best describes your opinion: "I have confidence in the left in governing the country," score = 0; "I have confidence in the right in governing the country," score = 0; "I have confidence in neither the left nor the right in governing the country," score = 1.

Authoritarianism Scale

This scale is built by scoring responses to the following items: "In thinking about school, can you tell me with which of these two opinions do you most agree: "School should give above all a feeling of discipline and effort," score = 1; "School should form above all people with open and critical minds," score = 0.

"The death penalty should be reestablished." — "completely or somewhat agree," score = 1; "completely or somewhat disagree," score = 0.

The overall additive index varies from 0 to 2 because someone may score 0 on both items, 1 on only one item, or 1 on both items.

Chapter 8

The Myth of Neoconservatism

Etienne Schweisguth

The thesis according to which the current evolution of values systems in French society is characterized by a trend of xenophobic, authoritarian, and traditionalistic neoconservatism reappears periodically in newspaper and political commentaries. According to this thesis, we are witnessing a return of traditional morals, of machismo, of authority, of nationalism, of xenophobia, and so on. It is our purpose here to show that nothing in recent trends allows for such a diagnosis. We also wish to show that the current evolution of values involves both a slow and continuous decline of traditional values and the growth of a long-term liberal and antiauthoritarian humanism. Certainly, since the 1980s we have seen an increased vote for the National Front, the French political party on the extreme right; it is true that the vote for the National Front corresponds in part to a world of particular values, more specifically to xenophobic attitudes, but we will attempt to show here that the electoral progress made by this party springs more often from political and social changes than from deep-rooted changes in value systems.

The Decline of Authoritarian and Traditional Values

In a previous article on the evolution of values in Europe as a whole (Schweisguth 1995), we were able to show that, in the area of sexual morality, the mechanism of change from one generation to the next was the source of a long-term decline in traditional values, and thus also a mechanism of increasingly wider acceptance of extramarital cohabitation, divorce, abortion, and homosexuality. The fundamental mechanism of this change in values is simply the fact of demographic evolution: older generations that carry traditional values disappear and are replaced by new generations that carry new values. Whatever the eventual circumstantial fluctuations in public opinion may be, such a mechanism acts like a steamroller: whenever statistical analysis brings this type of process to light, we know that we are faced with a strong, long-term tendency.

We also attempted to discover whether this mechanism of change in values across successive generations could account for the evolution of French attitudes toward authority. In order to address this issue, we made use of two studies, dating from 1978 and 1988, respectively, that examined the evolution of responses to the question of whether schools should above all else promote "the feeling of discipline and effort" or, on the contrary, should mold people "with alert and critical minds." At the time of these studies, the observable data did not allow us to conclude with certainty whether or not opinions on this subject evolved with succeeding generations. We certainly observed that a favorable response to "effort and discipline" was more common in older generations than in younger ones. It was easy to wonder, however, if this result did not simply translate into an effect of the life cycle: people are more favorable toward individual freedom when they are young, but they discover the virtues of authority as they grow older. Thus we noticed that when people were separated according to age in blocks of ten years, according to year of birth, the older the age cohort, the higher the percentage of responses favoring "effort and discipline": for example, from 1978 to 1988, the cohort of people born between 1951 and 1960 who gave this response rose from 35 percent to 48 percent; and the percentage of responses from people born between 1941 and 1950 went from 55 percent to 61 percent. We then could also defend another explanation of values change, that of values changing according to an effect of the life cycle. At the time, we were not able to distinguish clearly between these two hypotheses.

Today, thanks to two studies by CEVIPOF conducted at the time of the presidential election of 1995 and the legislative elections of 1997, respectively, we can observe the evolution of responses to the question of effort and discipline over nearly twenty years, from 1978 to 1997, with four measurements over this period of time. This time the results are not ambiguous at all. The fact that younger people are less favorable to authority than older people does not in any way link ideological evolution to aging. In fact, each new cohort of subjects from the very beginning favors a level of authoritarianism lower than that of the preceding generation, and each of these cohorts remains at that level, the subjects' views changing little as they age. If adherence to the principle of authority consistently increased with age, the percentages shown in table 8.1 on page 178 should rise steadily from the left to the right. All cohorts, however, from 1978 to 1988 show increasing percentages of favorable responses, relatively strong in certain cases, followed either by stability or by a decline in authoritarianism from 1988 to 1997.

TABLE 8.1. CHANGING PERCENTAGES OF PEOPLE WHO BELIEVE THAT "SCHOOL SHOULD GIVE ABOVE ALL A SENSE OF EFFORT AND DISCIPLINE"

Year of birth	*1978*	*1988*	*1995*	*1997*
1901–10	80	85		
1911–21	81	83	81	76
1921–30	73	79	74	75
1931–40	69	74	67	64
1941–50	55	61	56	55
1951–60	35	48	47	47
1961–70		34	39	41
1971–77			28	32

SOURCE: CEVIPOF National Election Surveys, 1978, 1988, 1995, 1997.

The growth in authoritarianism recorded between 1978 and 1988 in all the cohorts seems thus not to be a consequence of increase in age, but more so a circumstantial variation of opinion that affected the entire population. For example, note the effect of the statements of Jean-Pierre Chevénement, the minister of national education at the time, in praise of "Republican elitism." Whatever the case, the mass of data gathered hardly allows for argument in support of the thesis that authoritarianism increases with age.[1] If we examine the five cohorts studied from 1978 to 1997—that is to say the entire study population, which was born between 1901 and 1960—there is only one case in which adherence to the principle of authority is significantly higher in 1997 than in 1978: the cohort born between 1951 and 1960 went from 35 percent to 47 percent in its responses favoring a "feeling of discipline and effort." In the other cases, we notice either a decline of approximately 5 points between the study's starting and ending points (in the cohorts 1911-1920 and 1931-1940), perfect equality (in the cohort 1941-1950), or a nonsignificant statistical rise of 2 points (in the cohort 1921-1930).

Here is a remarkable confirmation of the thesis that there is a long-term decline of authoritarian values over successive generations. Naturally, the results presented in table 8.1 do not imply that it is impossible for this tendency to reverse itself in the future, with new generations one day becoming more authoritarian than earlier ones. The results do show, however, that the rate of adherence to the principle of "effort and discipline" declined between 1978 and 1997, dropping

TABLE 8.2. CHANGING PERCENTAGES OF FOUR INDICATORS OF CONSERVATIVE VALUES

	1978	*1988*	*1995*	*1997*
Effort and discipline	63	60	52	51
Monthly religious observance	18	16	13	13
Supporters of the death penalty		64	56	50
"There are too many immigrants in France":				
Agree completely		37	42	32
Agree somewhat		69	75	60

SOURCE: CEVIPOF National Election Surveys, 1978, 1988, 1995, 1997.

from 63 percent to 51 percent (see table 8.2); this cannot be attributed to a simple effect of method or to the changing nature of those polled. It is the effect of a movement at the base of society, which leads each new generation to reject more and more a morality based on submission and asceticism, in favor of one directed more toward hedonism and individual autonomy. The logic which has played a part in the evolution of our society since the end of World War II might be interpreted as one which pushes each new generation to take, when possible, a further step toward rejecting the constraints of tradition and authority. A reversal of this trend could occur only under the influence of some sweeping social change, of which we can see no sign.

Another indicator of the level of adherence to traditional values is the frequency of religious practice. Although this factor cannot in itself express the whole of religious sentiment, we know it is strongly associated with traditional political and moral orientations. A return to religion experienced a certain popularity in France several years ago. Large religious events, such as the gathering of youth celebrating the Pope's visit to France in August 1997, renewed speculation on this subject. If there is a return to religion, however, one thing is certain: it has not manifested itself by a return of the faithful to church. Religious practice has evolved in the same way as opinion with respect to "effort and discipline." It declines steadily as older generations, who are the most observant, disappear slowly and are replaced by new generations whose rate of regular observance (defined here as attendance at mass at least once a month) rarely exceeds 5 percent. Table 8.3 on page 180 thus shows an impressive stability in religious practice depending on year of birth, which contradicts the idea often put forth that people frequent church more as they grow older, in order to assure their salvation.

TABLE 8.3. CHANGING PERCENTAGES OF REGULARLY PRACTICING CATHOLICS

Year of birth	*1978*	*1988*	*1995*	*1997*
1901–10	29	30		
1911–20	25	28	25	38
1921–30	21	23	28	24
1931–40	20	21	20	22
1941–50	11	15	11	10
1951–60	7	8	8	8
1961–70		6	5	6
1971–77			6	5

SOURCE: CEVIPOF National Election Surveys, 1978, 1988, 1995, 1997.
NOTE: Regularly practicing = attends services at least once a month.

Let us establish once again that the decline of religious observance indicates a decline in traditional forms of religion, not necessarily a global decline in religious beliefs. This may be not a decline but a change in religion. For example, the current trend probably is not characterized by an increased number of people who reject all spiritual or supernatural beliefs. Thus the proportion of persons who believe in no single form of life after death does not vary according to age. This proportion remains extremely stable at approximately 30 percent, and this result was observed when the question of religion was asked in the studies of 1988 and 1995. It is the population that has some form of belief in the supernatural that casts doubt on traditional religious norms and beliefs, or abandons them in favor of new beliefs either within a reinterpreted Christian framework or within other frameworks such as Buddhism or reincarnation. In any case, such religious changes are essentially in keeping with a perspective of freedom of consciousness and the search for personal spiritual growth,[2] and they in no way constitute either a neoconservative return to dogma or a traditional rejection of religion.

The Slow Rise of Liberal Humanism Brought About by Higher Levels of Education

Thus far our new results have confirmed the conclusions of our earlier study: adherence to the principle of individual freedom, in opposition to those of authority and tradition, is progressing steadily in France (and, more generally, in Europe) because of the change in the values of succeeding generations. One could wonder, however, if this liberal evolution might simply boil down to a rejection of traditional norms and restrictions by individuals seeking personal comfort, a sort of amoral individualism. One could imagine also that the rise of this "individualism" might go hand-in-hand with, for example, a growing concern for individual security or intolerance toward foreigners.

Here again the available observations do not validate the thesis of conservative renewal. The studies done by CEVIPOF in 1988, 1995, and 1997 allow us to follow over time the evolution of answers to two questions, one concerning attitudes about the death penalty, the other concerning attitudes about immigrants. We must note that there is a strong correlation between the responses to these two questions. A person is six times more likely to agree completely that "there are too many immigrants in France" if he or she favors the death penalty. The strong relation between these two opinions may not be explained in any of the cases by the simple fact that a certain number of people live in neighborhoods characterized by both a strong immigrant presence and a high crime rate, because this correlation is found in all social milieux and in all sectors of public opinion. It is in line with what has been confirmed by all the studies done since the founding work of Adorno (Adorno et al. 1950): a close association between the tendency to devalue the members of the outgroup and the willingness to uphold radical sanctions with respect to those who do not respect the social norms. The questions concerning the death penalty and immigrants thus seem to lead us back to the same dichotomy: on one hand are those who believe that every human individual, no matter who he or she may be, has an intrinsic value and dignity that must be respected; on the other hand are those who believe that human individuals are not of equal value and that, consequently, those individuals lacking in value may legitimately become targets of the most extreme measures.

In contrast to the way we previously considered the evolution of opinion within certain cohorts, we now examine this same evolution among the French population as a whole. Whereas opinions favoring the death penalty rose noticeably during the 1970s and 1980s, it seems that more recently they have been declining, dropping from 64 percent in 1988 to 56 percent in 1995 and 50 percent in 1997. As to the evolution of xenophobic attitudes, the proportion of people who claim to agree that "there are too many immigrants in France" first rose from 37 percent in 1988 to 42 percent in 1995, then dropped markedly, falling to 32 percent in 1997, a level lower than it had been in 1988.[3]

At this more global level, nothing comes to light that confirms the hypothesis that opinions favoring the death penalty and hostile to immigrants are rising. We must use caution when working with such data. In the short term, variations in conjuncture about the evolution of opinions are sometimes of such an amplitude that they easily mask the long-term effects. If the evolutions that we have just mentioned do not support the thesis of neoconservatism, neither do they in themselves support the hypothesis of a long tendency toward rising liberal humanism. To test this, we must return to the method of analyzing cohorts according to year of birth.

Opinions about the death penalty and about immigration both depend strongly on the level of education of those questioned. The higher the level of education, the higher the levels of opposition to the death penalty and of tolerance toward immigrants. This is a deciding factor in the analysis of the evolution of opinion, since we know that the French population's level of education has increased enormously since World War II and continues to grow rapidly. Tables 8.4 and 8.5 show the evolution of cohorts distinguished between those who hold the Bac, or French high school diploma, and those who do not.

TABLE 8.4. CHANGING PERCENTAGES OF SUPPORTERS OF THE DEATH PENALTY

	Non–high school graduates			*High school graduates*		
Year of birth	*1988*	*1995*	*1997*	*1988*	*1995*	*1997*
1908–28	76	71	59	58	53	36
1929–42	74	70	62	52	34	29
1943–63	71	66	63	37	33	27
1964–70	58	69	63	36	37	39
1971–77		60	50		34	32
Total	72	68	61	42	35	31

SOURCE: CEVIPOF National Election Surveys, 1988, 1995, 1997.

An essential phenomenon appears: for the same level of education, belonging to either a younger or an older cohort has only minimal influence on opinions about the death penalty and about immigrants. In particular, among the portion of the population that has not received the Bac, only slight differences of opinion are noted between the very young and the very old. Among those who have received the Bac, more important differences occur: members of the generations living before the war tend to be more favorable to the death penalty and more reticent with respect to immigrants. However, these differences seem to have diminished in the past ten years, and, moreover, they have become less important than the gaps caused by educational level. Globally, in 1997, among

TABLE 8.5. CHANGING PERCENTAGES OF PEOPLE WHO AGREE COMPLETELY THAT "THERE ARE TOO MANY IMMIGRANTS IN FRANCE"

	Non–high school graduates			*High school graduates*		
Year of birth	*1988*	*1995*	*1997*	*1988*	*1995*	*1997*
1908–28	45	51	42	34	52	33
1929–42	46	60	47	35	35	22
1943–63	42	53	40	14	18	13
1964–70	40	49	40	13	16	12
1971–77		46	32		11	12
Total	43	53	41	19	20	14

SOURCE: CEVIPOF National Election Surveys, 1988, 1995, 1997.

those who have the Bac, 11 percent "agree completely" that there are too many immigrants, whereas 41 percent of those who do not hold the Bac "agree completely" with the statement. Also, among those who favor the reestablishment of the death penalty, 31 percent are high school graduates, whereas 61 percent never graduated from high school.

The long-term evolution of humanistic values seems thus to be intimately linked to the rising level of education among the French. If new generations are more humanistic than older ones, it is not only because of a generalized progress concerning norms of tolerance, but especially because newer generations have higher and higher proportions of people with education at least equal to that of the Bac. Perhaps the philosophers of the Enlightenment would see in all of this the realization of their dream. The development and diffusion of knowledge upsets the organization of Western societies, tending to instill universalistic humanist values as official norms. Our times seem far from those of Victor Hugo, who, one man against many, asked the Chamber of Deputies for the abolition of the death penalty. Today, after a long period of declining law and order in the 1970s and 1980s, public opinion in support of the death penalty perhaps is beginning to decline, having succumbed to the rising power of the discourse of the cultivated elite, whose voice is one with that of a growing highly educated population. Similarly, while for nearly twenty years immigration has been a major and controversial sociopolitical issue, it is striking that nearly all high school graduates born after World War II adhere to antiracist norms, preventing the rise of xenophobic values even among poorly educated members of the newer generations.

The National Front Vote and Xenophobia

The idea that the increase in the National Front vote necessarily is born of values hostile to universalist humanism undoubtedly derives from the strong adherence to these same values, according to many analysts. It is as if only voters who had broken away from humanist values and had gone over to the side of the transgressors, like Darth Vader discovering "the dark side," could vote for a party that so openly transgresses these values. But such an analysis relies on a peculiar optimism about human nature, in that it means believing that the French were not racist before Le Pen, and that if they are becoming racist, it is only because of economic or social difficulties, or because they are under the influence of one politician or another. France, however, cannot claim an idyllic past in which all citizens were ardent defenders of the "rights of man." Although antiracism is now established as an absolute norm for the intellectual elite, we cannot forget France's heavy heritage. Anti-Semitism and racism were publicly admitted without problem in France's past (one leftist party was openly anti-Semitic until the Dreyfus Affair), and the intervention of the law was necessary in order to keep these currents in check.[4]

In fact, an increasing number of very xenophobic voters is not the growth mechanism for the National Front vote; instead, FN growth relies on an increasing number of voters who are somewhat xenophobic. If progress for the National Front does not automatically mean growing xenophobia, neither does it follow that the National Front vote is unrelated to xenophobia and is nothing more than the product of economic and social dissatisfaction. On the contrary, the FN's influence is even stronger when correlated with the rising level of voters' adherence to xenophobic opinions. Among those who conform to antiracist norms—that is, those who disagree "somewhat or completely" with the idea that there are too many immigrants in France—the vote for the National Front is nearly nonexistent, below 2 to 3 percent. Among those who agree "somewhat," FN votes are approximately 10 percent, and 30 percent of those who "agree completely" vote for the National Front (see table 8.6). Thus xenophobia undeniably favors the National Front vote. Even a very high level of xenophobia, however, does not automatically ensure this political choice. The proportion of voters not voting for the National Front is 90 percent among moderate xenophobes and 70 percent among radical xenophobes.

In fact, analysis of the National Front electorate's sociodemographic evolution shows variations that reveal a logic that is both political and social, but that is in no way one of profound value changes among the French people. We know that

TABLE 8.6. CHANGING PERCENTAGES OF THE NATIONAL FRONT VOTE ACCORDING TO ATTITUDES TOWARD IMMIGRANTS

	"There are too many immigrants in France."		
	Agree completely	*Agree somewhat*	*Agree slightly or not at all*
1988	29	10	2
1995	28	9	2
1997	32	13	3

SOURCE: CEVIPOF National Election Surveys, 1988, 1995, 1997.

the National Front vote, which was initially and above all tied to the self-employed or to well-off wage earners, has assumed a more proletarian cast, so today the National Front has its greatest influence among the working class. We also know that it is gaining ground with young people. The CEVIPOF-SOFRES polls from 1995 and 1997 show more precisely that, compared to 1988, the greatest progress for the National Front has been among youth in the popular classes. If we consider those young people without high school diplomas, as presented in table 8.7, we see that in 1988, 18 percent of the cohort born between 1964 and 1970 (who were at the time of the study between the ages of eighteen and twenty-five) voted for the National Front.

TABLE 8.7. CHANGING PERCENTAGES OF THE NATIONAL FRONT VOTE ACCORDING TO YEAR OF BIRTH AND EDUCATION

	Non–high school graduates			*High school graduates*		
Year of birth	*1988*	*1995*	*1997*	*1988*	*1995*	*1997*
1908–28	14	9	13	19	13	16
1929–42	15	15	14	19	6	11
1943–63	18	20	19	7	7	9
1964–70	18	31	29	7	11	7
1971–77		30	30		12	11
Total	16	19	18	11	10	10

SOURCE: CEVIPOF National Election Surveys, 1988, 1995, 1997.

Seven years later, during the 1995 presidential election, this same cohort (then between the ages of twenty-six and thirty-one) saw a jump in its number of supporters of the National Front to 31 percent. During this same election, the new cohort of eighteen- to twenty-five-year-olds, born between 1971 and 1977 and voting for the first time, cast 30 percent of its votes for the National Front. These same two cohorts confirmed their solid support for the National Front vote at 30 percent during the legislative elections of 1997. In cohorts of older people—still among those with no high school diploma—the level of the National Front vote remained stable. If the increased National Front voting among young, non–Bac holders signaled a rise in xenophobia, this should mean that among this population there is a stronger proportion of "completely agree" responses to the question concerning the existence of too many immigrants. Instead, the reverse is true. In 1995 and 1997 these two cohorts remained less hostile to foreigners compared to older cohorts and, like all other groups, had a lower percentage of xenophobic responses in 1997 than in 1995.

This increased National Front vote among young non–Bac holders clearly seems to be not the result of a neoconservative wave, but rather a political expression of protest. In today's French society, being young and without a high school diploma often means unemployment, temporary and uncertain work, poor wages, and personal devaluation as one who has not succeeded. It means feeling rejected by society and being unable to secure one's rightful place. Youths who do not have their diplomas also manifest symptoms of a characteristic uneasiness. Whereas the suicide rate traditionally has been low among young people, it has risen, along with unemployment, since the 1930s, while conversely, the suicide rate of older people has dropped. Delinquency and incivility, which testify to a lack of acceptance of the rules of society, also mark this social group. In political terms, this group feels the least connected to and identified with the right or the left, and its members swing most easily from one camp to the other. The logic of this group's vote is that of opposition, of sanction voting against the majority that has not been able to resolve the country's problems. Such logic becomes clear if we follow the voting behavior of uneducated French youth in the elections of 1988, 1995, and 1997 (see table 8.8). In the presidential election of 1995 this group deserted the left in droves in favor of Chirac, whereas in 1997 it once again voted strongly for the left instead of the right, which was on its way out of power. This oppositional behavior manifested itself in votes for the National Front in both 1995 and 1997, for the moderate right in 1995, and for the National Front or the left in 1997.

It is easier to use political rhetoric to denounce the decline of values than to articulate the different explanatory factors for the National Front vote. Publications also sell better when the press announces the return of traditionalism or nationalism rather than the slow growth of antiauthoritarian, hedonistic, and humanistic values. An intellectual reflex that explains the electoral progress of a

TABLE 8.8. CHANGING PERCENTAGES OF THE VOTE AMONG NON-HIGH SCHOOL GRADUATES UNDER AGE FORTY

	1988	*1995*	*1997*
Left and Ecologists	52	41	53
Moderate right	30	33	19
National Front	18	26	27

SOURCE: CEVIPOF National Election Surveys, 1988, 1995, 1997.

political party by a change in values is easy to understand, but it means forgetting that a party's voters are always extremely diverse and that its total vote always reflects a combination of many different factors. In the case of the National Front, even if its voters distinguish themselves by the intensity of their common hostility toward immigrants, they are otherwise an extremely diverse group, with very divergent subgroups. Two large categories of voters can be distinguished:

1. The traditionalistic constituency of the National Front is made up of relatively old voters, most often practicing Catholics who belong more to the middle class than to the working class. They subscribe to the credo of economic liberalism as much as, if not more than, the voters of the moderate right do. By virtue of their familial and personal political orientation, they are part of the tradition of the right. Their vote may be interpreted as a manifestation of attachment to a natural order of things based on family, nation, individual merit, and authority. This has nothing to do with a rise in neoconservatism, but with the political radicalization of a traditional conservative ideology.

2. The populist constituency of the National Front is made up of young voters, who frequently belong to a working-class and very markedly de-Christianized milieu. The least that one can say about them is that economic liberalism is not their cup of tea: in their negative judgments on privatization or profit—giving priority to improving wage earners' salaries rather than to increasing the competitiveness of the French economy—they show themselves to be exactly like the voters of the left. Only a third of them claim to be for the right. For the so-called leftist Le Pen supporters (*gaucho-lepénistes*; see Perrineau 1997b), denunciation of the foreigner—whether immigrant or other European—has taken the place of denunciation of capitalism as the political expression of social discontent.

Of these two groups of voters, it is the latter that may find favor in today's France. Political leaders of both right and left have so far shown themselves incapable of solving the problem of unemployment, but the population apparently views it as the essential social problem, and it is certainly the one that plagues this group.

Chapter 9

The Influence of Political Scandals on Popularity and Votes

Jean-Dominique Lafay and Marie Servais

A political scandal is defined here as the indignation provoked in public opinion by the revelation that a politician, a political group, or a political institution has committed an action which is judged illegitimate, illegal, unethical, or shameful. This definition is purely factual. It implies no value judgment about either the reality of the charge or its justification, and it may correspond to many different situations: corruption and financial mismanagement, abuse of power and illegal decisions, acts that are considered to be shameful in personal life, and so on.

A very high number of such political scandals have erupted in France since the middle of the 1980s. The media have paid great and continuous attention to this subject. Several more or less exhaustive reviews of these scandals have been published in the press. A recent example is the long study "One Hundred French Scandals" by an important weekly magazine, *L'Express* (30 April 1998, 2443). In fact, this figure reflects only a selected sample of current cases that have not been judged in court. The cumulative number of political scandals for the past fifteen years is much higher. It has even been possible to develop a complete "dictionary" for them (Gaetner 1991). The degrees of seriousness of these scandals are very different, but their number in itself reveals the existence of a major phenomenon.

Indeed, the public and the press have been mostly interested in anecdotal facts, in judiciary developments, or in the personal consequences for some political leaders. The question of scandal is studied here from a more technical and positive point of view. First we show the theoretical interest of the subject, and then we evaluate the impact of political scandals on votes and on popularity.

Political Scandals as a Theoretical Problem

Even in well-institutionalized democracies, governments control important instruments that allow them to obtain money, to act illegally without sanctions, or to hide their errors. This means that there is an underground political market and government, similar to the underground economy (though much less studied). On the other hand, recent developments in the theory of economic policy have focused on the importance of expectations and credibility (see Blackburn and Christensen 1989). The economic theory of politics also has put a stress on the role of "trust" and/or "deference" in political and bureaucratic relations (Breton 1996; Buchanan and Vanberg 1989). How these opposite tensions are solved is central, and any theory of political scandals must logically begin by explaining the behavior of their voluntary "producers," that is, the politicians.

Revelation of a political scandal presents

1. high personal costs (related to trials, possible financial or penal condemnation);

2. a loss of credibility regarding future policymaking;

3. a reduced probability of political survival due to an expected loss of popularity.

The relevant question, then, is this: Why, in the light of such potential costs, do politicians rationally decide to bear the risk and to what extent? Technically, this question raises the problem of the equilibrium level of underground government.

The Equilibrium Level of Underground Government

Underground government can be considered as a special form of illegal rent seeking, so that the economic theories of rent seeking, of corruption, and of crime, which have developed extensively in recent years,[1] can provide interesting insights here. One may assume that politicians make a tradeoff between the expected benefits of a "dirty action," the probability of being discovered, and the costs incurred. The only factor peculiar to underground government concerns the structure of benefits and costs, which is very different from that of ordinary cases.

First, the potential gains are particularly high and lasting (notably in the form of rents). In some cases, they appear crucial to political survival (if, for example, no legal political-party financing has been defined, as in France before 1990). Also, the probability of being discovered varies a great deal through time, and from one country to another, according to the institutional setup. Third, very effective means exist for politicians to conceal their personal mistakes or voluntary "dirty actions," and the mistakes and "dirty actions" of those who act under their responsibility (namely, advisers, political staff members, bureaucrats). On this point there is a rhetoric of *raison d'État* (national interest), which, among the governmental staff, helps legitimate such concealment. Moreover, the critical efficiency of institutional checks and balances, the political opposition, and the media may be very different from one country to another.

Why a Scandal Breaks Out

If the government has perfect information, makes no error, and perfectly controls members of its formal and informal networks, and if there is no reaction lag, scandals will never emerge, simply because they will never overrun the governmental capacity of concealment. Some scandals are publicly disclosed because of expectational errors. In some cases, an unexpected shock will raise the need for concealment well above governmental capacities. In others, inadequate decisions will result from true expectational errors. A good example is the creation of the *Chambres régionales des comptes* (Regional Chambers of Accounts) in France in 1982, along with a law implementing a large decentralization. Many local politicians were expecting these institutions to be inefficient so that they could use and abuse their new local freedom. Unfortunately for them, these institutions had a bureaucratic interest in signaling their existence as efficient controllers. This was all the easier as past illegal decisions could not be erased and as it was difficult to change earlier habits. This is one of the main reasons why so many scandals appeared in France at the end of the 1980s and at the beginning of the 1990s.

The Dynamics of Scandals

Once they have exploded, political scandals will partially destroy the affected politician's initial stock of public credibility, trust, or deference. But they also will partially or totally destroy the interpersonal trust previously accumulated in corrupt or illegally behaving networks. Moreover, the capacity of those prosecuted or simply suspected to threaten others is strongly reduced. Hence, their secrets are less well kept, and scandals tend to snowball. In addition, suspected persons lose a sizable amount of their authority, that is, of their command over the instruments and networks at their disposal. Hence, implicated politicians have to defend themselves by using either new instruments and unfamiliar networks, or old ones that have become much less efficient (but to an unknown degree). It is not surprising that their defense may look awkward.

Reactions of Public Opinion

Once a scandal is disclosed, the public can withdraw its support for at least four different reasons:

1. It wishes to punish the guilty politicians or the government retrospectively.
2. Its prospective view of the trust, credibility, and deference attributable to the government may change, simply because a scandal corresponds to new information.
3. From a strategic standpoint, punishing is a way to send a warning signal to other politicians for the future.
4. For any given individual, the fact that he or she knows that the other people could withdraw their support makes the government less reliable in efficient policymaking.

The most immediate questions, those which the following empirical study directly addresses, are how much a scandal costs a politician, a government, or a political party in terms of popularity and votes, and whether these costs differ according to the type of scandal. It is clear that public opinion may have a different impact depending on whether a politician made an involuntary mistake or committed a deliberate action, whether the [presumed] culprit did or did not try to keep it secret, whether the [presumed] culprit was motivated by personal financial gain or by a more altruistic cause, such as party funding. The effect of a scandal also may differ according to its nature (financial and/or corruptive, resulting from lax public management or insufficient monitoring, involving an abuse of power, relating to a politician's personal life, and so on).

There also are additional interesting questions to be asked, notably those concerning the length of time that loss of popularity due to a given scandal lasts, the shape of the lag structure of this negative impact, and the resulting reduction of a given government's life expectancy. The possibility of cycles in the disclosure of scandals is also of interest. As for economic policy, there are theoretical reasons for electoral and partisan cycles in scandals (Alesina, Roubini, and Cohen 1997).

A rational politician with private information about a scandal involving a competitor has an interest in disclosing it during preelectoral periods.[2] Voters will have no time to forget such information before casting their votes, and its impact will be all the more important, given that vote intentions seem to be more sensitive and mobile during an electoral campaign (Gerstlé 1996). Moreover, if the incumbent loses the election, a burst of scandals may also be expected to follow, as the new government discovers the files of its predecessors.

In addition to the electoral cycle, a partisan cycle also may be expected. On one hand, politicians in the government have greater opportunities for scandalous behavior but more capacity to hide it. On the other hand, they have a greater capacity to discover the opposition's current scandalous behavior as well as its earlier infractions from a time when it was in power, that is, from a period when its behavior could be hidden more easily. As a result, there may be a significant partisan bias in the disclosure of political scandals, at the expense of the opposition. This conclusion is all the more likely with frequent changeovers of political power between political parties (or coalitions of parties). Even in this case, however, some factors will play in the opposite direction: governing politicians have more opportunities but are under closer scrutiny by the media.[3]

Finally, it is clear that a full theoretical model must be built that simultaneously explains the supply of potentially scandalous political actions, the number of those that will be brought to light, their time of disclosure, and the resulting political consequences. Though only the last question is of direct interest for the empirical study presented here, it is important to realize that it represents only one building block in a much bigger architecture.

Scandal as an Explanatory Variable of Political Popularity and Voting

For the past twenty-five years, research on the links between economic variables and political popularity or votes has been extensive and has achieved highly significant and internationally convergent empirical results (Lewis-Beck 1988; Lewis-Beck and Rice 1992). This clear confirmation of the influence of the economy on politics does not mean, however, that other variables cannot also have an impact. According to Nannestad and Paldam's (1994) authoritative survey of the literature, economic factors explain about one-third of the change in popularity or votes. Room for other, noneconomic variables then is rather large, and, not surprisingly, variables such as war (Vietnam for the United States and the Falkland Islands for the United Kingdom) or the rally-round-the-flag effect during international crises have been successfully introduced in several "popularity functions" (i.e., functions explaining the popularity indexes of governing authorities on the basis of several variables—inflation, growth, and unemployment, for example, being the most frequently used economic variables).

The first empirical measures of the influence of political scandals on popularity are linked to the strong decline in Richard Nixon's popularity observed during the Watergate scandal. To account for the shock caused by this event, J. Mueller (1970) introduced a dummy variable into his popularity functions for American presidents. Similarly, Fiorina (1991) measured the impact of the Watergate scandal on party identification, finding that Watergate had a strong negative effect on Republican Party affiliation for the lower-middle and middle income categories (between -5 and -10 points in popularity).[4] The problem with these results is that they are based on a unique event. The recent outbreak of scandals during the 1980s and 1990s in countries such as Italy and France has then at least one advantage: their great number permits a more robust statistical and refined analysis.

Indeed, this kind of study has intrinsic limitations. For example, we have no way of evaluating the potential for disclosure of political scandals (the effective amount of corruption, abuses of power, shameful individual behavior of politicians, and so on). Detailed information is, by definition, missing. For this reason, it would, for example, be very difficult to estimate the social cost of the underground government. For our present concern, however, this is not a real limitation. Because our interest focuses on the impact on popularity of the information that the public has at its disposal, only revealed political scandals will be taken into account.

The main difficulty in reality is only practical, that is, to have enough cases, and enough variability among them, to elicit useful estimates. There may be two pitfalls here. The country being studied may have such an efficient control mechanism that almost all corrupt or "dirty" actions are deterred, in which case there is nothing to study. Conversely, a country's control and audit institutions may be largely inefficient or even all but absent; in that case, politicians almost always escape unscathed, and political scandals are hardly ever brought to light. What is needed therefore is an "in-between" country, and France appears to meet this criterion, especially during the 1980s and 1990s. Although many scandals took place, France's control institutions and justice system have worked relatively efficiently to denounce and prosecute those involved.

The empirical study described in this chapter includes two different kinds of empirical analysis. The first measures the impact of revealed corruption and political scandals on voting in local elections. The second is based on a time series wherein the dependent variable is macropopularity of political parties.

The Impact of Political Scandals on Voting at the Municipal Level

The empirical analysis presented here is cross-sectional and corresponds to the estimation of a vote function for the June 1995 municipal elections in France. Disclosure of political scandals and corruption cases in France reached a peak at the beginning of the 1990s. During the 1989 municipal elections, only a few politicians had seen their campaigns hampered by such scandals. Six years later, in the 1995 municipal elections, the situation was quite different. For example, a national news magazine disclosed on the eve of the elections a confidential list of more than one hundred politicians involved—or suspected of being involved—in such cases, a large number of whom were running for reelection (*Le Point*, 10 June 1995, 186).

A previous study by Lafay and Jérôme (1991) demonstrated that three variables (of relatively equal importance) are significant for this type of ballot : (1) the percentage of votes obtained by the incumbent in the previous municipal election, (2) the results of the previous national election, and (3) the quality of the city management. Beginning with this model, we introduce an additional variable to test how the revealed scandals affect the incumbent.

The 1995 municipal elections are very interesting because they took place just a month after the presidential elections, so the observed difference in votes between the two types of ballots can be considered as a quasi experiment of the ceteris paribus influences of local factors (among which are the specific political scandals attached to candidates or local party teams). As no specific data on city management quality were readily available to us in connection with the 1995 elections (as they were for Lafay and Jérôme 1991), we used instead town-specific financial results, that is, per capita variations in city indebtedness and local taxes since the 1989 elections. The voting system for municipalities in France is a relatively complex two-ballot system.[5] But for our purpose, which was to measure the cost in votes of scandals, examining the first ballot was sufficient. Thus our dependent variable was the first-ballot result for the list of the incumbent mayor. The vote function to be estimated—by ordinary least squares—was, then, of the following form:

$$\text{VI95} = f\,(\text{VI89, VI89L, PRES95, TAXVAR, DEBTVAR, DEBTGR, SCAND})$$

To simplify, indexes for specific cities have been omitted in the different variables (for example, VI95 should be read $VI95_i$, where $i = 1 \ldots 92$).

VI95 = vote share of the incumbent on the first ballot in the 1995 municipal election in city *i*;

VI89 = vote share of the incumbent on the first ballot in the previous (1989) municipal elections in city *i*. The coefficient of this variable will measure fidelity in voting from one election to the other;

VI89L = VI89 if the incumbent in city *i* belongs to a left-wing party; = 0 if the incumbent belongs to a right-wing party. The degree of fidelity in voting may differ according to the party affiliation of the incumbent mayor. If the coefficient of this variable is positive, this means that the left-wing electorate has a higher fidelty than the right-wing electorate;

PRES95 = vote share of the left-wing candidate in the 1995 presidential election (second ballot) in city *i* if the incumbent belongs to a left-wing party;

TAXVAR = per capita variation in local taxes between 1988 and 1994 in city *i* (at 1994 prices)—positive (growth) or negative (reduction);

DEBTVAR= per capita variation in the city *i* indebtedness between 1988 and 1994 (at 1994 prices)—positive (growth) or negative (reduction);

DEBTGR = DEBTVAR if the city *i* indebtedness has grown or remained steady ($DEBTVAR_i \geq 0$); = 0 if the city *i* indebtedness has been reduced ($DEBTVAR_i < 0$). This variable introduces the possibility that debt increases and debt reduction are not judged symmetrically by the electorate. If the coefficient of this variable is negative (positive), then an increase in debt has greater (smaller) impact on vote than a debt decrease;

SCAND = 1 if a political scandal has been identified as affecting the incumbent or his or her local party team in city i, = 0 otherwise.

Data were collected for a sample of ninety-two large or medium-sized municipalities (population over 10,000 inhabitants) divided into two groups. The first group included thirty-three municipalities where revealed corruption cases and other political scandals were identified. The second group was a random sample of fifty-nine municipalities (from a total number of about one thousand) where no such scandals could be observed at the time of the election. In 1989 these two groups had very similar statistical features (see table 9.1).

TABLE 9.1. IMPACT OF POLITICAL SCANDALS ON MUNICIPAL ELECTIONS (IN PERCENTAGES)

	Vote share of incumbents with 1995 political scandals	*Vote share of incumbents without 1995 political scandals*
1989	51.5	49.4
1995	39.9	44.4

SOURCE: Direction Générale des Collectivités Locales.

NOTE: Mean percentage of votes for the incumbent at the 1989 and 1995 municipal elections—first-round ballot (sample of 92 cities with more than 10,000 inhabitants).

Based on this observation, we are entitled to consider both groups as belonging to a single population, and to assume that the disclosure of political scandals acted as an exogenous shock on some members of this population, the impact of which could be measured by the 1995 municipal elections.

The mean loss of incumbent mayors in cities with no disclosed scandals was 5 percent during the six years of their mandate. This illustrates a well-known phenomenon: the wearing effects of being in power (Paldam 1986). The mean loss of incumbent mayors in cities with political scandals was 11.6 percent. In some cases, it rose to 30 percent (Nîmes, for Jean Bousquet) or even 40 percent (Roissy-en-Brie, for Louis Reboul). The mean difference between cities with scandals and those without shows that the electorate heavily punished the incumbents. Indeed, not all the incumbent mayors in the cities with scandals lost, but important initial gains were necessary to avoid defeat (for example, Jacques Mellick at Béthune or Michel Mouillot at Cannes). Statistically, however, nearly half the mayors in scandal situations lost, while in cities without evident scandals, fewer than 24 percent were not reelected. (In the cities with evident scandals, 57.5 percent were reelected, as compared to 76.5 percent in the cities without scandals.)

The vote function estimated by ordinary least squares confirms the importance of the political cost of political scandals. According to the estimates reported in table 9.2 on page 198, the value of this loss is 7.6 percent. More generally, all the variables introduced in the equation are statistically significant at the .05 level (except TAXVAR), and the results suggest two broad remarks:

- First, concerning the basic local vote function, our estimates confirm the results obtained by Lafay and Jérôme (1991) in several respects, and bring to light new evidence on other points. As expected, the percentage of votes obtained by the incumbent is (positively) linked to his or her own perfor-

TABLE 9.2. VOTE FUNCTION FOR THE 1995 MUNICIPAL ELECTIONS (ORDINARY LEAST SQUARES ESTIMATES, DEPENDENT VARIABLE — INCUMBENT VOTE SHARE)

Independent variable	*Estimated coefficient*	*t-statistic*
Constant	3.97	(0.42)
VI89	0.30	(2.58)
VI89L	0.10	(2.15)
PRES95	0.43	(2.38)
TAXVAR	-0.08	(1.60)
DEBTVAR	-0.23	(2.27)
DEBTGR	0.27	(2.54)
SCAND	-7.60	(3.08)
$R^2 = 0.35$		
N = 92		

SOURCE: See table 9.1 on page 197.

NOTE: R^2 = the coefficient of multiple determination; N = the number of cities sampled.

mance in the previous municipal election (VI89), as well as to the local results of his or her political party or coalition in the latest national election (here, the presidential election, PRES95). The dummy variable introduced to account for a particular kind of partisan voting at the municipal level (VI89L) shows that left-wing incumbents benefit from more "faithful" voters than those of their right-wing counterparts. Still focusing on the basic municipal vote model, we find that raising per capita local taxes cost the incumbent some votes, whereas lowering taxes produced a gain in the same proportion (TAXVAR is statistically significant at .10, one-tailed test). More surprisingly, debt variations seemed to cause no such symmetrical effect: a reduction in city indebtedness (that is DEBTVAR < 0 and DEBTGR = 0) was beneficial to the incumbent in terms of votes, while an increase in the city debt was not on the whole prejudicial (since the coefficients of both of these variables tend to offset one another). Were this result to be confirmed, it would be evidence of an interesting asymmetrical, growth-biased, fiscal-illusion phenomenon at the municipal level.

- Second, regarding the specific focus of this analysis, namely the impact of revealed political scandals, that variable (SCAND) was found to be statistically significant, with the expected negative sign. On the whole, the disclosure of such scandals cost incumbents nearly 8 percentage points in votes. Therefore, in such a situation, the incumbent's reelection was severely hindered and could be achieved only because of strong initial gains, weak opposition, or other idiosyncratic factors.

The Impact of Political Scandals on Popularity at the National Level

There are several advantages in viewing the political impact of scandals from a national perspective. First, it allows us to study their influence on governmental machinery. Second, because such an analysis is grounded on time series, we can gain an idea via political indexes of the timing of responses to scandal shocks and can check for possible electoral or partisan cycles linked to their disclosure. Third, instead of using vote data, which add up to very small numbers because of the infrequency of elections, popularity indexes—that is, data which are collected monthly—can be substituted. This high number of observations allows a much more robust and detailed statistical analysis.

Several monthly popularity indexes have been published regularly in France since the 1960s and 1970s. Our estimates are based on the "Barometer" established by the SOFRES survey institute and published in the newspaper *Le Figaro.* We have chosen this monthly survey because it is the only one to have published popularity indexes of the political parties over a long period.[6]

No data were available on the place occupied by political scandals in the media, and hence on the information available to the public on this question. To solve this problem, the computerized database of the French daily newspaper *Le Monde* was used. This database includes all the articles published in this newspaper since 1987, with information about their date, length, format, and location (pages, number of columns, etc.). We did systematic research between 1987 and 1995 based on keywords related to political scandals. Figures 9.1 and 9.2 show the series constructed on the basis of this research. The total number of monthly lines published about political scandals is reported on the Y-axis (left-wing parties in figure 9.1 on page 200 and right-wing parties in figure 9.2 on page 201).

The graphs clearly show the outburst of scandals since the 1980s. The time profiles differ according to political parties: left-wing parties have been hit by scandal since the beginning of the period (1987), whereas the wave of scandals afflicting right-wing parties appeared much later (late 1992).

Table 9.3 on page 202 also shows that scandals broke out more frequently in the six-month period preceding the general elections in 1988, 1993, and 1995. These took the shape of either an increase in the number of "small" scandals or a

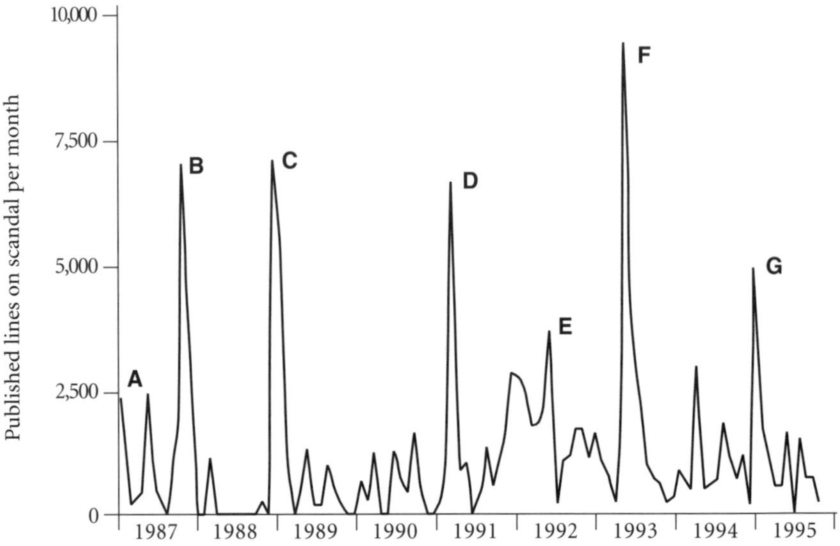

FIGURE 9.1 SCANDALS INVOLVING LEFT-WING PARTIES OR POLITICIANS

A Carrefour de Développement—Illegal funding of a nonprofit institution in charge of African development.

B Luchaire—Illegal arms sales to the Middle East.

C Pechiney—Insider-trading scandal involving people closely associated with President Mitterrand.

D P.S. (Emmanuelli, Urba, Sages)—Illegal party financing practices by the Socialist Party.

E *Sang contaminé*—Health minister and prime minister involved in a scandal concerning several cases of infection by the HIV virus following unsafe blood transfusions that had received authorization from the government.

F and **G** Tapie—Businessman, president of a soccer club, and former member of government involved in several scandals (tax evasion, fraudulent and illegal business operations, soccer player corruption).

revelation of some important ones involving, for example, the funding of political parties or a questionable use of state powers.[7] It is clear that since 1986, with the more frequent changeovers of political power between coalitions, the parties in power have had more and more difficulty avoiding this kind of trouble during critical political periods.

Analysis of the link between political scandals and the popularity of political leaders also shows that if they suffer a loss in personal popularity, the spillover effect on their party is quite limited. An example is the "Affaire Botton," in which the former mayor of Lyon, Michel Noir, was heavily involved. Noir's popularity was closely connected to the period of judicial development of this scandal,

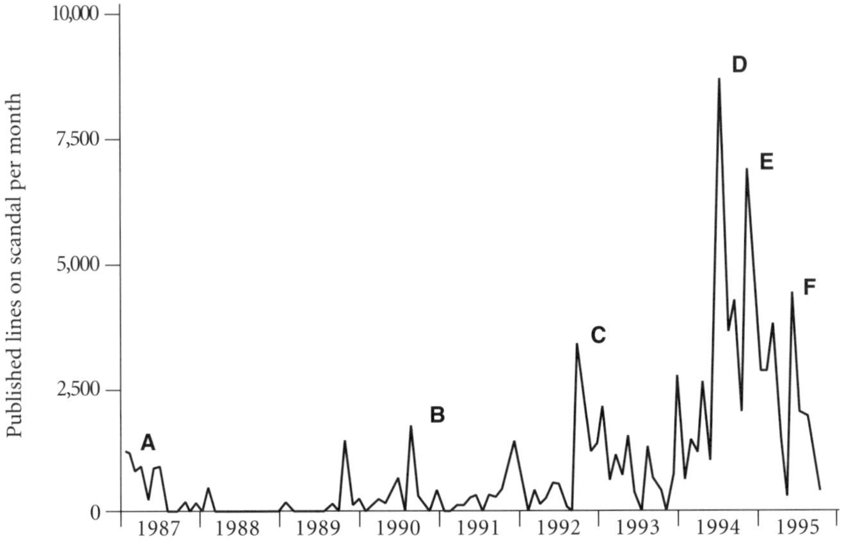

FIGURE 9.2 SCANDALS INVOLVING RIGHT-WING PARTIES OR POLITICIANS

A *Vrai-faux passeport*—The French ministry of the interior gave a passport to a bureau chief involved in the "Carrefour de Développement" scandal in order to allow him to avoid testimony.

B Médecin—The mayor of Nice was involved in corruption and illegal funding.

C Noir-Botton—Corruption involving people closely associated with the mayor of Lyon and former member of government, M. Noir.

D P.R. (Longuet), Carignon—Corruption and illegal party financing practices involving members of the Republican Party.

E HLM des Hauts de Seine—Corruption and illegal party financing operations by members of the Gaullist party.

F Juppé—The prime minister was involved in a scandal concerning illegitimate housing advantages gained in Paris by the city administration.

though not to the popularity of any of the right-wing parties. The same situation was observed in another well-known scandal involving a former left-wing minister (and businessman), Bernard Tapie. Though interesting, individual scandals are less decisive than those involving the parties as a whole, at least with regard to the general functioning of political institutions. For this reason, we have limited our empirical tests to the latter type of political scandal.

Technically, questioning the influence of scandals on party popularity is similar to testing credibility effects, except that it concerns, instead, "losses of credibility." Among the different methods available for tests (see Agénor and Taylor 1992), the simplest is to introduce additional proxy variables, such as those we

TABLE 9.3. SCANDALS IN THE PREELECTORAL PERIODS

	Lines about political scandals in Le Monde	
	Mean number per month	*Percentage increase over prior interval*
1. Presidential and parliamentary elections (May and June 1988)		
Prior period without elections (January 1987 to April 1988)	1,685	
During the six months preceding the elections	2,153	28
2. Parliamentary elections (March 1993)		
Prior period without elections (July 1988 to February 1993)	1,864	
During the six months preceding the election	3,784	103
3. Presidential election (May 1995)		
Prior period without elections (April 1993 to April 1995)	4,712	
During the six months preceding the election	7,517	60

SOURCE: *Le Monde,* issues published since 1987.

have computed using *Le Monde*'s database, into a popularity function. Because we are not interested in the impact of the other variables, popularity is assumed to be explained only by an autoregressive variable (popularity in the preceding month), by scandal variables, and by dummy variables taking into account the "honeymoon" effects that accompany any change in the governing party or coalition. As the scandal variables have a high probability of being really pure exogenous shocks, they are unlikely to be a source of bias.

Preliminary tests have shown that the results are more stable when the popularity function is formulated in differences (the left-wing/right-wing popularity difference being explained by the left-wing/right-wing scandal difference). Moreover, as the survey published at the beginning of each month (t) by *Le Figaro* in fact has been conducted by SOFRES at the end of the preceding month (t-1), all other variables are lagged by one month. Hence, the general form of the function is as follows:

$$EPOPUGD = f\,(EPOPUGD_{t-1}, ESCANGD_{t-1}, SCANTOT_{t-1}, EL8806, EL9303)$$

EPOPUGD:	difference between the popularity of the Socialist Party and the mean popularity of the right-wing parties (UDF and RPR) for the month *t*.
ESCANGD:	difference between the number of lines in *Le Monde* concerning left-wing scandals and the number of lines in the same newspaper concerning right-wing scandals (in thousands).
SCANTOT:	total aggregate number of lines in *Le Monde* concerning scandals in general, without party differentiation (in thousands).
EL8806:	dummy variable, with value 1 for the month in which parliamentary elections were held (June 1988), and zero otherwise.
EL9303:	dummy variable, with value 1 for the month in which parliamentary elections were held (March 1993), and zero otherwise.

The empirical results for the period ranging from February 1987 to January 1996 are given in table 9.4 .

TABLE 9.4. POLITICAL SCANDALS AND THE DIFFERENTIAL IN POPULARITY OF LEFT-WING AND RIGHT-WING PARTIES

Independent variable	*Estimated coefficient*	*t-statistic*
Constant	1.24	(2.21)
$EPOPUGD_{t-1}$	0.91	(29.30)
$ESCANGD_{t-1}$	-0.35	(2.26)
$SCANTOT_{t-1}$	-0.23	(1.77)
EL8806	8.86	(2.56)
EL9303	-14.33	(4.11)
$R^2 = 0.92$		
h = -0.89		
N = 108		

SOURCES: *Le Monde,* issues from 1987 to 1996; monthly "barometer" surveys of SOFRES.

NOTE: Ordinary least squares on monthly data, February 1987 to January 1996; dependent variable = popularity difference between Socialist party and right-wing parties.

The variables introduced in the equation are all statistically significant at .05 (except $SCANTOT_{t-1}$, which is significant at .10).

The autoregressive term ($EPOPUGD_{t-1}$) and the honeymoon variables (EL8806 and EL9303) are all, not surprisingly, highly significant.

The variable $ESCANGD_{t-1}$ (difference between the number of lines about left-wing scandals and the number of lines about right-wing scandals) has, as expected, a significant negative coefficient. According to the value of this coefficient, one might venture to say that a difference of three thousand lines in *Le Monde* about the left-wing parties (i.e., a bit more than three pages of this newspaper during a month) indicates a 1-percent decline in popularity. The more the left-wing party is beset by scandals (compared to a given value of right-wing scandals), the lower is its popularity differential with the right-wing parties.

Moreover, because the variable $SCANTOT_{t-1}$ (total aggregate number of lines concerning scandals) is significant, we can see that an increase of the total number of scandals is unfavorable to left-wing parties. It seems that a climate of scandal generates, all else equal, a demand for more "order," and, for this reason, an increase in the right-wing orientation of the electorate. About four thousand lines (four to five pages per month) on scandals in *Le Monde* corresponds to 1 point more of popularity for the right-wing parties. To illustrate this asymmetry, assume that, for a given month, the number of lines on scandals is 6,000, and that these scandals are only of left-wing origin. Then the loss in popularity for the left is 2 points because it is involved directly, and 1.5 points because the general level of unpopularity has increased, that is, a total of (2 + 1.5) points. In a parallel situation the right-wing parties would have lost only (2 - 1.5) points.

Two main conclusions can be drawn from these results: (1) at least in the domain of political scandals, the media seem to exercise effectively their "fourth estate" power, inflicting sizable popularity costs on the involved parties; (2) left-wing parties are hurt significantly more by political scandals than are right-wing ones. Some will see in this asymmetry an "injustice," others, an incentive to greater virtue.

One of the most interesting challenges for social scientists is whether they can study and empirically test assumptions on questions where data are unavailable or even nonexistent. From this point of view, the question of the link between political scandals and popularity or vote was particularly attractive, raising both theoretical and empirical technical challenges. The results about political scandals presented here remain rough, and the conclusions must be handled cautiously.

Nevertheless, on the basis of the French experience, they clearly demonstrate that political scandals have a sizable electoral effect. Furthermore, we suspect that such findings would be confirmed in a wider pool of democratic countries. Political scandals appear to have general, and important, electoral consequences. We think, however, that we have at least shown that the scientific treatment of this kind of problem is feasible and could lead to a much better understanding of our social universe. If we have inspired the reader to take even a small step in this direction, then we have not totally missed our major objective.

Acknowledgment—The authors thank particularly the political and documentation services of the newspaper *Le Monde.* Without their active support, this study could not have been achieved.

Chapter 10

The France That Doesn't Vote: Nonconsumption in the Electoral Market

Andrew M. Appleton

Since the law of 5 March 1848 established the practice of "universal suffrage" (at that time male) as the principal component of the individual stake in the national political community, participation in the electoral system has had a dual character in France (Garrigou 1992). This ambiguity is neatly summarized by the epithet inscribed on the cards issued to citizens upon registering to vote: "To vote is a right, it is also a civic duty." Unlike some democracies (Belgium and Australia, for example), France does not have compulsory voting. Nor does it have a tradition of "civic shame" like that persisting in Italy (where a substantial proportion of the electorate still falsely believe that voting is compulsory). Nonetheless, the notion of the vote as a civic duty continues to color perceptions of the mobilization of the electorate in France and carries a heavy negative connotation among French observers of electoral nonparticipation. In the wake of each election, much ink is spilled analyzing the extent and meaning of levels of nonparticipation.

In this chapter, we intend to lay out two different forms of nonparticipation in French elections, and examine each over the life of the Fifth Republic. The two kinds of nonparticipation that we will investigate are nonregistration and abstention. Although these two phenomena are quite different in character, they are not, we will argue, entirely discrete. Furthermore, although the lack of participation in the electoral process by a substantial number of eligible citizens in any given election may appear quite contrary to the consolidation of the Fifth Republic as a participatory democracy, we demonstrate that the aggregate figures often reported mask a much more complex reality. Our main contention in this chapter is that French citizens, rather than opting out of the electoral market altogether in greater numbers, actually have come to make use of nonparticipation as a strategic choice from election to election.

Nonregistration

Nonregistration has been a significant subject of attention in the United States, both among the public and within the academic world. Historically, registration laws were used to keep some potential participants, such as African Americans in the South, out of the system. Recent efforts to increase electoral participation in the United States have included federal legislation to open up the registration process (the so-called Motor Voter Law). Academics have seen voter registration as the first stage of what is actually a two-stage process of electoral participation; the thresholds established by state registration laws have a determinant impact on overall turnout levels in general elections. Thus voter registration is a topic that is relatively well documented and understood in America.

In contrast, there has been a relative dearth of information about registration in most European democracies, France included. Indeed, many European scholars appear to believe that the difference between the potential electorate and the actual electorate (i.e., the number of unregistered voters) is so negligible as to be trivial. Furthermore, the inattention to the topic also is derived from the fact that in many of these countries, the onus is on government to register individuals to vote, and to maintain the electoral registers. Thus it is assumed that the possible disincentives to register that have been the focus of study in the United States are simply irrelevant in the European context.

As we will discuss, both of these perceptions are fatally flawed in the case of France. In point of fact, French electoral law places the burden upon the citizen to set in motion the process of registration to vote. While the procedure is neither complicated nor spatially variant (as in the United States, where registration laws vary from state to state, even for federal elections), it is one that entails a certain cost to the individual. The only comprehensive treatment of French voter registration procedures published in English goes so far as to suggest that voter registration in France may be for the most part *more* difficult than in the United States: "in some respects, the French system of voter registration is more restrictive than the system employed in many populous U.S. states" (Pierce 1995, 111). Hence the second element of the prevailing myths about registration in France; the few studies that have been conducted uniformly indicate that at least one in ten eligible voters remains unregistered, perhaps more. The great difficulty, however, is to devise a methodology that can give a reliable estimate of the real number of nonregistered citizens.

The principle of universal suffrage was established in 1848 at the birth of the Second Republic; it was first practiced in the election of April of the same year. Suffrage was not extended to women until the Liberation in 1945, and 1946 was the first election in which women were eligible to participate. In 1974 the voting age was lowered from twenty-one to eighteen. Thus the right to register is accorded today to all those over eighteen years old who are in possession of civil and political rights (according to Article 3 of the Constitution of the Fifth Republic).[1] The only exception to this is the provision adopted in 1992 that citizens of the European Union have the right to vote in municipal elections. Periodically there has been discussion of allowing other immigrant noncitizens to vote in local elections; some cities (notably Amiens) have actually allowed resident aliens to participate in local voting, although this is not recognized under the constitution.

The electoral code mandates that citizens register to vote at the age of majority in the commune of their residence, or when a citizen moves from one commune to another. Registration takes place at the *mairie*, the center of political life at the local level. According to the code, registration is obligatory for all; however, the code imposes no sanctions for those who do not register. Unlike Great Britain, for example, there is no obligation upon government to register voters outside of this quasi-voluntary act. For some observers, this is tacit recognition of a distinction enshrined in French political life between "virtuous" citizens conscious of their social and political responsibilities and those who have no "civic conscience"; the French tradition recognizes that the duty to register and vote is obligatory for the former, but that democracy might actually lose more than it gains by compelling the latter to participate (Bréchon 1993).

That stated, the registration procedure introduces an immense amount of variance in the political context within which individual registration takes place, despite a nationally uniform electoral code. France is divided into over 36,000 communes of very different sizes, from a population of under ten to one of over one million. Demographic and territorial variation appears to have a tremendous impact on the distribution of nonregistration among the communes, with nonregistration being highest in large urban communes (Morin 1983; 1987). Pierce (1995) reports that in urban areas, the ratio of potential electors to registration places is much higher in France than in the United States, a further indicator that voter registration might involve more cost at the individual level in France than has previously been assumed.

Although registration takes place at the local level, a central electoral register is maintained by the National Institute of Statistics and Economic Studies (INSEE), which is intended to prevent double registration and voter fraud. It appears, however, that there is a certain incidence of double registration at any given election. In some cases, this might have spawned some systematic electoral fraud; for example, when the electoral rolls of Corsica were subjected to a rigorous purge in the early 1990s, the number of registered voters dropped by 25 percent, and in the subsequent regional elections of 1992 the region, traditionally one of the most abstentionist, miraculously became one of the most participatory (see Bréchon 1993; Subileau and Toinet 1992).

Registration requirements are also quite restrictive; "one must have lived in the town . . . for at least six months (or have been a local taxpayer for five years). . . . Geographic mobility is probably the most important nontechnical obstacle to voter registration, apart from motivation" (Pierce 1995, 113). The electoral law stipulates that a citizen may register to vote at any time during the calendar year, but the point at which registration takes effect differs by category of registrant. For those who have turned eighteen after February and for those who were naturalized during the previous year, registration can take effect virtually immediately, and they are eligible to vote in elections that same year. For all others (for example, those who have moved their place of residence), however, registration does not take effect until 1 March of the following year. Thus it is possible to envisage a situation in which a French citizen, following the technicalities of the procedure, finds him- or herself effectively disenfranchised for fourteen months.

The French voter registration system does differ markedly from that of the United States, however, in that registration in France is for all intents and purposes permanent, as long as the citizen continues to reside in the same commune and has not been not stripped of civil and political rights by judicial order. Pierce points out that in the United States, persistent nonvoters are often purged from the electoral rolls, the modal period of nonvoting being four years; in France, however, the authorities must have some independent reason to remove someone from the rolls (Pierce 1995). Local authorities do periodically send out new voter registration cards, and when these are returned by the postal service as undeliverable the practice is to open an investigation with an intent to update the electoral roll. Citizens who are to be removed may appeal, but the procedure is quite intimidating (Pierce 1995).

So what are the figures for nonregistration? Owing to the manner in which the central electoral register is compiled, and its lack of conformity with the main population database composed from census results, precise figures are impossible to obtain. Few systematic studies have been published, but what is remarkable is the consistency in the information conveyed by those that have. Two different approaches have been used to provide a relatively accurate estimate of the incidence of nonregistration. The first method essentially compares the number of registered voters contained in the central register with the eligible population, adjusting for methodological differences in data collection (Héran and Roualt 1995; Cluzeau 1992; Morin 1989, 1987, 1983; Levy 1978). The second approach is to gauge nonregistration from surveys (Mayer and Percheron 1990; Bréchon and Cautrès 1987; Percheron 1986). While the latter approach has demonstrably yielded biased estimates in similar studies in the United States, it does have the advantage that it potentially provides valuable sociological information about self-reported nonregistrants. Where there is bias in reporting levels from such survey data, it is almost certainly in the direction of underestimating actual levels of nonregistration (Pierce 1995).

Morin (1983) reported the level of nonregistration in 1982 as 11.3 percent of the eligible electorate, although he noted several sources of potential error. On the basis of a slightly different demographic sample, he gave a figure of 10.1 percent in 1986 (Morin 1987). Héran and Roualt (1995) reported the level of nonregistration as slightly over 9 percent in 1995, using a method similar to the earlier studies noted above. The differences in these levels might be accounted for by the study done by Cluzeau (1992), in which she noted a substantial wave of registration at the end of 1991. One further study undertaken by the Group for Interregional Ideas and Studies (GERI) estimated the portion of the unregistered electorate as rather lower than these figures: 7.5 percent in 1995, 5.5 percent in 1988, and 3.8 percent in 1981 (*Le Monde*, 11 May 1995, 6). This is worth noting simply to demonstrate the degree of variance in reports of nonregistration.

Perhaps the best study of nonregistration using survey data is that of Mayer and Percheron (1990), who combined data drawn from regional surveys conducted by the Interregional Political Observatory (OIP) and a French national election study conducted by the Center for the Study of French Political Life (CEVIPOF). The level of nonregistration detected by this method was reported as just over 9 percent. While Pierce (1995, 103) argues that "there is little reason, however, to accept that estimate at face value," it does compare very closely with the nonsurvey estimates presented above. Nonetheless, it seems safe to suggest that Morin's original (1983) conclusion is still a good summation of the levels of nonregistration in France; one potential voter in ten is, at any given time, likely to be in an ineligible position to vote.

Who are the nonregistrants? According to one observer, Françoise Subileau, nonregistration is primarily a result of weak "social insertion" (interview in *Le Monde*, 6 May 1997, 10). Social insertion is a concept that has been used to describe the degree to which individuals are integrated into their social context, generally through the mediation of institutions such as voluntary and religious associations, trade unions, family, and even marriage. Weak social insertion is generally highest among certain groups such as recent immigrants, the young, those of lower socioeconomic status, and those living in peripheral areas.

Support for this view was found in the study by Héran and Roualt (1995), whose data showed that only 75 percent of the young register to vote before they are twenty years old. In addition, they showed that renters are less likely to register than homeowners; however, their data did not support the contention that citizens who were born outside of France (a good proxy for immigrants) are registered in lower numbers than their French-born homologues. Percheron (1986) concurred with the age-related findings quoted above, while she found no difference in registration rates between men and women. A series of BVA surveys conducted between December 1984 and May 1985 found that of the 9 percent of potential voters who were unregistered, 43.1 percent were under twenty-five years old and 28.5 percent were in the twenty-five to thirty-four age bracket (*Le Matin*, 30 September 1985, 5). Cutting the data a little differently, INSEE estimated that 33.1 percent of the under twenty-five age bracket were not registered in 1986 (*Le Monde*, 2 January 1988, 9). The BVA surveys showed that nearly 60 percent of the nonregistered were located in towns of over 100,000, with 28.3 percent of them in the Greater Paris area. There was a small difference in terms of workforce participation, with those active in the workforce constituting 41.6 percent of the sample, as compared to 47.9 percent inactive. These surveys found little significant difference between the unregistered in terms of partisan leanings, with 39.1 percent of them declaring that they had no party preference.

The weak social insertion model has been challenged by some, however. Pierre Bréchon, responding directly to the *Le Monde* interview with Françoise Sublieau, claimed that a substantial proportion of nonregistration may actually consist of what he terms an excess of insertion; namely, those who are highly mobile and who may suffer from the static assumptions built into the French voter registration system (interview in *Le Monde*, 21 May 1997, 7). Elsewhere he supports the view of the Centre d'Information Civique (CIC) that there are perhaps not one but three categories of nonregistered voters (Bréchon 1993). These are, respectively, the highly mobile, the weakly inserted, and the "anarchists." The first category is composed of those who tend to move often for job-related reasons and who tend to have higher educational and sociocultural levels than the national average. The third category is smaller than the other two; it consists of those who have made their nonregistration a conscious rejection of the political institutions of the French system.

Despite these different views, it does appear that nonregistration is beginning to be taken a bit more seriously as a problem of public policy. At the end of the 1980s, several associations, including SOS-Racisme, France Plus, and the CIC, undertook a concerted campaign to increase registration levels among the young, particularly those living in urban areas and of immigrant extraction. As part of this campaign, the former (and very popular) minister of culture, Jack Lang, undertook a registration campaign in thirty of France's largest towns (*Le Monde*, 2 January 1988, 9). Prominent figures were enlisted to help; for example, the actor Gérard Dépardieu revealed that he had never actually voted in his life, but went to register his name on the electoral roll. The CIC, which was established in 1967 as part of an effort to increase political participation in France, periodically releases reports on the problem of nonregistration and has consistently argued for a liberalization of the registration laws.

To summarize, we may conclude that the nonregistration of potential voters is a significant and underreported component of the French electoral process. When participation is discussed in terms of abstention versus casting a ballot, the figures need to be adjusted downwards by at least 10 percent in order to provide a more accurate picture of the true levels of voting (Appleton 1995). Although nonparticipation, even when so adjusted, remains lower than in the United States, it is rather more significant than is generally understood. It is to the second form of nonparticipation introduced above, namely abstention from voting, that we will turn next.

Abstention

Studies of electoral participation in the United States have tended to emphasize at least three different groups of factors that lead to nonvoting, or abstention. The first of these factors is socioeconomic status (SES). It has been amply demonstrated that those of lower SES—less educated, younger, poorer, minority citizens—will be more likely to abstain from voting than others, ceteris paribus.

Studies emphasizing SES have shown the influence of education over turnout to be dominant among the SES variables traditionally examined (Wolfinger and Rosenstone 1980). A second approach to the problem of participation emphasizes psychological factors, including party attachments (Campbell, Converse, Miller, and Stokes 1960) and interest in politics (Verba and Nie 1972). The third approach to nonparticipation places the emphasis on contextual factors that affect individual behavior. Context has been variously interpreted as a set of institutional factors (e.g., Jackson 1995), or a set of social factors (e.g., Teixeira 1992). As we shall see, there is some evidence to show that each of these three approaches can provide some explanation of abstention in France, while all of them contain important limitations.

Whatever the explanation for the decision to abstain from the vote at the individual level, the fluctuations in the aggregate level indicators of abstention have been a constant source of preoccupation among observers of French electoral behavior. In the legislative elections of 1997, as noted by Elisabeth Dupoirier (*Le Monde*, 29 May 1997, 11), abstentionists constituted the largest single block of eligible voters in France; out of the potential electorate, 9.1 percent voted for candidates of the sitting right-wing majority, 10.6 percent voted for the left-wing opposition led by Lionel Jospin, and 12.5 percent abstained from the vote altogether. Dupoirier further pointed out that this was not a new phenomenon, but actually the third consecutive election in which abstentionists formed the largest block of eligible voters. In contrast, Anne Muxel characterized the 1997 level of abstention as "the sign of a malaise in the party system, if not an overall rejection of politics" (*Le Monde*, 5 June 1997, 12). In the wake of three successive electoral consultations in 1988 that witnessed record highs in the numbers of those who did not vote (34 percent in the legislative elections, 50 percent in the municipal elections, and 63 percent in the referendum on New Caledonia), one editorial lamented that "we can once again invoke the specter of the Americanization of French political life" (*Vendredi*, 3 March 1989). (Needless to say, "Americanization" is automatically understood in Gallic parlance to be rather bad!)

Yet the normative implications of seemingly higher rates of abstention have not always been viewed so negatively. Pierce (1995) pointed out that even after adjusting for the problem of nonregistration, French abstention rates are lower than those in the United States. Similarly, data from European elections suggest that France is not to be considered as having an abnormally high abstention rate in comparison with other nations. One French observer, J.-L. Parodi, portrayed the high abstention rates of 1988 not as a portent of bad things to come but rather as "attesting to the calming down of the political climate" (*Quotidien de Paris*, 29 June 1989). In this view, a certain level of nonparticipation is "normal" and represents more a satisfaction among voters with the operation of the political system than the rejection implied in the statements quoted earlier.

The rates of abstention in seven different kinds of elections (presidential, parliamentary, cantonal, referendum, European, municipal, and regional) over a thirty-year period are summarized in table 10.1. What is evident from these data is that there is no clear trend of rising abstention in French elections, despite some high rates in particular ones. In order to gain a clearer picture of the pattern of electoral abstention, it is necessary to disentangle these data and examine them by election type: national, local, European, and referendum. As we shall see, election type and frequency have an important impact on the rate of abstention; in other words, institutional context affects the rates at which citizens turn out to vote.

As in the United States, presidential elections in France witness higher levels of turnout than do others. The direct election of a president with important executive powers is an event that draws citizens into the electoral process. Typically four out of every five registered voters in France head to the polls at the first round to cast their votes in this kind of election. The highest rate of abstention in the first ballot of a presidential election over the life of the Fifth Republic was recorded in 1969 as 22.4 percent, marginally higher than the 22 percent recorded in 1995. An interesting feature of the presidential election in France is that turnout generally increases at the second ballot in the runoff between the top candidates; this has been true for all four presidential elections since the 1960s. The highest abstention rate recorded in a presidential election was in the second ballot of the 1969 election, in which Georges Pompidou, the heir of de Gaulle, defeated Alain Poher, a center-right candidate. That abnormally high rate of abstention is explained by the lack of a candidate from the left, which led many Socialist and Communist supporters simply to refrain from participating in the runoff ballot.

In legislative elections, the picture is rather different. Until 1981, first-ballot abstention rates in parliamentary elections approximately mirrored those of presidential elections, with consistent participation rates of over 80 percent of registered voters. In 1981, however, the abstention rate soared to almost 30 percent; it fell to 21.9 percent in 1986[2] but has exceeded the 30-percent mark in all three subsequent parliamentary elections. It should be noted that abstention rates at the second ballot, just as in presidential contests, have been lower than those of the first (with the exception of the 1967 and 1968 elections). Thus, with abstention rates in legislative elections greater than 20 percent in five successive elections over

TABLE 10.1. ABSTENTION IN FRENCH ELECTIONS, 1965–98 (PERCENTAGE OF REGISTERED VOTERS NOT VOTING)

	Presidential		*Parliamentary*	*Cantonal*			*Municipal*	
	1st round	*2d round*	*1st round*	*1st round*	*Referendum*	*European*	*1st round*	*Regional*
1965	15.25	15.67						
1966								
1967			19.08					
1968			20.04					
1969	22.41	31.14			19.86			
1970				38.20				
1971							24.80	
1972					39.75			
1973			18.76	46.60				
1974	15.77	12.66						
1975								
1976				34.70				
1977							21.10	
1978			16.88					
1979				34.60		39.29		
1980								
1981	18.91	14.14	29.13					
1982				31.57				
1983							21.60	
1984						43.27		
1985				33.29				
1986			21.90					22.10
1987								
1988	18.62	15.93	34.26	50.87	63.10			
1989						51.10	27.20	
1990								
1991								
1992				29.34	29.49			31.30
1993			30.80					
1994				39.64				
1995	22.00	20.58						
1996								
1997			32.04					
1998				39.60				42.00

a sixteen year span, and four out of the five elections witnessing nonparticipation rates of nearly 30 percent or more, it is tempting to conclude that French legislative elections have lost their character as mobilizing events.

The temptation to view the rise in abstention beginning in 1981 as a permanent phenomenon must be tempered, however, by considering the conjunction of circumstances that predominated during each election. In 1981, 1988, and 1997, each of the elections in question followed a tactical presidential dissolution of the National Assembly. In 1981 and in 1988, the dissolution followed closely in the wake of a presidential election and was the means by which the newly-elected president (Mitterrand both times) established a working majority in the legislature. In 1997 the dissolution of the National Assembly was a move by the president, Jacques Chirac, to try to prolong the life of a right-wing majority in the legislature (elected in 1993) up to the time France was to move to a single European currency.[3]

In addition, voter fatigue is a potential explanation for some of the rise in abstention over this period. Since the late 1970s, two additional kinds of election have been added to the French political calendar. In 1979, the first direct elections were held for the European Parliament (elected every five years on a fixed cycle), and in 1986 the twenty-two regional assemblies became subject to selection by universal suffrage. Furthermore, room had to be found in this already crowded schedule for two referenda, the 1988 referendum on New Caledonia and the 1992 one on the Maastricht Treaty. Thus the apparent rise in abstention from legislative elections may have been a product of institutional and conjunctural factors rather than a deep-seated rejection of the system as whole.

Three different types of local elections can be considered in discussing patterns of electoral participation. The first of these are regional elections, held every six years in the twenty-two regions of France, beginning in 1986. That year, the regional elections were held coterminous with the legislative elections, and the abstention rate was just slightly higher for the regional elections at 22.1 percent than the 21.9 percent for the legislative elections. In 1992 the regional elections were joined with the first round of the cantonal elections, in an attempt to stimulate turnout; nonetheless, the abstention rate rose to 31.3 percent of the registered electorate. Similarly, in 1998, when the regional elections were paired once again with the cantonal elections, abstention was yet higher, at 42 percent. The single-ballot proportional representation system used in the regional elections does not allow for a comparison between rounds; however, turnout was marginally less in all three cases than for the elections with which they were paired. Thus it does not appear that regional elections by themselves are particularly mobilizing, at least as measured by turnout.

Cantonal elections select members of the ninety-six departmental councils (*conseils généraux*). The system used is the same constituency-based two-ballot mechanism employed in legislative elections, although the constituencies are much smaller in size. Councilors are elected for six-year terms, although only half of each council is elected each time; thus cantonal elections are held every three years, although comparisons should be made across six-year cycles for consistency. The average rate of abstention over the course of the Fifth Republic in this type of election has been about 37 percent; the record was set in 1988, when it rose to over 50 percent in a year of great voter fatigue. In fact, nonparticipation rates in the latest series of cantonal elections (1994 and 1998, 39.6 percent and 39.6 percent) do not appear to be significantly different than in earlier equivalent contests (1970 and 1973, 38.2 percent and 46.6 percent).

Municipal elections, held every six years, are used to select the members of the town councils in France's more than 36,000 communes. Municipal elections have consistently experienced the highest levels of electoral mobilization of all three types of local election, with abstention rates never exceeding 30 percent. In general there is a direct correlation between the size of the commune and the rate of abstention; rural communes are characterized by a very high rate of electoral participation in municipal elections compared to other communes (Bréchon 1993). Looking only at larger urban communes, however, Hoffman-Martinot (1992) concluded that variation in participation rates for municipal elections could not be explained solely by population size.

The abstention rates for European elections are much higher than for the other election types already discussed. In the first European election of 1979, 39.3 percent of the registered electorate refrained from casting a vote; this rose to 43.3 percent in 1984 and to 51.1 percent in 1989. Although these rates are much higher than nonparticipation rates in national or local elections, they are lower than for some other European countries, notably Britain, Denmark, and the Netherlands. Finally, the four referendums that have been held since 1969 have provided contrasting results in terms of nonparticipation. The regional reform of 1969 had a high rate of participation (over 80 percent), while that on the constitutional status of New Caledonia marked an all-time high for abstention (over 63 percent). Each of these figures can effectively be explained by conjunctural dynamics. In the first case, the high degree of electoral mobilization was in large part a product of the perception that the referendum was a plebiscite on the leadership of General de

Gaulle. In contrast, the low turnout for the referendum of 1988 can be ascribed mainly to the position taken by the political opposition at the time, which advised voters to abstain.

The data on abstention for these seven different elections types thus defy easy interpretation and demand the careful consideration of conjunctural forces in order to be placed in context. Nonetheless, Bréchon (1995) did suggest—following J.-L. Parodi—that the electorate is, in general, more mobilized in some periods than in others. He argued that there is little evidence of a sustained increase in abstention that could be viewed as a sign of French depoliticization; he concluded, "Universal suffrage is not sick. Voting is in fact a well-internalized democratic norm" (Bréchon 1995, 29).

So what do we know about abstention at the individual level in France? Sublieau and Toinet (1993) provided a comprehensive treatment of the phenomenon of electoral abstention, using a combination of survey data and a careful examination of electoral records (*listes d'émargement*) in selected voting districts in Paris. The second of these techniques permitted them, through a careful comparison of attendance records for successive elections, to build a history of electoral participation for each individual registered to vote in those voting districts. The surprising finding they reported is that the number of chronic abstainers—that is, those who are registered but simply do not participate in several successive elections—actually is very small, estimated at about 1 percent of the sample. Elsewhere, they estimated the number of those who abstained in both rounds of the presidential and legislative elections of 1988 at 13 percent; this figure is the same for the equivalent elections of 1981 (*Le Monde*, 22 June 1988, 10). Thus, they argued, the study of abstention at the aggregate level tends to mask the true nature of the phenomenon. In reality, there is far less stability from election to election (or even between rounds of the same election) in terms of the division between voters and nonvoters than is suggested by many observers.

The same kind of analysis was performed by Morin (1989) who concluded that, across four kinds of elections involving seven ballots between 1988-89, the proportion of consistent abstentionists in his sample was only about 8 percent. Although this figure is somewhat higher than the 1 percent suggested by Sublieau and Toinet, several factors must be taken into account. The elections Morin studied included presidential, parliamentary, and municipal ones, in addition to the 1988 referendum, while Sublieau and Toinet examined only legislative elections. The inclusion of the 1988 referendum, with its 63-percent abstention rate, certainly increased the probability that members of his sample would have abstained at least once;[4] in addition, holding four elections in rapid succession would appear to raise the possibility of voter fatigue and thus the probability of voters lapsing into consistent abstention. Héran and Roualt (1995) found that the number who abstained in both the presidential and municipal elections of 1995 was about 11 percent of their sample.

Despite the differences in these figures, they all reveal that the category of abstention does not simply contain one homogeneous group of persistent nonvoters. Morin (1989) argued that three groups could be distinguished within his sample: the persistent abstainers; the assiduous voters (those who vote in all elections); and the majority, who participate in the electoral process depending on the conjunction of circumstances. The latter category he estimated at 60 percent of his sample: 37 percent who voted in three of four elections, 15 percent who voted in two, and 8 percent who voted in only one. Assiduous voters thus outnumber persistent abstainers by four to one, Morin argued, although three out of five registered voters decide to participate based on conjunctural factors.

We may object, of course, that the majority group may be overinflated by the inclusion of an atypical electoral event, such as the referendum on New Caledonia, which saw such a high rate of abstention. The dynamics of the referendum appear to be rather different from other events included in Morin's study. One detailed examination of the referendum, based on a survey of 508 citizens who abstained, argued that those who refrained from voting could be classified into five groups (*Le Monde*, 9 November 1988, 7). The first of these groups, about 19 percent of the sample, was composed of those who abstained out of political opposition. Eighteen percent chose not to participate because they rejected the mechanism of the referendum (direct democracy). Nearly 34 percent claimed that they felt no enthusiasm for the issues at stake. Twenty-one percent saw themselves as essentially satisfied with the system. The remaining 8 percent were classified as those who persistently abstained because they were not integrated into the political system.

Thus, although variation in participation depends on both the time period and the kinds of election studied, it appears clear that the proportion of the electorate who can be classified as persistent nonvoters is actually smaller than aggregate level statistics intimate. Even more importantly, there is little evidence to suggest that persistent nonvoters are becoming a larger group within the French electorate. Where the figures do seem to show a rise in abstention at the aggregate level (which, as we have suggested, is not at all clear), it can plausibly be accounted for by an increase in the proportion of those who generally vote but who may sit out any particular election for circumstantial reasons. This proposition can be examined by looking at the sociological picture of abstention in recent French elections.

Bréchon (1993) advanced the notion that there are really three different groups contained in the aggregate-level indicators of abstention. The first he called a social abstention, that is, one linked to individual insertion in society. The second he termed an antipolitical abstention, namely one arising from individual judgments about the nature of the political system and self-efficacy. The third category of abstentions was that of conjuncture: the nature of the election, the political context, and the mobilizing capacity of the political party system.

As discussed, the decision to abstain from the electoral process because of an insufficient insertion into society (i.e., a low individual SES) has been shown to be influential in shaping patterns of abstention in the United States. What about France? Pierce (1995) claimed that SES was not linked to abstention in presidential elections; indeed, he argued for a slight but detectable *negative* relationship between SES and electoral participation. In other words, those of lower SES may be more mobilized, at least in presidential elections, than those of higher SES. This he attributed to (a) the mobilizing capacity of parties of the left (particularly the Communist Party) among the working classes, and (b) the higher rate of registration in France than in the United States. Other evidence would not lead us to endorse this negative relationship notion, but there are signs that SES is less determinant in France than in the United States.

TABLE 10.2. REGISTERED VOTERS ABSTAINING IN LEGISLATIVE ELECTIONS, BY AGE (IN PERCENTAGES)

Age category	*1993*	*1997*
18–24	32	40
25–34	30	43
35–49	19	34
50–64	19	30
65 and older	23	33

SOURCE: SOFRES.

Age is one factor that all agree has an impact upon electoral participation. Héran and Roualt (1995) showed that abstention is highest among the young and that it decreases with age. Table 10.2 displays figures from the last two legislative elections, which show abstention (in the first round of voting) by age category.

The data indicate that nonvoting was higher among the twenty-five to thirty-four age group than among the eighteen to twenty-four age group. This disparity can be explained, however, by the much higher rate of registration among the former group; more in the eighteen to twenty-four category did not participate, but the figures for abstention do not take into account the patterns of nonregistration discussed previously. It must also be noted that participation dropped off in the oldest age bracket, largely because physical limitations prevented the elderly from casting their votes.

The urban/rural cleavage also seems to have an important effect on patterns of participation. In an ecological analysis of abstention, Dupoirier found that abstention in the 1997 legislative elections (first round) was 6 percent higher in urban constituencies than in predominantly rural ones, and 5 percent higher in the first round of the 1993 legislative elections (*Le Monde*, 29 May 1997, 8). The study by Morin (1989) cited earlier indicated that the portion of the abstentionist electorate he described as persistent (8 percent) did not vary by age or socioprofessional category but by urbanization, with higher rates of persistent abstention in more urban areas. Bréchon (1993) argued that abstention is lower in both more rural communes and smaller communes (with, of course, a high degree of correlation between these two).

The data on the relationship between socioprofessional category and abstention are much more nuanced. Morin (1989) found that assiduous voters (those who vote all the time) were more likely to have a higher socioprofessional status; however, persistent nonparticipation was not linked to socioprofessional status. The ecological data supplied by Dupoirier did not suggest a relationship between socioprofessional status and abstention (*Le Monde*, 29 May 1997, 8). Looking at the same elections, however, Muxel detected a higher rate of nonparticipation among workers than among salaried employees (*Le Monde*, 5 June 1997, 7). Héran and Roualt (1995) suggested that abstention may be higher among manual workers, particularly those who are unemployed; in contrast, they also found that so-called "mobile" socioprofessional groups tended to abstain in local elections at a rate three times or more higher than farmers. Bréchon (1993) argued that abstention is linked to lower SES; he suggested elsewhere, however, that abstention may also be higher among those with "excess" social insertion (*Le Monde*, 21 May 1997), that is, the same highly mobile categories identified by Héran and Roualt (1995).

There also is a limited amount of evidence to show that educational level is correlated with electoral participation. Héran and Roualt (1995) emphasized the importance of education in distinguishing between those who vote and those who do not; within the 20 percent of their sample of 38,500 registered voters and 225,000 citizens (identified from the census) who were either nonregistered or who abstained in both rounds of the presidential and municipal elections of 1995, the rate of nonparticipation among those with a high school diploma or higher degree was 12 percent, while it was 29 percent among those without a diploma. Without providing any hard data, Bréchon (1993, 30) stated that "the more education one has, the less one abstains."

It thus can be concluded that SES has an impact upon abstention, albeit in a more restricted fashion in France than in the United States. The antipolitical abstention, the second of the categories noted by Bréchon (1993), has been vigorously debated among observers of French electoral politics. At the outset, it must be noted that there is potentially a great overlap between this group and the first; political apathy is, a priori, likely to be higher among those with lower SES, which makes it difficult to discern the direction of causality. If by an antipolitical abstention we mean one motivated by a lack of interest in politics generally, then the data do not supply much evidence that such a relationship exists. The number of French who declare themselves to be very or somewhat interested in politics has been relatively stable throughout the Fifth Republic (about one-third of survey respondents). Ranger (1993) concluded that interest in politics did not wane between 1978 and 1988; furthermore, Platone (1993) noted that confidence in political institutions rose over that same period.

Ultimately the relationship between antipolitical sentiment and abstention rests more than anything else on voters' perception that political parties are failing to perform a mediating role between civil society and the political institutions of the republic. Thus one account attributed a significant proportion of abstention in 1997 to the lack of clear ideological choices offered and the weakening of ideological ties between parties and voters (*Le Monde*, 22 May 1997, 6). Platone (1993) demonstrated that while confidence in political institutions may have risen slightly during the 1980s, those with the lowest degree of public support are political parties. The number of "*affaires*" (cases of political corruption or influence trading) that wracked the political system in the late 1980s and early 1990s may have reinforced the feeling among some segments of the electorate that (1) parties do not matter very much in terms of differences in policy outputs, and (2) the French political system remains dominated by a self-interested elite. Abstention may be the logical recourse for some who share such sentiments; however, the explosion of small parties and political groups outside of the traditional parties also has provided a channel of mobilization for those who reject the politics of the status quo.

A note might be added to this last point. As the number of candidates has multiplied in recent years, so too has abstention risen in legislative constituencies with large numbers of candidates. This has remained so for some time, even during the 1986 elections held under proportional rules. *Le Figaro* attributed abstention levels in that year to "dissonance" produced by large numbers of electoral lists outside the main parties (11 August 1987, 3). In 1997 the number of candidates during the legislative elections set a record under the Fifth Republic (6,243 candidates in 577 constituencies), which coincided with the comparatively high level of abstention already discussed (*Le Marianne*, 26 May–1 June 1997, 13). Grunberg also attributed high levels of abstention in 1997 to the record number of candidacies (*Libération*, 24 May 1997, 3). We must caution, however, that the number of candidacies tends to vary proportionally with the degree of constituencies' urbanization, which in turn is strongly related to the socioeconomic profile of the electorate within constituencies. Therefore, the relationship between abstention and the number of candidacies may be more an artifact of socioeconomic status than the direct one implied by the data.

The last form of abstention identified by Bréchon (1993) is that of conjunctural forces. Of course we may object that this is a reductionist argument that explains away all abstention that cannot be accounted for by the longer-term underlying forces analyzed earlier. It does seem probable, however, that certain institutional and political factors in France make conjunctural abstention more prevalent than it might be elsewhere. There are several aspects of any election that are often cited as influencing the uniqueness of the conjunctural forces at work on the electorate: the number of elections taking place in any given period, the timing of legislative elections, the issues at play in referenda, the platforms of the political parties, the partisan sympathies of the voters in relation to the balance of political forces at the aggregate level, and the possibility that a party or movement has issued a call for tactical abstention.

Much of the work cited here has demonstrated that the number of persistent abstainers is rather low; therefore, the motives of those who abstain intermittently are likely to be specific to given elections. Where many elections have succeeded one another within a short period (such as in the late 1980s), abstention has tended to be relatively high. Some evidence exists that voters are prone to voter fatigue; that is, they are less likely to mobilize when more demands are forced on them. The Ministry of the Interior has recognized this fact, and from time to time has changed the election calendar by postponing certain types of elections for a short period of time. On the other hand, the ministry has also seen fit to experiment with holding simultaneous elections (for example, the regional and cantonal elections in 1992) in order to stimulate turnout. Election timing also is important in explaining abstention in legislative elections; where those elections have resulted from a dissolution of the National Assembly by the president, abstention has tended to be higher (e.g., in 1981, 1988, and 1997).

Finally, conjunctions of circumstances affect individual mobilization depending on prior partisan sympathies. In general, turnout tends to increase for the second ballot of French elections, that is, during the decisive round. But in constituencies where there is either (a) only one candidate remaining at the second round, or (b) two candidates from one side of the ideological spectrum (left or right), abstention is likely to be higher in that round. The corollary, of course, is that mobilization tends to be highest where competition is strongest and the possibility of a narrow outcome exists (Héran and Rouault 1995). However, competition does not mobilize voters equally across the socioeconomic spectrum; it has been shown, for example, that when there was a possibility in the municipal elections of 1995 that a commune would fall to the left, the upper socioprofessional groups were mobilized to turn out in the second round at a higher rate than their lower socioprofessional counterparts would in situations where the right was likely to gain control of the municipal council (Héran and Rouault 1995).

Ultimately, then, most observers agree about the differential nature of nonparticipation in French elections. It is relatively safe to conclude that (1) persistent nonparticipation is much lower than suggested by aggregate figures and the popular press, (2) much of the apparent rise in abstention in recent years is a consequence of the growth in conjunctural abstention, and (3) while weak social insertion may account for some abstention in all of the three categories described above, the increasing mobility of French society may also have an impact upon higher levels of abstention because of excess social insertion. Thus it can be suggested that while the traditional models of voter participation that have been found to be determinant in patterns of mobilization in the United States have some correlation with the French case, they explain only one part of a complicated dynamic.

Conclusion

As we suggested at the outset, the popular press in France in recent years (continuing a long republican tradition emphasizing the act of voting as a civic duty) has bemoaned the apparent rise in nonparticipation among French voters. Since its foundation in 1967, the CIC has attempted to highlight the problem of nonparticipation and has even awarded the Civic Trophy to the commune with the highest rate of electoral participation in any election. In recent years, the CIC has joined the chorus of those who believe that nonparticipation is on the rise and that a high level of electoral nonparticipation threatens the stability of French democracy. With its involvement in registration campaigns and in voter mobilization efforts, the CIC has been a siren voice of those who fear electoral nonparticipation.

Yet, as we have shown, not all the data bear out these dire warnings. It is true that nonregistration probably is a larger problem in France than has sometimes been assumed, and that it is highest among the young and those with weak social insertion. Yet the evidence also suggests that the restrictive registration laws disbar many who have high levels of mobility and social insertion. These laws, enacted in a different era, when geographical mobility was less prevalent and society more static, could quite easily be changed to ease the problem of nonregistration. Furthermore, although registration is lowest among the young, evidence shows that the majority of those who do not register on their eighteenth birthday do so not many years thereafter. Nonregistration apparently is not increasing in France (indeed, the data presented here indicate it may have declined marginally). Where campaigns have been undertaken to increase voter registration, they appear to have been quite successful, lending credence to the notion that nonregistration, while a tangible problem, also may have a policy solution.

As we have also shown, the phenomenon of nonparticipation through electoral abstention is more complex than the aggregate figures generally used in the popular press would allow. This is not to deny that some abstention in any given election is a product of political marginality, disinterest, or lack of incentives to participate. Yet the proportion of the overall electorate that persistently refuses to participate in elections is relatively low and does not appear to be getting much larger. More common is conditional abstention, that is, the increasing propensity of some French voters to sit out one round of an election, or one election in a series, because of conjunctural factors. Some of the institutional reasons people fail to vote also have relatively simple policy solutions; for example, the timing of elections and the rhythm of the electoral cycle can be manipulated.

The lack of incentive to participate has no simple policy solution at the political party level, however. Where parties fail to provide clear-cut ideological differences or distinctive policy programs, or otherwise to link civil society to the process of government, the individual voter may be tempted to resort to electoral nonparticipation. French parties historically have been weak (with the exception of the PCF), and their capacity to mobilize given electorates has been poor. Yet, even here, there is no overwhelming evidence that such weakness will lead to a rise in irredeemable abstention. For example, in the right-wing landslide of 1993, 19 percent of those who had voted Socialist in the previous legislative elections in 1988 did not vote (*L'Express*, 22–28 April 1993, 15). Yet the PS was returned to power in 1997 largely on the basis of its capacity to mobilize support on the center-left. Thus the dropoff in party mobilization in any particular election appears to be much more conjunctural than long-term.

Overall, electoral nonparticipation remains an issue that raises normative concerns within the republican tradition, although it is inevitable. While much of the nonparticipation in French elections in recent years can be explained by factors other than the French voter's complete rejection of the system and of the desire to participate within that system, it is also inevitable that it will continue to be seen in that light by many commentators in the French media.

Chapter 11

Do the Parties Matter?

Kay Lawson and Colette Ysmal

There is, of course, a sense in which parties obviously still matter in every democratic nation, including France. Even though interest groups, political consultants, the media, the candidate, and the candidate's entourage now also engage in many of the activities formerly more clearly the domain of parties, parties continue to provide essential organization, expertise, financial resources, and signifying labels. They still "structure the vote," and we are not yet ready to abandon them.

In another sense, however, it is less clear that parties still matter in western democracies, including France. When we take the position that parties matter to the extent that they are still serving, as they always claim to do, as agencies of linkage between citizens and the state, then we have reason to be less certain. There are various ways in which parties have established that linkage in the past—by permitting members a large say over internal affairs as well as over candidate selection and the formulation of issues (*participatory linkage*); by paying close attention to voter interests, formulating their programs accordingly, and making a serious attempt to carry out those programs when gaining office (*responsive linkage*); by making their own decisions independently but seeking nonetheless to educate as well as to persuade the electorate (*educative linkage*); and so forth (see Lawson 1980). The factors enfeebling parties as agencies of linkage are also well known and widespread in modern democracies (see Katz and Mair 1995).

Separating the Variables

The French political system has long been seen as exceptional, however, and France has been identified as a nation in which parties have remained stronger than elsewhere as agencies with power of their own, still capable of providing significant linkage to the state (Wilson 1988). But is this still true? In order to answer this question, we treat five important factors that are more and more often confounded: (1) popular opinion regarding the issues of the day, (2) the campaign offer of the parties, (3) the vote, (4) the capacity of winning parties to carry out their programs and achieve desired ends once in office, and (5) popular opinion regarding the parties.

Of these five distinct factors, the third, the vote, has not only received by far the greatest scholarly attention; it has often been taken to represent the first, the second and/or the fifth, and sometimes the fourth as well. Nevertheless, we cannot really tell by how they vote what voters' opinions on the issues are, nor what the parties offered in the campaign, nor even what the voters think of the parties. None of these factors is synonymous with any of the others. We cannot assume that when a party wins it is because the voters' stands on the issues—including their opinions regarding what issues matter most—have been reflected in the campaign offers of the parties they chose, that voting for the candidates of a particular party means approving of that party, and that therefore all we need to know are voters' opinions and the voting results. If these assumptions were well-founded, they would be confirmed when we actually looked at the parties' issue positions or at the voters' opinions of the parties, including the ones they have voted for themselves. Unfortunately, however, we seldom if ever find such tidy matching up. We also cannot safely extrapolate either the party offer or the level of voter satisfaction with parties from voter's issue stances and the voting results. Nor is it correct to assume that voters' evaluation of particular elected officials' performance in office can be equated with voter evaluation of the parties to which those officials belong (but to which they in fact may have little or no sense of loyalty, particularly after achieving victory).

The tendency we sometimes have to conflate the nonconflatable may be owing in part to the fact that in every partisan election there is, inevitably, a winning party, a party that does better than the others.[1] Victory is a positive phenomenon and seems to carry with it other positive phenomena. We tend to forget that although democratic politics produces winners, it does not ensure that voters will not all be losers. Even voters who find they have supported winning candidates may, and often do, remain disappointed with the choices that had been offered to them.

Another reason for our occasional confusion may be the heightened interest of voters in issues in recent years, a phenomenon particularly noteworthy in the United States, but also remarked in France (Cayrol 1998, 97). Caring about issues is not the same as knowing how the parties stand on the issues, however, nor is it even the same as voting on the issues. Voters may be completely wrong in the certainty that particular candidates or parties agree with them on the issues; they may also base their votes on candidates' personalities or other factors that have nothing to do with the issues that matter to them. And candidates may distance themselves early in the campaign from their parties' published programs.

Thus it is our intent to examine these key factors individually and to confront as objectively as possible the question of the relationships among them, in the case of France. We consider first what the most important issues in France are today, according to the voters. Then we examine what issues the major parties present in their campaigns, concentrating on the two most powerful parties, the Rally for the Republic (in alliance with the Union for French Democracy) and the Socialist Party. We offer a brief review of voting results (treated in far greater detail in other chapters in this book), then examine to what extent the party programs of the winning parties have been implemented and to what extent victorious candidates have pursued very different policies from those promised by their parties. Finally, we consider how French voters evaluate the parties.

If we find that the parties' campaigns respond to the voters' interests, that the winners carry out party promises, and, finally, that the voters express approval of the parties they have supported, we must conclude that linkage by party—at least linkage of the responsive type—is still strong in France, and that French parties do matter. If the answers go in the opposite direction, or are mixed, the final evaluation must vary accordingly. First, however, we offer a brief review of recent French party history.

Parties in the Fifth Republic: A Strong Response to a Strong Attack

When Charles de Gaulle returned to power in 1958, one of the conditions he posed was that he should not be required to negotiate the details of that return with any of the leaders of existent political parties. Thus it is not surprising that when a new constitution was written to the general's specifications, it offered France a quasi-presidential system, one giving the president far greater power and Parliament—the natural home and preferred arena of parties—considerably less.

The parties were definitely weakened by the new terms of the Fifth Republic, just as de Gaulle had intended. Whatever functions the public may assign parties, however, their purpose is the pursuit of power. If the locus of power shifts, so will parties, and certainly French parties have been no exception. The new constitution presented them with a difficult challenge. It left open the possibility of *cohabitation*, that is, of a presidency controlled by one party and a Parliament controlled by another (or by an alliance of parties on the opposite side of the political spectrum from the president). At the same time, it left considerable power over domestic affairs in the hands of the prime minister, meaning that when that official and the president were in disagreement, the prime minister and Parliament would assume greater importance in the balance of power. The parties could not, therefore, simply turn their attention entirely away from Parliament—it still mattered, very much, which party or parties held legislative power. Yet at the same time, there was no question but that the presidency had become the most important office. Under the constitution (which, after a 1962 amendment, called for the direct election of the president) and the majoritarian electoral system (two ballots, the second between the two leaders on the first) any party seriously interested in power now had to have at least one credible candidate for the presidency, a program with broad appeal, a well-developed and well-financed national organization, and the ability to form strong second-ballot alliances with other parties and candidates.

These requirements forced the parties to move toward coalition politics and at the same time preserve individual competitive capacities (for the legislative contests and for the first ballot in the presidential election). The Gaullists (successively labeling themselves the Union for the New Republic, the Union for the Defense of the Republic, the Union for the Defense of the Fifth Republic, and the Rally for the Republic) and the Union for French Democracy (the UDF, itself an alliance of component parties) were the first to master the new arts of quasi alliance, and between them they controlled the new system for its first twenty-three years. Under the leadership of François Mitterrand, however, the Socialists slowly but surely caught up, taking power in 1981 by forming a weak but sufficient alliance with the Communists. By the 1986 legislative elections the pendulum was ready to swing (part-way) back, and Gaullist-UDF victory in Parliament initiated the first period of cohabitation, 1986 to 1988. Mitterrand's reelection to another seven-year term in 1988 gave him the right to call for new legislative elections and the power to win a new leftist majority, but the latter evanesced in 1993, when the next legislative elections again produced a right-wing Parliament. Cohabitation number two lasted until the 1995 presidential elections, when RPR candidate Jacques Chirac won the presidency. Right-wing dominance of both bodies lasted only until 1997, however, when the new president, aware that his side's popularity was in precipitous decline, took the risk of dissolving the legislature a year ahead of time—and lost the bet that it might thereby still be possible to renew the majority of the right-wing alliance. Cohabitation number three began, therefore, in 1997, with Chirac still in the presidency and Socialist leader Lionel Jospin as the new and remarkably popular prime minister.

The ability of the RPR-UDF alliance, and then of the Socialist-Communist alliance, to adapt to the new constitution has been impressive. Within these alliances, the RPR and the Socialists have been the most adept, the UDF always hampered by its lack of internal unity and the Communists by all the woes that particular partisan identity is heir to, especially since 1989. Both the Gaullists and the Socialists took new names and gave themselves new leaders, new organizations, and new tactics during the 1970s. Although both still require electoral aid from alliance partners, they are clearly the two major parties of France.

Both parties have, however, encountered serious problems as a result of maintaining the centrist politics that the strongly majoritarian system now requires. The Communists and Ecologists, key members of the leftist coalition, make divisive demands from within; the far-right National Front attracts an ever-greater percentage of French voters away from the center right, and disagreement regarding how to respond to this challenge has produced serious conflict within both the RPR and the UDF. Nor is the problem simply a matter of internal divisiveness; abstention is on the rise, and among those who do vote, the major parties have been steadily losing support (Gaxie 1997). Among them, the PS, the RPR, and the UDF took 78 percent of the vote in 1981, 75 percent in 1988, but only 60 percent in 1993, and 58 percent in 1997 (Ysmal 1999).

Nevertheless, centrism remains the order of the day. Although it carries with it the risk of alienating not only more of the active members of each coalition but also more of the general public, veering to either side would be likely to produce even greater loss.

Do these conditions suggest that the leading French parties now matter less and less as agencies of linkage? Certainly they are not and never have been strong agents of *participatory* linkage: the French have never been strong partisans and the parties have never offered the rank-and-file membership strong opportunities to help shape programs, choose candidates, or otherwise take a decision-making part in party affairs. But they have been important in the past as agencies of *responsive* linkage. Are they still? To answer this question, we must begin by considering what the interests of the voters are.

Interests of the Voters

The most important issue in France is, and has been for many years, that of unemployment. Eighty-four percent of the French polled at the beginning of the 1997 electoral season listed it as one of the nation's most important problems. The five next most important issues to the voters were social protection (52 percent), the struggle against social inequalities (52 percent), education (45 percent), security (44 percent), and the fight against corruption (40 percent). Issues with lower but still significant scores were: fighting clandestine immigration (37 percent), improving salaries (37 percent), the environment (35 percent), fighting racism (34 percent), the deficit (32 percent), the good functioning of institutions (32 percent), and integrating immigrants who are in irregular situations (30 percent). Building Europe was a prime concern for 29 percent, the fight against inflation mattered to 27 percent, and the influence of France in the world was named by 25 percent (Cayrol 1998, 100).

The same poll also discovered a strong readiness on the part of the voters to "modernize France and make her always more competitive," and a modest majority (50 percent versus 37 percent) favoring the development of Europe, but it uncovered as well a marked reluctance to pursue either of these goals at the cost of continued austerity. Change was acceptable, but only on condition that the French "social model" be preserved (Cayrol 1998, 102-7). According to Roland Cayrol, the voters were not interested in choosing between "free enterprise or the state, socialism or liberalism, individual initiative or collective responsibility, Europe or the nation, archaism or modernity"—on the contrary, they wanted the opposites to be reconciled, they wanted to move toward the inevitable modernity but still improve employment, keep education free and obligatory, and guarantee a fair minimum wage, social security, and a decent retirement (pp. 105-6).

Programs of the Parties

French political scientists often complain today that the parties do not really formulate serious programs any more and that the programs they do offer are too similar to one another. The general public, as we note later, tends to agree. In the legislative elections of 1993, key themes did stand out, however, and the positions of the parties—or at least of their candidates—on each were known. These issues included protecting the French social security program, solving the housing crisis, providing employment, strengthening the franc, reversing the decline of French agriculture, and reforming the tax system. The parties' positions were not distant from one another on these matters, but positions were taken nonetheless. One noteworthy exception to this readiness to engage the issue was the silence maintained by the Socialists on the question of privatizing industry, while the RPR, in its common platform with the UDF, stressed the need to continue vigorous privatization (Chaussebourg and Ferenczi 1993, 32-45).

In presidential elections it is more difficult to speak of *party* programs, since although such documents make their appearance, they are always more clearly the manifesto of the leader/candidate than of a collective organizational effort. This rule was slightly bent in 1988 when the Socialist Party made an effort to distinguish itself as a separate entity from its candidate, François Mitterrand, by stressing specific accomplishments of Socialists—all Socialists, not just the man seeking reelection as president (Lawson and Ysmal 1992, 113).[2] Nevertheless, by 1995 the Socialists were less concerned to distinguish themselves in any way from candidate Lionel Jospin, and the RPR showed itself more tightly linked than ever to Jacques Chirac, giving him its almost unanimous support in the bitter contest he waged with Edouard Balladur for the support of the "classic right." The issues most stressed by the candidates were fighting unemployment and maintaining social services, and the differences among them had more to do with the specificity than the substance of their promises. Although Chirac set up thirty-three study groups on various issues, the key theme of his campaign was simply that profound change was essential and that he was the man to bring it about; the key quality was its strongly populist tone and style. Former economics professor Jospin, on the other hand, offered extremely specific proposals for turning the economy around (Mauduit 1995, 18).

The circumstances surrounding the 1997 legislative campaign—and the programs presented by the parties—were unusual. To begin with, although legislative elections were not expected until the spring of 1998, the Socialists took the trouble in late 1996 to formulate a new economic program and to present a number of very specific proposals to the French people. This program was not, according to opinion polls, particularly well received. At the same time, polls were showing signs of serious disappointment with the Chirac presidency and the performance of Alain Juppé as his prime minister. Taxes and the rate of unemployment were both going up, not down, and the wonderful promises that had been made during the 1995 presidential campaign (albeit always sloganistically, with few if any details about how such marvels were actually to be achieved) were not being kept. The RPR-UDF coalition began to believe it would not be possible to retain control of the legislature if they waited until 1998. The constitution gave the president the power to dissolve Parliament, and although this power had never before been overtly used for purely political reasons other than immediately after the election of the president, there was nothing to prevent Chirac's calling for new elections a year ahead of time simply because they might be easier to win now than later. The Socialists had saddled themselves with a new set of propositions that had limited appeal and no doubt would find it difficult to change them overnight. The moment, it seemed, was ripe.

A program that seems unimpressive when presented in the cold light of daily political routine, however, may shine much more brightly in the reflected light of electoral struggle. Once the dissolution was declared, the situation changed rapidly. The RPR and UDF stressed the need to "continue." They assured the electorate that a program of continuing economic liberalization would in fact bring about the desired ends (protecting social security, reducing unemployment, and so on). They offered nothing new, and no conclusive evidence that movement in the hoped-for direction was in fact taking place. The Socialists, on the other hand, had their new economic program ready. In addition to promising to put an end to excessive privatizations and to keep threatened social services in place, they offered a very specific set of proposals regarding unemployment: they would, they said, create 750,000 jobs for young people over the next five years (the normal legislative term of office). Half of these jobs would be in the public sector, with an emphasis on *emplois de proximité*, that is, jobs giving serious help to the old, the young, the handicapped, the homeless, and similarly disadvantaged groups. Furthermore, they promised to reduce the work week to thirty-five hours.

Although the Socialist program was more precise (and, as events were to prove, more appealing) than that of the RPR-UDF, it should nonetheless be pointed out that there were contradictions and elements of vagueness on the left as well as on the right. The 1997 campaign was marked by a singular lack of reflection on the problems implicit in any attempt to strike the right balance between accepting the dictates of economic globalization and protecting cherished social benefits. Neither side risked facing up to the possibility that there were no easy answers, that perhaps difficult and politically unacceptable choices would have to be made. Other issues were discussed—corruption, immigration, the deficit—in which voter interest was relatively weak (Cayrol 1998, 99-100). Otherwise, both sides tended to promise, with greater or lesser specificity, that a balance between meeting immediate social needs and long-term modernization needs was in fact possible. The greater emphasis of the Socialists on the former clearly provided a closer fit to the bargain the French hoped to be able to strike (pp. 107-10).[3]

The Vote

Although electoral results cannot tell us all we need to know about the connections parties establish between citizens and the state, they certainly represent a crucial link in the process. The exact results of the 1995 presidential elections and the 1997 legislative elections are analyzed at length in other chapters; here (see tables 11.1 and 11.2) we simply remind readers of the most important figures (brief mention of the 1998 regional elections are made in the conclusion).

TABLE 11.1. 1995 PRESIDENTIAL ELECTION: VOTE SHARE, BY CANDIDATE

	First ballot, 23 April 1995		*Second ballot, 7 May 1995*	
Candidate	*Number*	*%*	*Number*	*%*
Laguiller	1,615,653	5.3		
Hue	2,632,936	8.6		
Jospin	7,098,191	23.3	14,180,644	47.4
Voynet	1,010,738	3.3		
Balladur	5,658,996	18.6		
Chirac	6,348,696	20.9	15,763,027	52.6
Villiers	1,443,235	4.7		
Le Pen	4,571,138	15.0		

SOURCE: Ysmal 1996, 331-45.

TABLE 11.2. 1997 LEGISLATIVE ELECTIONS: VOTE SHARE, BY PARTY

Party	*First ballot results*	*Seats (per parliamentary party)*
Extreme left	644,051	
Communists	2,523,405	36[a]
Socialists	5,977,045	250[b]
Ecologists	1,738,287	33[c]
Other left	713,082	
RPR	3,983,257	140[d]
UDF	3,617,440	113[d]
Other right	1,679,369	
National Front	3,800,785	
Extreme right	26,759	
No party affiliation	5	

SOURCE: Perrineau and Ysmal 1998, 307, 330.

a. Includes two affiliated members.

b. Includes eight affiliated members.

c. Includes other leftist members in a group known as the Radical, Citizen, and Green Group (RCV).

d. Includes six affiliated members.

For reasons already discussed, legislative elections are normally stronger indicators of party strength than are presidential elections, but in 1995 the two candidates who made it to the runoff, Jospin and Chirac, both owed their strong showing in larger part to the unflagging support of their respective parties. Legislative election results tell us about party strength in two ways: votes and seats. The number of votes each party receives indicates its support among the electorate, but the number of seats it has will determine its ability to influence the course of government. Where there are two ballots, the first ballot gives the clearer view of voter support for each party. (The capacity of the electoral system to translate the former fairly into the latter is, of course, a key factor in establishing effective linkage between the citizen and the state, but as that system is not something a party normally has within its control, we leave that aspect out of our discussion here.)

As the legislative vote goes, so goes the possibility of forming a government. The RPR did not win sufficient seats to be able to form a governing coalition with the allies it was willing to accept; the Socialists did not win an adequate number to be able to rule alone, but they were able to form a governing coalition with the Communists and the Ecologists.

Policies Followed

Electoral results are, at least for the victors, like the end of a fairy tale: the hero party wins the blushing voter bride and the delighted couple confidently plans to live happily ever after. But postelection results tend to be more like real life: problems may develop.

The victory of the RPR and the UDF in March 1993 meant a second period of cohabitation and, furthermore, one that would take place, as had the first (1986-88), in the last two years of a presidential term. Chirac's losing candidacy for the presidency in 1988 had convinced the parties of the right and their leaders that during this period it would be better to be as cooperative as possible and demonstrate their ability to manage the business of government rather than to attempt to introduce serious reforms in the directions they might desire. The French do not accept reforms lightly, and those that are unpopular may well be greeted with strikes and demonstrations by the various affected groups. In the mid-1990s such a response could in turn lead to the remobilization of the parties of the left and their supporters.

This reasoning—combined with Chirac's decision to reserve his own energies for preparing for a third presidential campaign—caused the right-wing alliance to turn to Edouard Balladur, a man whose personal style was marked by the spirit of conciliation and compromise. As prime minister, Balladur made little attempt to put into effect the program that had been presented to the voters in the 1993 campaign. He did, however, relaunch the program of privatization that had been "frozen" by Mitterrand in the period of Socialist hegemony, 1988-93. In an attempt to reduce the influence of the National Front, several laws were passed regarding clandestine or "excessive" immigration: the code governing citizenship was modified, identity checks were increased, those found to be in France illegally were sent back to a frontier or even to their countries of origin in chartered planes, and such measures were carried out by the administration with no possibility of appeal through the judicial process. The anti-immigration policies actually adopted were, however, much more moderate than those promised in 1993 when Charles Pasqua, as the new minister of the interior, spoke of "zero immigration" and the immediate expulsion of any illegal immigrant.

The government made no effort to carry out proposed projects of governmental reform or to limit the number of civil servants; it attempted no fiscal reform. In the struggle against unemployment, it simply continued the policies of the Socialists, giving aid to enterprises that created jobs, offering training programs to the unemployed, and allocating additional unemployment benefits to those in the greatest need. All reference to reforming the system of social protection was banished, including any mention of shifting to private insurance companies for health or pension purposes.

After victory in 1995, Chirac and his new prime minister, Alain Juppé, also were hesitant to put campaign promises into effect. This time, as we have seen, the task was eased by the vagueness of the campaign offer. Nonetheless, throughout his 1995 campaign, Chirac had denounced the "social fracture" of France and insisted on the need for reintegrating the neediest and most disadvantaged into the national community. Little had been said about what this meant in practice, but there was at least a hint, if only in the discreet silence maintained throughout the campaign on the subject, that the right was ready to back away somewhat from its policies of maintaining a strong franc, of aligning French currency with the German mark, and of reducing the public deficit to the extent required by the Treaty of Maastricht. Indeed, in his first address as prime minister, Juppé declared that the priority would be on employment rather than on reducing the deficit, and the structure and composition of the first cabinet did, in fact, indicate an interest in addressing social questions, naming, for example, a minister in charge of social interaction and a minister for solidarity between the generations.

The turnabout of the government was, however, swift and complete. Before the year was out, the new slogan had become "reduce the public deficit to reduce unemployment." Heavy budget cuts were made in the areas of education, justice, culture, and social affairs—in fact, in the very areas of greatest importance to the poor and disadvantaged. A new tax to cover the deficit in the social security system was introduced. Although the campaign rhetoric had included the idea that "maintaining a French style of public service" should be inscribed in the constitution, by November the government was openly considering privatization of the telephone, postal, and transportation systems. A new system of private pension funds was established to take the place of financing retirements (in the private sector) by employee and employer contributions, which had always been set by the state. Income taxes were reduced, especially for higher-paying categories (the highest possible tax was to be reduced from 56.8 percent of income in 1996 to 47 percent in 2001). In April of 1997 Juppé called for further tax cuts to "favor the creation, development and transmission of business" (Gaxie 1997).

The ability of the new Jospin government to carry out the Socialist program is more difficult to evaluate, since it has, at this writing, been in power for less than a year. Certainly the program itself was less demanding than that which burdened the Socialists who came to power in 1981 (their programmatic mission being nothing less than to "break with capitalism"). It was less ambitious, less utopian, and the chances that it could and would be put into effect were therefore better. In fact, several laws have been voted or at least introduced in its first ten months that clearly are related to the program: the reduction of the workweek to thirty-five hours as a means of reducing unemployment, the law to reduce homelessness and other forms of what the French term "exclusion," the reform of the judicial system (making it more independent of the other branches of government and more egalitarian in its operation), and specific measures necessary to keep the promise of more employment for the young. It is true, however, that already one can note some tendency on the part of the PS and the government to twist the meaning of words slightly in order to appear faithful to its promises. Having announced, for example, that there would be no more privatizations, but then deciding that in fact some degree of privatization would be necessary to respond to the exigences of the new Europe-wide conditions of competition within certain public services, they have created the term "*prise de participation*" ("touch of participation") to describe what is in fact the partial privatization of the airline Air France and of the French telephone system France Télécom.

The new government has also found it difficult to keep its campaign promise to dismantle the anti-immigration laws passed by the previous government. The Socialist Party has given up the idea of completing rewriting all immigration law (some of which dates back to 1945, much of which has been so consistently modified as to be now incoherent and incomprehensible). It has not been able to reestablish *jus soli* (right of citizenship by fact of birth on French soil) but has lowered the age at which a person born of foreign parents in France may claim French citizenship, and it has eliminated the need for parental approval as well as the requirement that the applicant make a "solemn declaration" of his or her desire to assume the responsibilities of citizenship. It has moved also very slowly indeed toward the promised "regularization" of the status of clandestine immigrants who lack official papers.

The PS and the government in power are also faced with delicate choices regarding the distribution of wealth, especially as the French economy is once again in a period of growth. Should the fruits of such growth be directed toward reducing budget deficits and the national debt, per the demands of Maastricht? Or would it be better to raise salaries and social benefits for the neediest, thus improving the conditions of life, in particular in the French suburbs, and, perhaps, lowering thereby the overheated political temperature in these arenas of discontent?

In sum, one can say that the PS—and its Communist and Ecologist allies in the new coalition government—have paid attention to the interests of their voters and are trying to respond to their expectations. How well they will succeed remains to be seen.

Voters' Assessment of Parties in Government

French voters have watched all these developments with interest and often with deep concern. The contradiction between the presidential program offered by the RPR (and by the UDF after the first-ballot loss of Balladur, the candidate to whom that party had earlier given its rather hesitant and clearly ineffectual support) in 1995 and governmental practice afterwards, combined with the fact that both parties moved with no apparent hesitation from supporting Chirac I (1995 to September 1996) to supporting Chirac II (September 1996 to May 1997), led to a serious drop in the credibility of the parties and the leaders of the right. There has in fact never been so rapid a drop in the popularity of a newly elected president and his prime minister: in June 1995, 55 percent of the French had a "good opinion" of Chirac and the approval rating for Juppé was 52 percent; six months later the figures had fallen to 37 and 31 percent, respectively (Ysmal 1996, 342, 345).

At the same time that right-wing credibility was dropping, that of the left was on the rise. During the electoral campaign of 1997, opinion polls indicated that the left in general and the PS in particular was seen as more efficacious than parties on the right regarding almost all the important social issues: the struggle against inequality, the ability to guarantee social protection, and the defense of the interests of one's own social category (Cayrol 1998, 108-10, 115-16). The single exception at this time was in the fight against unemployment: 28 percent of the respondents saw the left as stronger here, while 33 percent favored the RPR/UDF coalition; however, the very low scores of both sides suggest that, in fact, in this most important domain the French no longer believed the promises of any party.

The policies followed in the first few months of the new Socialist government, largely focused as we have seen on these same matters, produced signs of voter satisfaction, to judge by the approval ratings for the prime minister and his party. Between June 1997 and March 1998 the approval rating for the Socialist Party remained at 54 percent, while the percentage of the French who "felt confident in Lionel Jospin" varied but never fell below 54 percent (see table 11.3).

TABLE 11.3. SURVEY RESPONDENTS WHO "FELT CONFIDENT IN LIONEL JOSPIN" (IN PERCENTAGES)

Survey date	*Percent*
June 1997	63
July 1997	66
Aug 1997	62
Sept 1997	62
Oct 1997	58
Nov 1997	57
Dec 1997	59
Jan 1998	54
Feb 1998	56
Mar 1998	68

SOURCE: SOFRES polls.

Concluding Comments

Do French parties still matter? Can they still be seen as important agencies of linkage between citizen and state? How strong is the chain of connection running from voter concerns to party programs, to the actual vote, to policies followed in government, and, finally, to voters' assessment of the parties? By looking at each of these subjects separately, and avoiding the trap of taking the vote itself as a sign of the nature of all the others, we are in a better position to assess the quality of linkage provided by French parties today.

Obviously, the parties do still matter. The concerns of French voters find expression in the major parties' programs. Although in recent years these concerns have been given much more detailed and substantive expression in the programs of the parties of the left, Chirac's ability to convey the impression of strong personal commitment to resolving these problems was, at least for the duration of the campaign, a sign of partisan responsiveness. The vote was consistent with programmatic persuasiveness at the time of the elections.

Subsequent performance of the parties in power has, however, been less impressive in linkage terms: the right has abandoned its promises with startling alacrity, especially after 1995, and the left is not always able and/or willing to do exactly what it said it would. French voters are no fools: they pay attention, they assess, they change their vote. Young voters, workers, and unemployed persons who voted for Jacques Chirac in 1995 in response to his theme of "social fracture" moved to the left in 1997, according to postelection surveys by SOFRES. Satisfaction with the performance of the left is reflected in the support that side of the spectrum received from the young, higher and middle-level management, and white-collar workers in the regional elections of March 1998. On the other hand, lower-paid workers increased their vote for the extreme parties of left and right (4.4 percent for the former, its best score in legislative elections under the Fifth Republic, and 15.5 percent for the National Front). The Socialists have not kept all their promises (yet?); the very groups that should, in theory, be the core of their support show serious signs of defection. Postelection analyses will show how consistent these results are with actual voter assessment of the parties. Overall, however, the linkages running from citizen to state, via party, have not disappeared. There are weaknesses. Parties do not always do what they say they will do, or even try very hard to do so. Voters' assessments, especially during ever-more-mediatized campaigns but also after observing governments in action, may be far from infallible. Overall confidence in the parties as public institutions has certainly been in decline. The chain is not made of iron; the links must constantly be repaired. But the general assessment leans to the positive: French parties matter.

How have the French been able to maintain this level of significance for their parties? Four reasons come to mind, one constitutional, and three owing to the ways in which French law does and does not regulate French political parties.

First, despite the personalization of power that has accompanied the new importance of the presidency, and, to a lesser extent the prime ministership, the

French Parliament remains a powerful institution, and one in which parties matter. Three periods of *cohabitation* have made that clear. The parties still have an arena they can control, as parties, and from that arena they can reach out to control the exercise of power. It remains plausible for parties to formulate serious programs and choose candidates who promise to be guided by them. They may no longer be able to control the fine details of policy, but they can send those whom they choose to do the job, and they can pull them out if they do not give satisfaction.

Second, there are no nominating primary elections run by the state and open to the general population, which wrest from the party its most precious freedom and most valuable asset, the right to choose its own candidates. The proposal of Gaullist Charles Pasqua that some form of primary election be established by the state in France indicates either that he is unaware of the dangers it poses or that he sees it as a way for Gaullist candidates, who have a strong and often badly managed tradition of self-selection, to be even more free of the programmatic constraints of their party. In any case, this proposal has so far received little positive response, even within that party.

Third, the French allow considerable free media time to candidates, forbid paid advertising on television, and put limits on campaign spending. Of these interrelated conditions, the most important is clearly the prohibition of paid advertising on television. Paid ads almost inevitably become the chief content of campaigns where they are allowed and there is no reason to believe that the French—difficult, individualistic, ever-rational though they may be—could not be transformed into mere watchers and buyers.[4]

Finally, the internal affairs of parties are largely unregulated in France. Campaigns are regulated, but parties are not. No one says what form their internal organizations must take (and indeed they take many different forms), who can serve on their executive bodies, who may choose them, or what their duties shall be. The French may not have a great deal of respect for intermediary organizations, and particularly not for parties, but they do know something about the real meanings of freedom of expression. Like most Europeans, they find it all but unbelievable that Americans have outlawed parties from participation in local elections. It is easy to form a new party in France, and although new parties do not win seats easily, the runoff electoral system used in most elections and the limited use of proportional representation in others do give them a chance to make their point. In recent years, the National Front and the two Green parties have made their way into local and national seats of office.

A constitutional and legal system that ensures the freedom and significance of parties, while holding in check that of the media, is a system in which parties will inevitably be stronger than one that privileges the rights of the media over those of political organizations. When organizations can be formed to represent and present all points of view, even those most antithetical to a people's cherished traditional values, the political system demonstrates thereby its ability to bring its most serious problems and disagreements into a democratic arena and battle them out. Such a system is one in which parties still provide linkage between citizen and state. Such a system is one in which the parties matter.

Abbreviations

BVA	Brûlé Ville Associés (Brûlé Ville Associates—polling)
CAP	Common Agricultural Policies
CDS	Centre des démocrates sociaux (Center of Social Democrats)
CERES	Centre d'études, de recherches, et d'éducation socialistes (Center for Study, Research, and Socialist Education)
CEVIPOF	Centre d'étude de la vie politique française (Center for the Study of French Political Life)
CFDT	Confédération française démocratique du travail (French Democratic Confederation of Labor)
CFTC	Confédération française des travailleurs chrétiens (French Confederation of Christian Workers)
CGT	Confédération génerale du travail (General Confederation of Labor)
CIC	Centre d'information civique (Center of Civic Information)
CIDSP	Centre d'informatisation de données sociopolitiques (Information Center for Socio-Political Data)
CNI	Centre national des indépendants (National Center of Independents)
CNIP	Centre national des indépendants et paysans (National Center of Independents and Peasants)
CNPF	Conseil national du patronat français (National Council of French Business)
CRAPS	Centre de recherches administratives politiques et sociales (Center for Administrative, Political, and Social Research)
CSA	Conseils sondages analyses (Consulting, Polls, Analysis)
CSG	Contribution sociale generalisée (Generalized Social Contribution)
DM	Deutsche mark
EC	European Community
ECB	European Central Bank
EDC	European Defense Community

EEC	European Economic Community
EMI	European Monetary Institute
EMS	European Monetary System
EMU	Economic and monetary union
ENA	École nationale d'administration (National School of Administration)
ERM	Exchange Rate Mechanism
ESCB	European System of Central Banks
EU	European Union
FEN	Fédération de l'éducation nationale (Federation of National Education)
FLN	Front de libération nationale (National Liberation Front)
FN	Front national (National Front)
FNSEA	Fédération nationale des syndicats des exploitants agricoles (National Federation of Farmers' Unions)
FO	Force ouvière (Workers' Force)
Fr	Francs
GATT	General Agreement on Tariffs and Trade
GDP	Gross Domestic Product
GE	Génération ecologie (Ecology Generation)
IFOP	Institut français d'opinion publique (French Institute of Public Opinion)
IGC	Intergovernmental Conference
INSEE	Institut national de la statistique et des études économiques (National Institute of Statistics and Economic Studies)
IPSOS	IPSOS OPINION (IPSOS opinion polling)
JDD	Journal du dimanche (Sunday Journal)
LCR	Ligue communiste révolutionnaire (Revolutionary Communist League)
LDI	La Droite indépendante (The Independent Right)
LO	Lutte ouvrière (Workers' Struggle)

MDC	Mouvement des citoyens (Citizens' Movement)
MDR	Mouvement des réformateurs (Reformers' Movement)
MPF	Mouvement pour la France (Movement for France)
MRG	Mouvement des radicaux de gauche (Movement of Left Radicals)
NATO	North Atlantic Treaty Organization
PCF	Parti communiste français (French Communist Party)
PLN	Parti de la loi naturelle (Natural Law Party)
PPL	Parti pour la liberté (Party for Liberty)
PR	Parti républican (Republican Party)
PRS	Parti radical-socialiste (Radical-Socialist Party)
PS	Parti socialiste (Socialist Party)
PSU	Parti socialist unifié (Unified Socialist Party)
RMI	Revenue minimum d'insertion (minimum income)
RPF	Rassemblement du peuple français (Rally for the French People)
RPR	Rassemblement pour la république (Rally for the Republic)
SFIO	Section française de l'internationale ouvrière (French Section of the Workers' International)
SOFRES	Societé française d'enquêtes par sondage (French Society of Survey Investigations)
UDF	Union pour la démocratie française (Union for French Democracy)
UDR	Union des démocrates pour la republique (Union of Democrats for the Republic)

Notes

Chapter 1

1. In 1997 the PS claimed 111,000 registered members, and the Socialists accounted for 119 (out of 388) mayors of towns with more than 20,000 inhabitants (of which 70 had more than 100,000).

2. On the official roles of his two brothers, his two sons, his sister, and various cousins, see Cole 1994, 107-11.

3. In the European elections of 1994, Mitterrand was said to have supported Bernard Tapie, head of the Left Radical ticket, which cut deeply into the vote for the Socialist slate headed by Rocard.

4. Toward the end of his presidency, there were widely circulated revelations about his daughter, born to his mistress.

5. Poll of 24-26 January 1995 and 12-13 February 1996, in SOFRES 1996, 318-19.

6. For example, his failure to prevent the Gulf War; to insert France as a partner with Washington in Arab-Israeli negotiations; to arrest the reunification of Germany; to stop the disintegration of Yugoslavia; and to match Germany's investments in the ex-Communist countries of Eastern Europe.

7. Jospin's loyalty to his friends and associates was said to work to his detriment on occasion. He has continued to support Jean-Marc Ayrault, the chairman of the PS parliamentary group, despite Ayrault's reputed ineffectiveness.

8. On the evolution of that relationship, see Mercier and Jérôme 1997, 125-41.

9. Chevènement, a founder and leader of the Franco-Iraqi Friendship Society, had been a supporter of Saddam Hussein, whom he considered a secularist (and therefore "progressive") Arab leader.

10. That strategy was to produce certain problems; for instance, when Dominique Voynet was offered a cabinet position, she proposed other names, because the abandonment of her Assembly mandate (required under the incompatibility clause [Art. 23]), would have meant relinquishing it to her PS alternate and thus result in the loss of a crucial parliamentary seat for the Green party that she headed. Ultimately she acceded to the importunings of Jospin, who wanted a known personality as minister of the environment.

11. So named after Charles Pasqua, the Gaullist minister of the interior in 1995, and Jean-Louis Debré, who succeeded him in 1997.

12. On rational choice (issues) versus other determinants, see Lewis-Beck 1993, 1-13.

13. The CGT and FO rejected the offer, while the *Confédération française démocratique de travail* (CFDT), the largest truckers' union, accepted it as the best it could get; Gayssot, "speaking as a CGT member and a minister [*sic*]" presented the agreement in a favorable light.

14. Hue had been successful in convincing Jospin and most of the French public that the brand of communism of the PCF he led had nothing to do with the Stalinism of the former Soviet Union, whose record of mass murders had just been restated in the best-selling *Livre noir du communisme: Crimes, terreur, et répression,* ed. Stéphane Courtois (Paris: Laffont, 1997).

15. Several of the (now powerless) "old elephants," including Jack Lang, have severely criticized that policy and called for a boycott of Iran, but they are voices crying in the wilderness.

16. Guigou suggested that a "dialogue" be maintained between the justice minister and state prosecutor, in order to prevent inaction or obstruction by the latter for his own political reasons (Demonpion 1997).

17. According to a public opinion poll of political attitudes among youth in the spring of 1996, 58 percent of the respondents thought that the state did not intervene sufficiently in economic affairs, and only 20 percent felt that it intervened too much (figures for sympathizers of the left were, respectively, 57 and 22 percent, and for sympathizers of the right, 48 and 18 percent) (Witkowski 1996, 177).

Chapter 2

1. A few days later, Laurent Fabius offered this concise slogan, full of imagery: "Juppé in power, get ready for disaster!"

2. During the *7/7* show on 20 April, he said, "The president of the Republic is not the issue in these general elections."

3. On 11 June, Eric Raoult, minister of the Juppé government, evoked the name of Philippe Séguin—"why not Prime Minister" after the election—before a press release in which he claimed to be "proud to be a Secretary for Alain Juppé."

4. One episode illustrates rather well the climate in which Juppé campaigned. Wanting to behave as "government leader," the prime minister chose to go to every region to "help" candidates. The deputy and mayor of Toulouse, Dominique Baudris, declined this "help;" strangely enough, other candidates also were absent during Juppé's visits. As *Libération* comically stated on 16 May: "When Juppé comes their way, the candidates run away." Four days earlier, *Libéra-*

tion had commented on a poll that was encouraging for the government: "Government on the rise, in spite of Juppé."

5. Pasqua tried to make his differences heard within the government, especially regarding social issues and the construction of Europe. He stated on 26 April, "There won't be any 'new momentum' without new policies," and he asks the president "to consult with the people when the time comes" on Europe, that is, on the change of currency to the euro.

6. Describing for *Le Monde* the launching of the government campaign by Juppé on 22 April, Jean-Louis Sceaux noticed that when surrounded by the highest-ranking members of his government, the prime minister "assumes the role of the chief of government. . . . Thus freed of all competition, M. Juppé could, the very day after the dissolution of government, assume the role of undisputed chief of governing parties, now out of power" *(Le Monde*, 24 April 1997). One of Juppé's political mistakes probably was to symbolize "undivided power," because of his many responsibilities. As Raphaëlle Bacqué noticed, "Prime Minister, RPR president, mayor of Bordeaux, president of the Bordeaux Urban Community? Only Jacques Chirac, Prime Minister of the first cohabitation and Mayor of Paris, had a similar profile. But never did a man with as much power as Alain Juppé have to suffer as much from its disadvantages. For this excess load of mandates quickly turned out to represent in the eyes of the people a concept of unshared power." Bacqué, Hors Matignon, *Pouvoirs* 83 (1997): 59-64.

7. Interview with *Paris-Match*, 15-21 May 1997. In spite of this "support," the rivalry between Juppé and Séguin shows up in a latent way and on several occasions during the campaign. Juppé, on 13 May, publicly asked an enigmatic question: "Is it better to have a big jovial man who does not know his files, or a skinny one, not so jovial, who knows them?" Knowing their rivalry and their very different physical appearances, this very unfortunate question led the media to speculate: did Juppé have Séguin in mind (although the latter is not known to be "jovial")?

8. Study done on 29 and 30 April 1997, and published in *Le Point*, 3 May 1997, 50.

9. Gerstlé 1998. The analyses developed here come in part from reading this chapter. I want to thank Jacques Gerstlé for letting me read it before it was published by Science Po Press, and I also thank him for his advice.

10. François Mitterrand speaking during the televised debate with Jacques Chirac, between the two ballots of the presidential election, on 28 April 1988. See "L'election presidentielle," 24 April-8 May 1988, *Supplement aux Dossiers et documents du Monde* (May 1988), 64.

11. The presidential announcement of the dissolution was reprinted in *Le Figaro,* 16 May 1988, 6.

12. Said during the 14 July 1996 televised interview, printed in *Le Monde,* 16 July 1996, 6.

13. This theme of the "interest of the country" is part of the speech by Jean-François Mancel (then secretary-general of RPR) on 22 April 1997: "Granted, the four precedents since 1958 have all been linked to a social and political crisis. . . . But resorting to a dissolution should by no means be exclusively linked to these two reasons, in content and form. To pretend otherwise is not only to adopt a limiting point of view, but also to defend an erroneous analysis. For the only real reason, in spirit, is the concern for and the interest of the nation. It is this sole preoccupation which guided Jacques Chirac's choice." This discourse caricatures efforts to justify the dissolution. One can read this text on the Internet at http://www.rpr.org/Legislatives/Savoir/texte.html. One can also find on this site the text of the presidential discourse (21 April 1997) with the title "Une dissolution dans l'intérêt de la France."

14. This rhetoric is interesting: the president tries to adopt as his own the legitimate question that his decision brings about, which is, why did he refuse to dissolve the Assembly earlier?

15. In other words, it would have five years from the time of the dissolution until the 2002 presidential election.

16. Choosing to publish this address in fourteen newspapers of the local press shows Chirac's desire to revert to the style of his messages during the 1995 presidential campaign. The national press (*Libération,* for example), probably judged too "Parisian" and reaching a limited "target," nevertheless got hold of the text of the presidential address and published it . A controversy about this mode of communication (conducted by some newspaper owners who had not been chosen by Chirac to publish his address) partly muddled the way it was received.

17. Alluding to the French "social model" allowed Chirac to return to the theme of "social division": "this is the only way for us to act more efficiently against an intolerable unemployment rate and an unacceptable social division." Chirac thus tried to prove that he had not forgotten the promises he made during the 1995 electoral campaign, in which the "fight against social division" occupied a central position. By doing that, he stressed in a paradoxical way the tactical aspect of the dissolution: "If the majority in power supported the government loyally" (21 April speech), and if the struggle against "social division" remained an important aspect of the government's actions, what could be expected of a disso-

lution called in the hope that it would allow voting by the same majority in the National Assembly and the same kind of policies?

18. Jospin was careful to adopt a different strategy than that of the president, declaring that his address would be sent to all newspapers of the national and local press, and that it would be up to them to publish it or not. His address was published on 9 May by many newspapers. In addition Jospin published two discourses to develop his social and economic platform in *Libération* on 16 and 17 May 1997.

19. This probably was an indirect allusion to Chirac's 1995 presidential campaign, orchestrated mainly by denouncing the "only way of thinking."

20. There is a sentence at the end of the speech that makes one wonder: "I wanted, by provoking general elections, to recapture the national energy to lead, to convince and to give the nation a strength it was losing." This sentence, a little enigmatic, raised some comments during the end of the electoral campaign. Some did not hesitate to put forward hypotheses dealing with political psychology, or even psychoanalysis. The newspaper *Libération*, for example, asked some psychoanalysts for their opinions. Emmanuelle Hamou summed up the question that she was asked in the following words: "Freudian slip alluding to a personal failure or expression of an unspeakable desire for a new cohabitation?" The answers to this question bring little relevance to a political science perspective. Nonetheless, the question asked is interesting because of what it reveals about the political climate of the electoral campaign; see Hamou 1997. The day after the presidential intervention, Jospin spoke of an "incredible confession of failure, as if he himself was feeling this loss, like blood running out, a loss of energy. This appeared to me as a major acknowledgment of defeat concerning the first two years of his term." Heard during the "Journal de 20 heures" on France 2, printed in *Libération* on 28 May 1997, 2.

21. It is a six-page document, a synthesis of what the UDF and RPR were going to offer separately for the 1998 general elections.

22. The Socialist Party's program had been presented to the press as early as 18 March, but with the intent of getting ready for the 1998 elections.

23. More precisely, the program of the Socialist Party states four conditions for the single currency: (1) the countries that founded Europe or those that became "Europe's pillars" (Italy, Spain, Great Britain) shall not be excluded, (2) "Europe must be social and political," (3) creation along with the European Central Bank of a "European economic government," (4) balanced parities among the euro, the dollar, and the yen ("to prevent any monetary dumping").

24. After a meeting at the "Mutualité," a symbolic place for the left wing in Paris.

25. On 16 December 1996, during the 29th Congress of the Communist Party (PCF), Robert Hue alluded to the Popular Front. As early as 16 January 1997, Jospin suggested "a contract of orientation between the left wing parties and the ecologists," thus answering the idea of "a basis of common agreements" considered by Robert Hue during the 29th Congress of the French Communist Party. The Socialist Party (PS) finally concluded separate agreements with the PCF (29 April) and the Greens (30 April; an agreement with the 1998 general elections in mind had already been reached on 23 March 1997). In terms of agreement for the elections, the PS and the PCF would present their respective candidates for the first ballot, and then apply the "republican discipline" for the second ballot (withdrawing in favor of the left-wing candidate with the best results after the first ballot). The agreement for the elections between the PS and the Greens would have single candidates for about thirty constituencies; all in all the Greens would have 413 candidates, among which 20 were supported by the PS (the Greens would not have any candidates against the PS in 79 constituencies). Besides, Jospin agreed, as early as 22 April, on an "election pact of nonaggression" with Jean-Pierre Chevénement, the president of the Movement of the Citizens (MDC): The PS would not run candidates against four representatives of the MDC, who had been voted into power, nor against Roland Carraz (MDC in Cote d'Or). In return, the MDC would not run candidates against the PS candidates who had been elected, or against Raymond Forni in Belfort. A similar agreement was reached with the Radical Socialist Party. Finally the PS, PCF, and Radical Socialist Party decided on one candidate in five constituencies, where the influence of the far right was strong.

26. During the PCF national council on 25 April, Robert Hue stated: "We suggest defining the main points of the Communist contribution to the series of policies that could be started after the ballots of 25 May and 1 June, should the left wing and the forces of progress, the ecologists, be voted into power and decide to take up the government to implement policies sure to bring real change. Which is, as I point out, by the way, the condition that there be Communist ministers. Change will only happen, as we all know, if there are Communist ministers. . . . I want to stress that our participation in a leftist government is not on the condition that our policies are put into place, but on the condition that the policies that would be put into place would radically break away from those of the right-wing parties, and be leftist." This declaration, as well as the text of the PCF program, may be found on the Internet at http://www.pcf.fr/legislatives/.

27. The FN program had been presented, with the 1998 general elections in view, during the FN congress in Strasbourg on 31 March 1997. Besides the usual

program put forward by the FN (family, immigration, protectionism), Le Pen wanted to add some social policies to his program, the FN considering itself as "the first party for the workers in France" since the presidential election of 1995.

28. The Independent Right (LDI) seemed taken by surprise by the announcement of the dissolution. Philippe de Villiers obviously had a hard time finding his place in the electoral campaign, and the LDI results showed on the evening of the first ballot that, besides a consultation about Europe, there was no political space in France for a party to the right of the moderate right. LDI had 510 candidates in the general elections (420 MPF and 90 CNIP). On 4 May de Villiers stated that he intended to make the first ballot of the election "a referendum on euro, a referendum on Europe." He added: "We want the right wing to have right-wing policies." In addition, he published an address in *Le Monde* in which he denounced the dissolution as a maneuver to "dissolve the debate on euro," and he organized the three themes of his program in a hierarchy: "What is at stake today is the nation; either France becomes involved on the Euro road of no return, that is, an integrated, federal Europe led from Berlin and Frankfurt, or it decides to build 'another Europe,' in which it chooses not to give up its own sovereignty." *Le Monde*, 29 April 1997, 18.

29. This "liberal turn" was the object of internal debates within the right wing and the entourage of the executive following the disastrous estimates of the *Note on Perspectives* from the budget management, given to the prime minister at the end of March and soon known by the press. The budget estimates filled the period prior to the dissolution and the beginning of the electoral campaign with debates on France's ability to "qualify" for the change of currency. This yearly estimate assessed the public deficit for 1997 at 3.7 or 3.8 percent—far above the 3 percent of the GDP required for the change of currency in the Treaty of Maastricht. This estimate came with recommendations for drastic cuts in public spending and social costs. On the reactions of Chirac's entourage and on the different conclusions that this entourage drew from this estimate ("liberal turn" or not), see the journalistic analysis, which is well documented, by the political section of *Libération*: "Histoire secrète de la dissolution, Le Service Politique de Liberation" (Paris: Plon, 1997), 74-80. Alain Madelin, who was in favor of a "redefinition of the perimeter of the state," is said to have uttered on 19 April, two days before the announcement of the dissolution: "It's done for, nothing is going to happen."

30. To no avail, one could say, for as soon as his 20 April interview on the televised show *7/7*, Jospin chose to denounce "hardcore capitalism." Jospin took

great advantage of the "hesitations" among the right wing about the hypothesis of a "liberal turn" during the period immediately preceding and following the announcement of the dissolution. He put a lot of stress in his campaign on the theme of "the turn of a screw" awaiting voters after a possible right-wing victory.

31. Séguin's intervention in this meeting marked his entering the campaign. He was opposed to the dissolution, and many observers had stressed his silence since 21 April. About this meeting and Séguin's remarks, see *Libération*, 30 April 1997.

32. Séguin stated in an interview in *Marianne* (19-25 May): "I try hard to give a meaning to the dissolution and to look for its chief usefulness: to get ready for 1998."

33. François Hollande, interview in *La Tribume-Desfosses*, 6 May 1997. Hollande specified to *Le Monde* that the PS wished for France Télécom to remain 100 percent public, and that he had no intention of privatizing enterprises such as the CIC. On the other hand, Hollande did not exclude a few transfers of minority interest for some enterprises in which the state only holds a weak percentage (see *Le Monde*, 7 May 1997, 6).

34. The television channel TF1 had suggested from the beginning a "debate of the four" on 20 May, five days before the first ballot. This suggestion was rapidly accepted by Juppé and Leotard, then by Hue, but Jospin quickly declined. For the right wing, it was a matter of showing "M. Jospin and M. Hue side by side, since they want to govern together," as Juppé stated. The theme of PCF archaism and of the "socialist-communist alliance" was not absent from the electoral campaign.

35. The address published in the local press on 7 May had a similar effect. According to a survey by Louis-Harris conducted 10 May 1997, 79 percent of the people polled had not read this address, and 63 percent of those who had read it did not find the chief of state convincing.

36. Considering the French electoral system, one estimates that the difference of one point (in the percentage) can mean the gain or loss of thirty seats. In spite of the caution taken in the many predictions about seats, these turned out to be very difficult to assess. About the question, see Gauthier 1997. Also see Mechet 1997, 58-64.

37. This percentage is the same as the one the BVA survey came up with on 25 and 26 April 1997.

38. IFOP-JDD predictions: monthly surveys done by IFOP for the *Journal Du Dimanche* from national samples representing the French population above 18 years of age. The surveys can be checked on the Internet at http://www.ifop.fr/archives/barojdd/.

39. Gallup-*l'Express* survey, done on 7 and 8 November 1996, according to a national sample representing the population of at least 18 years of age.

40. See the report of this survey in *Le Nouvel Economiste*, 25 April 1997, or in *Le Monde*, 27 April 1997. The CSA/*Le Nouvel Economiste* survey was conducted according to a national sample of 1,005 people.

41. As well summarized in Jaffré 1998.

42. Le Pen gave his voters the list of the candidates of the moderate right wing to be punished, and in a meeting, gave his supporters the cardboard head of Catherine Trautman, mayor of Strasbourg. During the National Front Congress in Strasbourg, the mayor of this city had organized various symposia and demonstrations against the National Front.

43. See the very enlightening assessment of the 1996 public opinion in Grunberg and Dupoirier 1997, 153-66.

Chapter 3

1. Nevertheless, by 1984, only 11 percent of FN voters expressed party preferences for either the Communists (1 percent) or the Socialists (10 percent). For details, see Schain 1996.

2. This analysis generally agrees with that in Martin 1996, 20-23.

3. CSA Study 9662093, crosstabulations of CHAB and RS12.

4. See the analysis by Nonna Mayer of the phenomenon of "gaucho-Lepénisme" in *Le Monde*, 29 May 1997, 10.

5. Survey results are from CSA, *Les Élections Legislatives du 25 mai 1997*, 18. My thanks to the director of CSA, Roland Cayrol, for making this survey available to me. The SOFRES/CEVIPOF postelection survey indicates a transfer of 3.7 percent from the PCF and 2.5 percent from the PS.

6. The percentages for the CGT, CFDT, and FO appear to have declined from 1995, from 7 percent, 6 percent, and 16 percent, but risen for the CFTC, from 5 percent. See "Le Front National à l'assaut des entreprises," *L'Expansion*, 6-19 March 1995, 44.

7. In fact the percentages are highest for CGT and FO (54 and 53 percent), and lowest for CFDT (42 percent). See CSA Study 9662093, crosstabs of Q4 and RS10. These figures appear to have declined since 1994 for the CGT and the CFDT (from 63 and 49 percent).

8. *Interco-Flash-CFDT*, 4 January 1996. The two unions (the FNP and the FPIP) had survived a challenge before the Conseil d'Etat.

9. See *Le Monde,* 29 May 1996; also see *Rapport CRIDA 97* (Paris: CRIDA, 1996), 65-67. CRIDA, the Centre de Recherche d'Information et de Documentation Antiraciste, has now issued three reports on racism, antisemitism and the extreme right in Europe.

10. These elections have been challenged in the courts by the trade union organizations. See *Le Monde,* 10 January 1998, 1.

11. These and other early moves by the government are documented in *The European,* 21-27 July 1995.

12. Implementation of the Schengen Accords was formally delayed until the end of the year, a procedure that was permitted under the accords. See *Le Monde,* 18 July 1995. Implementation was then further delayed, with the French government citing as its reason the inability of the Benelux states to control the movement of drugs across their frontiers, and has now been only partially implemented. *Le Monde,* 26 March 1996.

13. The basis for this approach is contained in Weil 1997, 47-48. Also see the commentary in *Le Monde,* 31 July 1997, 6.

14. In anticipation of the regional elections in March 1998, possible negotiations with the resurgent National Front were bitterly debated by both the right and the left. See *Le Monde,* 2 December 1997, 6.

15. Exact numbers are hard to verify, since many FN candidates—as in previous elections—presented themselves as "divers droite" or "indépendants." See *Le Monde,* 21 June 1995; and *Libération,* 19 June 1995.

16. In the second round, the presence of the FN resulted in 97 three-way races, and 20 four-way races, almost all in large towns and cities. See *Libération,* 19 June 1995.

Chapter 4

1. The Communists were excluded from participating in power in the Fourth Republic because of their pro-Soviet Cold War positions. The Gaullists "excluded themselves" because General de Gaulle, their leader, refused to accept the institutions of the Fourth Republic.

2. Removing many of the most important obstacles to renewed European action (the "British check" problem, and expansion to Spain and Portugal, most notably) and nominating Jacques Delors to the presidency of the European Commission opened new European prospects.

3. The fact that European economies turned upward during the same years, for the first time in a decade, helped as well.

4. The cost, perceived as short-run, was aligning French economic and monetary policy with that of the Germans, a tradeoff that would sustain the Franco-German "couple" through the different phases of European construction (in particular through to the EMU already on the table in 1988, with the appointment of the Delors Committee, which drew up the EMU's initial blueprints).

5. Altogether too little scholarly attention—in contrast to discussion in the elite press—has been paid to the huge political problems posed by the need to reform the deep structures of national political economies constructed during the postwar boom. "Exogenizing reform" through Europe and, it must be added, through the conscious creation of newly liberal and global macroeconomic policy regimes, were strategies by national actors to create settings in which national "hands were tied" by transnational commitments and structures that would have the effect of obliging reform.

6. No government was responsible to it, and it had no policy-relevant opposition and majority. Its members, elected by universal suffrage only since 1989, tended, once in Strasbourg, to "go native," adopting the same sense of mission as the commission—that furthering European integration was a good in itself.

7. This was, in large part, because Europe was considered "foreign affairs" by member states and therefore was well shielded from direct scrutiny by the discretion granted national executives in foreign policy.

8. His misunderstanding of events leading to German unification was symbolic of the real trouble that followed. Mitterrand made a series of major strategic mistakes in his second term, in domestic as well as foreign policy.

9. The Gaullist strategy had shifted resources massively toward an independent nuclear deterrent targeted on Eastern Europe and the Soviet Union, plus conventional forces that were integrated into this deterrence posture. The original hope was that European allies, particularly the Germans, would be seduced towards greater cooperation with the French, and away from reliance on the Americans and NATO. Events of 1989 left this strategy in a cul de sac. France thereafter tried to generate a "Common Foreign and Security Policy" (CFSP) from the EU at Maastricht to achieve similar ends, but this has come to little as well. In the meantime the dramatic change in France's economic circumstances in the 1990s, in part due to the EMU, has meant a lack of funds for any serious reconversion of French forces to meet the new and different missions of the post–Cold War period, let alone to underwrite new strategic capacities to pursue these missions independent of the United States and NATO.

10. The "1 for 1" conversion of ostmarks for Dmarks was the economic culprit.

11. The CFSP turned out to be largely empty words, again to the chagrin of the French. The Germans also got a substantial increase in Euro-parliamentary power.

12. The RPR and the UDF won 82 percent of the seats, 474 of 577. The reason was the collapse of the left. The right-left voting ratio soared to 60-40 percent. The Socialist vote in the first round dropped from 34.8 percent in 1988 to 17.4 percent in 1993, and the PCF dropped from 11.3 percent to 9.1 percent. The National Front had also begun to make serious inroads among workers.

13. For the most part, it involved the "mutual surveillance" of member-state monetary, financial, and budgetary policy, with an eye to inciting convergence.

14. The 1994 elections to the European parliament ran true to earlier form. Europe, the pretext for the elections, was obscured by the substance of domestic French politics. The elections were less a sequel to the 1992 referendum than a prelude to the 1995 presidential campaign. There were important results, to be sure. Michel Rocard's prospects for the presidency were destroyed, and protest voting increased (Gaffney 1996; Lodge 1996; Perrineau 1995b).

15. For a superb review of these problems, see Cameron 1996.

16. Resuming nuclear testing in the South Pacific in time for the fiftieth anniversary of Hiroshima was an exemplary touch. The new president then startled the usually staid G-7 meetings in Halifax, Canada, by his direct, not to say indiscreet, manner of speaking. At the Cannes European Council in June 1995, he concluded what had been a dismal French presidency of the EU Council of Ministers by voicing loud complaints against Italian monetary policy, including a final press conference in which, said one journalist, he "broke every rule in the diplomatic book."

17. It is very difficult to understand what Chirac was up to. He obviously knew that it would not do to turn immediately to new austerity after promising the exact opposite. He may even have believed that major new cuts could be avoided. The Germans would be the ones to call the shots as the EMU approached, and it was conceivable, given German eagerness to promote further European integration, that they might be willing to soften the Maastricht criteria to make things easier for the French. Any such thoughts were dashed completely when Chirac met Helmut Kohl at Baden-Baden for the semiannual Franco-German summit at the end of October 1995. Kohl, with the Bundesbank and his own grumpy electorate to worry about, was firm: France was not to sabotage movement to the EMU by its lax policy.

18. Juppé's plan split the French left and labor movement. The CFDT's leader, Nicole Notat, actually approved of the plan, as did a wide range of centrist elements, such as Michel Rocard of the Socialist Party. This gave rise to another typical Gallic spectacle, the public petition campaign displaying intellectual quarrels, with one group rallying around the distinguished left Catholic journal *Esprit* in favor of the plan, and another group, led by Pierre Bourdieu, against the plan.

19. Most of the strikers went out initially to protect their own special privileges—retirement at the age of fifty for railroad engineers, for example, or early retirement and lower pension contributions for civil servants—but this did not diminish the depth of resentment that the strike produced.

20. Just prior to the 1997 elections, 27 percent were satisfied with Juppé, and 61 percent were unhappy. Chirac's numbers were 31 percent and 56 percent (Le Gall 1997).

21. Chirac actually proceeded with some skill in the area of defense reforms, particularly in a geopolitical sense. Trying to get back into NATO within the perspective of creating a genuine European pillar was a shrewd redefinition of older Gaullist concerns, for example, even if the Americans were wise to the maneuver and stopped it in its tracks. Abolishing conscription and moving towards a volunteer military made sense, for example, but it would also cost jobs and create more unemployment. The reform was proposed in February 1996. Chirac left open the question of whether conscription should be replaced by "civic service." The huge cost of anything even remotely universal meant that civic service was a nonstarter, however.

22. It raised all kinds of hackles in Brussels at the European Commission, however, because of its unorthodoxy. French success at creative bookkeeping also encouraged others, including Italy, to seek such one-time items to move closer to the Maastricht criteria.

23. Muddle also characterized the administration's other economic policies, in-cluding privatizations and defense industry rationalization.

24. Strong credibility would be needed to discourage speculators. German resolve was strengthened by the prospect of Spanish, and particularly Italian, EMU membership.

25. Once a government went above 3 percent it would have to put money "on deposit" at the European level. It would forfeit this money if high deficits continued. Fines were to be calculated at .2 percent of GDP plus .1 percent for every percentage point of deficit above 3 percent.

26. Chirac also lost considerable control over his own party, the RPR. Philippe Séguin became secretary-general soon after the elections, indicating that a successor generation was taking over.

27. The FN's vote demonstrated its growing ability to attract support across the political spectrum, including from the left (Le Gall 1997, 20; Perrineau 1997b). During the campaign, Le Pen had intimated on several occasions that a victory of the left might be preferable to that of the Chirac majority, a call that opened up serious divisions inside the FN. Then the FN held its ground in a large number of second-round elections, which became *triangulaire* in consequence. This was clearly to deprive the moderate right of its ability to use the electoral law as a multiplier.

28. The "pluralist" alliance supporting Jospin gave Robert Hue, the relatively new Secretary General of the Communist Party, an important opportunity to undertake major reforms in the PCF's strategy and culture. PCF ministers thus would be expected to cooperate with Jospin's policies in order to cope with Europe, even though the party's long-standing positions might be in contradiction with such cooperation.

29. Grunberg (1997) presents evidence that correlates "universalist" attitudes and positive positions on Europe. Universalist attitudes themselves correlate with high educational attainment and/or higher social standing.

30. Jospin's willingness to retreat had another motive. His accepting the growth and stability pact meant that the "Club Med" countries would be expected to maintain good financial and budgetary practices in the future. Jospin had campaigned on the need to include these countries, particularly Italy, in the EMU, and allowing the famous "pact" to go forward would reassure the Germans about France's presence in the EMU. In the medium term, the presence of Italy and Spain in the EMU would provide the French with needed allies in the struggle against German demands.

31. A number of member states (mainly small ones such as Belgium, Austria, Denmark, and Sweden) had, along with France, put employment policy papers on the table during the IGC discussions, but little would have come of them were it not for the elections in the United Kingdom and France and the Jospin demonstrations just prior to the Amsterdam European Council. For an excellent review, see Goetschy 1997. On the Amsterdam Treaty more generally, see Dehousse 1997.

32. The operative treaty clause for coordination is a new Article 128. This coordination will be done in ways similar to those promoting the EMU convergence criteria. Each year the commission will present the Council of Ministers

with a report and a proposal for "employment guidelines." The council will then recommend broad lines of policy and specific targets. Progress will be regularly monitored. The guidelines will then have to be explicitly incorporated in national economic action plans drawn up by member states in a multiannual perspective. Unlike the EMU situation, however, there will be none of the compulsion that flows from a final goal and deadline.

33. Of course, everything depends upon the precise meaning of employment policy. Here the words become important, because there is considerable conflict about how to create employment. Employers and some governments want greater labor market flexibility. Some other governments, unions, and other groups want security optimized through the processes of change and more job creation. The dispute, centering on the meaning of the word "employability" in 1997, essentially was about the mix of liberalism and state intervention, and passive versus active labor market policies. These issues are far from resolved.

34. The insertion of a new but vague text in the final stages of Amsterdam to give special treatment for "public services" provided another example beyond employment policy (EU 1997a, 26).

35. The tough monetarism begun by the left in the mid-1980s meant that France easily satisfied the other criteria on cumulative deficits, inflation levels, currency stability, and interest rates.

36. A list would include youth "animators" in troubled urban areas (including schools), aids for the elderly ("meals on wheels" and like activities) and the handicapped, conflict mediators in cities and public transportation systems, tour leaders for *randonnées*, and workers to help rehabilitate France's "national cultural heritage" in particular, treasured old buildings.

37. The most frequently mentioned idea is an "annualization" of hours to give employers greater short-term scheduling freedom, but there will be other proposals.

38. The law will apply first to all employers of over fourteen workers, who will be required to comply by reducing workweek hours to thirty-five by the year 2000. Smaller businesses will be given an additional two years. The government will provide financial subsidies to employers until the final date to facilitate transition. It also determined that overtime work up to thirty-nine hours must be remunerated at 125 percent.

39. Initial union discussion about the conference indicated that these pathologies were alive and well. The CGT wanted higher wages, plus the thirty-five-hour week, with no cut in salaries. The FO wanted the same and, in addition, was dead

set against negotiating hours annualization (and, presumably, other forms of labor market flexibility). The CFTC said that it would cooperate as long as lower- and middle-level wages were not reduced. The CFDT, in contrast, denounced in advance "thirty-nine hours' pay for thirty-five hours' work." Nicole Notat felt that this position sought a "fake working class victory," which would not create jobs. To her, the problem was to bring the "excluded" into the labor force. The CFDT was open-minded about negotiating new "flexibility" and accepting prorated wage reductions for lower hours.

40. This was, no doubt, to limit the extent of actual change which occurred.

41. The government handles this issue by arguing for shorter-run wage reductions that would be earned back over time, but dealing with unions in competition with one another about such things will test its capacities.

42. It will be interesting to watch over time how this burden-shifting plays out in the broader politics of social protection. With health-care expenses taken up by general revenues, the issue of their cost will become central in discussions about the level of taxation. Moreover, because of administrative changes carried over from the Juppé Plan, decisions about the taxation level will be made by Parliament, with parity deliberations excluded from the discussion. In the medium term this could cause more trouble for the French welfare state.

43. These ideas have been culled from the "second left" of the 1960s and 1970s, in particular its Christian components, tempered during the Mitterrand years by recognition of difficult economic constraints and the importance of Europe. Jacques Delors's ideas loom particularly large; indeed, Delors forecast much of the new government's approach in an important article published even before the election victory was clear (Delors 1997).

44. Evidence of this is abundant. The complicated discussions at the Luxembourg European Council around the matter of the "Eurocouncil" (Euro-X)—the informal committee formed to supervise the coming of the euro, and composed of initial EMU members—were really about "economic government." The employment policy discussions we have reviewed provide more substance. Preliminary debates about a "code of fiscal good conduct" to prevent "tax-dumping" within the EMU move in the same direction.

Chapter 6

1. This type of alliance is often referred to as a "primary" to suggest a similarity to the American nominating primary. A significant difference is that electorates in American primaries are restrained or restricted.

2. Studies of the elections held in the 1960s did not even distinguish between the support of the Independent Republicans and the Gaullists (Goguel 1963; 1971; 1983, 500-503; Lancelot and Weil 1971; Lancelot and Lancelot 1971). Colliard (1972, 207-234) raises the difficulties of distinguishing between the Gaullists' and the Independent Republicans' electoral support in the sixties. Converse and Pierce (1986, 30, 32, 38, 114-15, 189, 218, 262-63, 266, 435-36) stress the similarities in the sixties between the two. Analyzing the results of the 1973 election, Charlot (1973, 81-144) found the Independent Republicans and the Gaullists sharing the same electoral fate. See also Hayward and Wright 1973.

3. French candidates for the National Assembly run with a *suppléant* or stand-in. Since government ministers must resign their seats in the National Assembly, the *suppléant* can immediately replace the minister. The *suppléant* can also replace the deputy who dies or who is elected to an incompatible office such as the Senate.

4. The ability to hold more than one local office, as well as the office of deputy, is due to the peculiar French practice of *cumul des mandats*. Efforts to limit the practice were made in 1985, without great effect. The Jospin government plans to make a new effort to limit the practice of accumulating electoral mandates.

5. Others in the Front's leadership ascribed it more bluntly to his fear of being defeated as he had been in 1993. Le Pen himself ascribed it to his need to be prepared for the presidential election that was sure to follow the RPR-UDF defeat, an explanation that even his followers found amusing (Mano and Birenbaum 1997, 186-191).

Chapter 7

1. The data used come from a postelection poll by SOFRES/*Libération*/CEVIPOF/CIDSP-Grenoble/CRAPS-Lille, taken by phone from 26 to 31 May 1997, from a national sampling (3,010 persons) representative of the registered electorate, and also from previous polls by CEVIPOF, concerning the legislative elections of 1978 and the presidential elections of 1988 and 1995 (Capdevielle et al. 1981; Boy and Mayer 1993; Boy and Mayer 1997a). The declared votes were viewed as a function of actual results from the first round, except for the analyses of logistic regression, which were carried out with the raw data for reasons of statistical validity.

2. See the postelection polls by CEVIPOF from 1978, 1988, and 1995.

3. Only 9 percent of regularly practicing Catholics consider that "extramarital sex" is "a sin," a figure that increases to 17 percent concerning homosexuality,

and 28 percent concerning abortion (poll by CSA/*Le Monde, La Vie, L'Actualité religieuse dans le monde,* and *Forum des communautés chrétiennes,* based on a national sampling representative of people age eighteen and older (1,014 persons).

4. Profession was determined by asking an open question, written in plain language then precoded by the poller according to the criteria of INSEE nomenclature. For the three polls, the codes were regrouped according to the classifications of the new nomenclature.

5. The available data—from questioning National Front voters on their votes in the previous election, as was done in a detailed contextual analysis carried out in cantons or communes—show that the Communist contribution to the National Front candidates has always been marginal (Platone and Rey 1996). The decline of the Communist vote began well before the electoral breakthrough of the National Front and was mainly to the advantage of the Socialist vote. If there is a crossover from the Communist vote to the National Front vote, it takes place most likely after intermediate steps, that is, casting a non-Communist vote for the left, or abstention. As Jérôme Jaffré noted, "There is a phenomenon of functional substitution between the two powers in the French political system" (Jaffré 1986, 229). Especially among young people, it is not necessarily the former Communist voters who give their votes to the National Front, but they have the same social and cultural profile as those who used to vote for the French Communist Party, when it still represented between 15 and 20 percent of the electorate.

6. Based on professional activities of households in 1989 and average gross figures from domestic, professional, and personal real estate property in 1988 (Fall and Lattès 1993, 351; Malpot, Pacquel, and Verger 1993, 386).

7. Based on the SOFRES/*Le Nouvel Observateur* poll, from 21 March to 5 April, with a national sampling representative of French people (2,300 persons) of voting age (Platone 1993, 47).

8. This is mentioned in Grunberg and Schweisguth 1983 and Mayer 1986.

9. A number of young people with degrees explicitly chose the public sector over the private sector in order to avoid having to get involved in the worker/boss conflict.

10. This phenomenon has already been stated by Singly and Thélot (1988, 179ff).

11. For more on the symmetric evolution of American wage-earning middle classes, in the shift of their support from Republicans to Democrats beginning in 1968, see the interesting study by Hout, Brooks, and Manza (1995).

12. The exact text of the questions that we rapidly summarize here is given in the appendix.

13. This is in reference to the meaning given to this term in Adorno et al. 1950, 151-52.

14. According to a poll by SOFRES/*Le Monde* conducted just before the legislative elections (25-26 April 1997, with a national sampling of 1,000 persons representative of the population age eighteen and over), more than a third of the voters trust neither the left nor the right in governing the country, and expect nothing to come from either victory.

Chapter 8

1. In contrast, these results are compatible with a minimalist conception of the effects of life cycles, which considers that a limited change in values may occur when passing from youth to adulthood. For the cohort born between 1951 and 1960 (between the ages of eighteen and twenty-eight in 1978), only 35 percent adhered at that time to the principle of effort and authority, with a much higher percentage (48 percent) agreeing ten years later. Similarly, the cohort born between 1961 and 1970 (between the ages of eighteen and twenty-eight in 1988) saw its responses in favor of authoritarianism rise from 34 percent to 39 percent from 1988 to 1995. This hypothesis of a limited change in values, as one goes from irresponsible youth to adulthood with its many burdens of responsibility, is completely plausible. Nevertheless, it has nothing to do with the hypothesis of a continual evolution of values as one grows older.

2. This does not consider the phenomenon of sects, which at any rate affects less than 1 percent of the population.

3. That this evolution is characterized by a decrease in xenophobia beginning in 1995, which occurred after a period of increase, is attested by other sources. The polls by CEVIPOF show exactly the same evolution concerning other indicators of xenophobia. The polls carried out by SOFRES for the Commission on Human Rights (*La Commission consultative des droits de l'homme*) denote the same evolution: in the French population, feelings of agreement with Jean-Marie Le Pen's ideas concerning immigrants were on the rise until 1995, after which such sentiment declined.

4. The truth is that, since the 1980s, the problem of xenophobia manifests itself differently than in previous times. The members of the outgroup are no longer "foreign workers," as before, men living alone who had jobs and who lived in housing designated for foreigners. Now there are entire families, who often have French citizenship and who live among families of French origin who are of the same social class. These immigrants encounter difficulties caused by unem-

ployment, racial discrimination, and other problems of living in diverse communities. They are frequently associated with disorder and insecurity. Also, more than in the past, the so-called "old French families" (les Français de souche, French "blue bloods") frequently manifest xenophobic reactions. What we mean by saying there is no progression of xenophobia is that the intensity of xenophobic reactions today is less than it used to be. To use a medical metaphor, we could say that today more people "have a fever," but instead of fevers of 104°F as in earlier times, they have temperatures of 101°F.

Chapter 9

1. The pioneering works are Tullock 1967 and Krueger 1974 for rent-seeking theory; Rose-Ackreman 1978 for corruption theory; and Becker 1968 for crime theory. See also Klitgaard 1988, 1998; Cartier-Bresson 1997; Lafay and Lecaillon 1993 for references.

2. The ethical and philosophical aspects of this question are not of concern here.

3. In a full model, the media would have to be introduced as a central actor. For example, (serious) newspapers, as rational agents, aim at maximizing their long-term actualized profit (or, more simply, at maximizing their current profit under a "survival" constraint). For this reason, they have to take into account the interest generated by their subjects (congruence with the preferences of the public), and also the necessity to preserve a minimum degree of credibility (truth in reporting). This last point is all the more important now that information is becoming increasingly contestable (largely because of globalization), and this pushes information suppliers to be more cautious and to establish recognized professional norms. These factors indeed have serious consequences.

4. The Watergate effect was, however, nonsignificant for the lower income category, and it seems to have been costly not for the Republicans but for the Democrats in the upper-middle (-5) and upper (-14) income categories.

5. A minimum percentage of votes is required to be allowed to run for the second ballot. Alliances between first-ballot lists for the second ballot are possible. The list arriving in first position at the second ballot benefits from a premium of seats to obtain a majority.

6. The question asked about the political parties was this: "Do you have a good opinion or a bad opinion or no opinion about the (Communist Party, Socialist Party, Ecologist Party, UDF [right-wing centrist party], RPR [Gaullist party], National Front [extreme right party])?"

7. Notably, during the test period, "Affaire Carrefour du développement," "Vrai-faux passeport d'Yves Chalier," and "Affaire Schuller-Maréchal."

Chapter 10

1. The provision relating to civil and political rights means that about half a million potential electors are excluded from the electoral rolls at any given time. Once an individual has been convicted and a sentence has been passed that includes the deprivation of civil and/or political rights, the government statistical service INSEE is charged with the responsibility of removing that individual from a central electoral register. However, the procedure is complicated and leads to a significant disparity between the theoretical and actual numbers of those excluded under this provision.

2. As discussed later in the chapter, the parliamentary election of 1986 was conducted under a one-ballot, proportional representation system, which was changed back to the two-ballot constituency-based system for the 1988 elections.

3. The failure to obtain that majority was an astounding defeat for Chirac and must qualify as one of the great political blunders in recent French history.

4. It should be noted that he demonstrates that 52 percent of the abstentionists in the referendum voted in all of the other elections (Morin 1989).

Chapter 11

1. That is, until the day independents begin to win elections regularly. For now, however, even when less than delighted with the choices offered them by the parties, voters are still more likely to vote for partisan candidates when given the choice between them and one or more independent contestants.

2. In 1988 Mitterrand ran a largely issueless and nonpartisan campaign, stressing his readiness to "open to the center."

3. This interpretation is borne out by the fact that voters who shifted from Chirac in the 1995 presidential race to a candidate on the left in 1997 distinguished themselves from those who remained loyal by being far more favorable to "solidarity" than to "private enterprise," far more lukewarm regarding the construction of Europe, and far more favorable to the reduction of the workweek to thirty-five hours (Cayrol 1998, 115).

4. Although their evaluation of the results is different from ours, Lynda Lee Kaid and Christina Holtz-Bacha (1995) give strong evidence of these points in their study.

References

Aaronovitch, Sam, and John Grahl. 1997. "Building on Maastricht." In *The Question of Europe*, ed. P. Gowan and P. Anderson. London: Verso.

Adorno, Theodor W., Else Frenkel-Brunswick, Daniel J. Levinson, and Nevitt R. Sanford. 1950. *The Authoritarian Personality.* New York: Harper & Row.

Agénor, P.R., and M.P. Taylor. 1992. "Testing for Credibility Effects." *IMF Staff Papers* 39, no. 3: 545-71.

Alesina, A., N. Roubini, and G.D. Cohen. 1997. *Political Cycles and the Macroeconomy.* Cambridge, Mass.: MIT Press.

Allègre, C. 1996. "La Gauche entre deux élections." In SOFRES, *L'État de l'opinion 1996*, ed. O. Duhamel and P. Méchet. Paris: Seuil, 31-48.

Appleton, A. 1995. "Parties under Pressure: Challenges to 'Established' French Parties." *West European Politics* 18, no. 1: 52-77.

Aubry, Martine. 1997. *Il est grand temps . . . .* Paris: Albin Michel.

Barthez, Alice. 1996. "Une Agriculture en mutation." *Données sociales 1996.* Paris: INSEE, 466-75.

Becker, G. 1968. "Crime and Punishment: An Economic Approach." *Journal of Political Economy*, March/April, 169-217.

Bergougnioux, A., and G. Grunberg. 1992. *Le Long Remords du pouvoir.* Paris: Fayard.

Bezat, J.-M. 1997. "Le Gouvernement est divisé sur la semaine de trente-cinq heures." *Le Monde*, 28-29 September.

Birenbaum, Guy. 1992. *Le Front National en politique.* Paris: Balland.

Blackburn, K., and M. Christensen. 1989. "Monetary Policy and Policy Credibility." *Journal of Economic Literature* 27, no. 1: 1-45.

Bougereau, J.-M. 1997. "Cocos d'amour." *Nouvel Observateur*, 18 June.

Boy, Daniel, and Jean Chiche. 1997. "Les Électeurs campent sur leurs positions." *Libération*, 13 May.

Boy, Daniel, and Elisabeth Dupoirier. 1986. "Le Poids des petits candidats." In *1981: Les élections de l'alternance.* Paris: Presses de la Fondation Nationale des Sciences Politiques.

Boy, Daniel, and Nonna Mayer. 1997a. "Secteur public contre secteur privé: Un nouveau conflit de classe." In *Les Modèles explicatifs du vote*, ed. Nonna Mayer. Paris: l'Harmattan, 111-32.

———, eds. 1997b. *L'Électeur a ses raisons.* Paris: Presses de Sciences Po.

Bréchon, P. 1993. *La France Aux Urnes: Cinquante ans d'histoire électorale.* Paris: La Documentation Française.

Bréchon, P., and B. Cautrès. 1987. "L'Inscription sur les listes électorales: Indicateur de socialisation ou de politicisation?" *Revue française de science politique* 37, no. 4: 502-25.

———. 1997. "La Cuisante Défaite de la droite moderée." *Le Monde*, 29 May.

Breton, A. 1996. *Competing Governments.* Cambridge, England: Cambridge University Press.

Buchanan, J.M., and V. Vanberg. 1989. "A Theory of Leadership and Deference in Constitutional Construction." *Public Choice* 61, no. 1: 1-28.

Burban, Jean-Louis. 1993. "The Impact of the European Community on French Politics." In *France and EC Membership Evaluated*, ed. F.-G Dreyfus, J. Morizet, and M. Peyrard. London: Pinter.

Butler, David, and Donald Stokes. 1966. *Political Change in Britain.* New York: St. Martin's (2d ed. 1974).

Cameron, David. 1996. "National Interest, the Dilemmas of European Integration and Malaise." In Keeler and Schain, *Chirac's Challenge.*

Campbell, Angus, Philip E. Converse, Warren E. Miller, and Donald E. Stokes. 1960. *The American Voter.* New York: Wiley.

Campbell, Peter. 1965. *French Electoral Systems since 1789.* Hamden, Conn.: Archon Books.

Camus, Jean-Yves. 1996. *Le Front National: Histoire et analyses.* Paris: Editions Olivier Laurens.

Capdevielle, Jacques, Hélène Meynaud, and René Mouriaux. 1990. *Petits Boulots et grand marché européen: Le travail démobilisé.* Paris: Presses de Sciences Po.

Capdevielle, Jacques, Elisabeth Dupoirier, Gérard Grunberg, Etienne Schweisguth, and Colette Ysmal. 1981. *France de gauche, vote à droite.* Paris: Presses de Sciences Po.

Capdevielle, Jacques, and Elisabeth Dupoirier. 1981. "L'Effet patrimoine." In Capdevielle et al., *France de gauche, vote à droite.* Paris: Presses de Sciences Po, 169-227.

Cartier-Bresson, J., dir. 1997. *Pratiques et contrôle de la corruption.* Paris: Montchrestien.

Carton, D. 1995. "Lionel Jospin croit en sa 'force tranquille.'" *Le Monde, Dossiers et Documents: L'Élection présidentielle 1995.*

Cautrès, Bruno, and Antony Heath. 1996. "Le Déclin du vote de classe: Une analyse comparée en France et en Grande-Bretagne." *Revue internationale de politique comparée* 3, no. 3 (December): 541-68.

Cayrol, Roland. 1998. "L'Électeur face aux enjeux economiques, sociaux et europeens." In Perrineau and Ysmal, *Le Vote surprise.*

CEVIPOF. 1990. *L'Électeur français en questions.* Paris: Presses de Sciences Po.

Cezard, Michel, and Françoise Dussert. 1993. "Le Travail ouvrier sous contrainte." *Données sociales 1993.* Paris: INSEE, 202-11.

Charlot, Jean. 1970. *Le Gaullisme.* Paris: Armand Colin.

———. 1971. "Les Préparatifs de la majorité." In *Les Élections de mars 1967.* Paris: Armand Colin.

———. 1980. "The Majority." In *The French National Assembly Elections of 1978,* ed. H. Penniman. Washington, D.C.: American Enterprise Institute.

———. 1988. "The End of the Majority." In *France at the Polls, 1981 and 1986,* ed. H. Penniman. Durham, N.C.: Duke University Press.

———, ed. 1973. *Quand la Gauche peut gagner.* Paris: Editions Alain Moreau.

Chaussebourg, Anne, and Thomas Ferenczi. 1993. *Élections legislatives: La droite sans partage.* Paris: Le Monde.

Chenu, Alain. 1993. "Une Classe ouvrière en crise." *Données sociales 1993.* Paris: INSEE, 476-85.

Chiche, Jean, and Elisabeth Dupoirier. 1993. "Les Voies contrastées de la reconquête électorale: L'électorat de la droite moderée en 1993." In *Le Vote sanction,* ed. Philippe Habert, Pascal Perrineau, and Colette Ysmal. Paris: Presses de la FNSP/Dept. d'Études Politiques du Figaro.

Chiche, Jean, and Nonna Mayer. 1997. "Les enjeux de l'élection." In Boy and Mayer, *L'Électeur a ses raisons,* 219-38.

Chirac, Jacques. 1978. *La Lueur de l'espérance: Réflection du soir pour le matin.* Paris: La Table Ronde.

Clark, T., Seymour Martin Lipset, and M. Rempel. 1993. "The Declining Political Significance of Social Class." *International Sociology* 8, no. 3 (September): 293-316.

Cluzeau, C. 1992. "Les Inscriptions sur les listes électorales en 1991." *Insée première* 187 (March): 1-4.

Cohen, Elie. 1986. "Les Socialistes et l'économie: De l'âge des mythes au déminage." In *Mars 1986: La drôle de défaite de la gauche,* ed. Elisabeth Dupoirier and Gérard Grunberg. Paris: PUF, 71-96.

Coignard, S., and M.-T. Guichard. 1996. "14 Ans d'intrigues à l'Élysee." *Le Point*, 27 January, 37-41.

Cole, A. 1994. *François Mitterrand: A Study in Political Leadership*. London: Routledge.

Cole, Alistair, and Peter Campbell. 1989. *French Electoral Systems and Elections since 1789*. London: Gower.

Colliard, Jean-Claude. 1972. *Les Républicains Indépendants*. Paris: Presses Universitaires de France.

———. 1979. "Le Parti giscardien." *Pouvoirs* 9: 115-29.

Colombani, J.-M. 1997. "Le Pacte social et moral de Lionel Jospin." *Le Monde*, 21 June.

Converse, Philip E., and Roy Pierce. 1986. *Political Representation in France*. Cambridge, Mass.: Harvard University Press.

Dalton, Russell, Scott Flanagan, and Paul Beck, eds. 1984. *Electoral Change in Advanced Industrial Societies*. Princeton: Princeton University Press.

Darley, Diana, and Dominique de Fleurian, eds. 1992. *Dictionnaire national des communes de France*. Paris: Albin Michel.

Dehousse, Franklin. 1997. *Les Résultats de la conférence intergouvernementale*. Brussels: CRISP, Courrier Hebdomadaire, No. 1565-66.

Delors, Jacques. 1997. *Réflections et propositions pour un nouveau modèle de développement*. Paris: Fondation "Notre Europe."

Demonpion, D. 1997. "Les Coulisses de la Commission Truche." *Le Point*, 12 July, 42-45.

Dogan, Mattéi. 1996. "Classe, religion, parti: Triple déclin dans les clivages électoraux." *Revue internationale de politique comparée* 3, no. 3 (December): 515-40.

Dolez, B. 1997. "Le Gouvernement Jospin." *Regards sur l'actualité* 233 (July-August): 3-11.

Duhamel, A. 1997a. *Portrait d'un artiste*. Paris: Flammarion.

———. 1997b. "La Bataille." *Libération*, 17 October.

Dunleavy, Patrick, and Christopher T. Husbands. 1985. *British Democracy at the Crossroads*. London: Allen and Unwin.

Dupin, E. 1991. *L'Après-Mitterrand: Le parti socialiste à la dérive*. Paris: Calmann-Lévy.

Dupoirier, Elisabeth. 1997. "La Coalition sortante a perdu la bataille de la mobilisation," *Le Monde*, 29 May.

EU. 1993. EC Commission. *Growth, Employment and Competitiveness.* Luxembourg: EC.

———. 1997a. European Union. *Treaty of Amsterdam.* Luxembourg: EU.

———. 1997b. European Council. *Presidency Conclusions, Extraordinary European Council Meeting on Employment, Luxembourg, 20 and 21 November 1997.* Brussels: 24 November.

Fall, Madior, and Gérard Lattès. 1993. "Les Revenus des ménages par catégorie socio-professionnelle." *Données sociales 1993.* Paris: INSEE, 350-62.

Fauvelle-Aymar, Christine, and Michael S. Lewis-Beck. 1997. "L'Iowa donne l'opposition gagnante." *Libération* 4978 (23 May): 15.

Faux, E., T. Legrand, and G. Perez. 1994. *La Main droite de dieu.* Paris: Seuil.

Favard, E. 1997. "Jospin, l'art du comment." *Les Echos,* 21-22 November.

Fleury, Christopher J., and Michael S. Lewis-Beck. 1993. "Anchoring the French Voter: Ideology versus Party." *Journal of Politics* 55, no. 4 (November): 1100-1109.

Fieschi, Catherine, John Shields, and Robert Woods. 1996. "Extreme Right-Wing Parties and the European Union." In *Political Parties and the European Union,* ed. J. Gaffney. London: Routledge.

Fiorina, M. 1991. "Elections and the Economy in the 1980s: Short- and Long-Term Effects." In *Politics and Economics in the Eighties,* ed. A. Alesina and G. Carliner. Chicago: University of Chicago Press.

Fitoussi, Jean-Paul. 1995. *Le Débat interdit: Monnaie, Europe, pauvreté.* Paris: Arléa.

Flood, Christopher. 1997. "Euroscepticism in the Politics of the British and the French Right: A Comparison." Paper presented at the annual meeting of the American Political Science Association, Washington, D.C.

Franklin, Mark, Tom Mackie, Henry Valen et al., eds. 1992. *Electoral Change: Response to Evolving Social and Attitudinal Structures in Western Countries.* Cambridge, England: Cambridge University Press.

Frears, J.R., and Jean-Luc Parodi. 1979. *War Will Not Take Place.* London: C. Hurst.

Friend, J.W. 1993. "Mitterrand's Legatee: The French Socialist Party in 1993." *French Politics and Society* 11, no. 3 (Summer): 1-11.

Gaetner, G. 1991. *L'Argent facile: Dictionnaire de la corruption en France.* Paris: Stock.

Gaffney, John. 1996. "France." In Lodge, *1994 Elections to the European Parliament.*

Gaffney, John, and Lorna Milne, eds. 1997. *French Presidentialism and the Election of 1995*. Aldershot: Ashgate.

Garrigou, A. 1992. *Le Vote et le vertu: Comment les français sont devenus électeurs.* Paris: Presses de la FNSP.

Gauthier, Nicole. 1997. "Sondages: Les projections en sièges trés aleátoires," *Libération*, 3 May.

Gaxie, Daniel. 1997. "Les Partis politiques et la représentation des intérêts sociaux." Paper presented to the Congress of the International Association of Political Science, Seoul, 21 August.

Gerstlé, J. 1996. "L'Information et la sensibilité des électeurs à la conjoncture." *Revue française de science politique* 46, no. 5: 731-52.

———. 1998. "Dissolution, indifference, retrospections: Les vicissitudes d'une campagne de temps court." In Perrineau and Ysmal, *Le Vote surprise*, 56-75.

Giesbert, F.-O. 1996. *François Mitterrand: Une vie*. Paris: Seuil.

Goetschy, Janine. 1997. "L'Emploi et le social dans le Traité d'Amsterdam: Rattrapage, consolidation ou percée?" CNRS working paper. Nanterre: Travail et Mobilités, URA, CNRS 1416.

Goguel, François. 1963. "Le Référendum du 28 octobre et les élections du 18-25 novembre 1962." *Revue française de science politique* 13: 289-314.

———. 1971. "Analyse global des résultats." In *Les Élections législatives de mars 1967*. Paris: Armand Colin.

———. 1983. "Les Élections législatives des 23 et 30 juin 1968." In *Chroniques électorales*. Vol. 2. Paris: Presses de la FNSP.

Gowan, Peter, and Perry Anderson. 1997. *The Question of Europe*. London: Verso.

Griffiths, Richard T., ed. 1993. *Socialist Parties and the Question of Europe in the 1950s*. Leiden: E.J. Brill.

Groux, Guy, and Catherine Levy. 1993. *La Possession ouvrière: Du taudis à la propriété (XIX-XX siècle)*. Paris: les Editions de l'Atelier.

Grunberg, Gérard. 1997. "Les Français veulent-ils l'Europe." Paper presented at the annual meeting of the American Political Science Association, Washington, D.C.

Grunberg, Gérard, and J. Chiche. 1995. "Le Regain socialiste." In *Le Vote de crise: L'élection présidentielle de 1995*, ed. P. Perrineau and C. Ysmal. Paris: Presses de la FNSP, 189-211.

Grunberg, Gérard, and Elisabeth Dupoirier. 1997. "L'Angoisse devant l'avenirs." *Pouvoirs* 81: 153-66.

Grunberg, Gérard, and Pascal Perrineau. 1997. "Défiance, déprime: Radiographie du vote sanction contre Chirac." *Libération*, 3 June.

Grunberg, Gérard, and Etienne Schweisguth. 1981. "Profession et vote: La poussée de la gauche." In Capdevielle et al., *France de gauche, vote à droite*, 139-67.

———. 1983. "Le Virage à gauche des classes moyennes salariées." In Lavau, Grunberg, and Mayer, *L'Univers politique des classes moyennes*, 351-77.

Guillaumat-Tailliet, François, Jean Jacques Malpot, and Véronique Paquel. 1996. "Le Patrimoine des ménages: Répartition et concentration." *Données sociales 1996*. Paris: INSEE, 354-70.

Habert, Philippe. 1989. "Le Choix des électeurs au printemps 1988." *SOFRES. L'État de l'opinion*. Paris: Seuil, 67-93.

———. 1992-93. "Le Choix de l'Europe et la décision de l'électeur." *Commentaire* (Winter).

Habert, Philippe, and Alain Lancelot. 1996. "L'Émergence d'un nouvel électeur?" In *Le Nouvel Électeur*, ed. Philippe Habert. Paris: Vinci, 21-58.

Habert, Philippe, Pascal Perrineau, and Colette Ysmal. 1992. *Le Vote éclaté*. Paris: Presses de la FNSP/Figaro Etudes Politiques.

Haggard, S., J.D. Lafay, and C. Morrisson. 1995. *The Political Feasibility of Adjustment in Developing Countries*. Paris: OECD.

Halimi, S. 1997. "La Mélopée des contraintes et les leçons de l'histoire." *French Politics and Society* 15, no. 3 (Summer): 1-8.

Hamou, Emmanuelle. 1997. "Le Discours de Chirac: Lapsus ou acte manqué?" *Libération*, 29 May.

Hayward, Jack, and Vincent Wright. 1973. "Presidential Supremacy and the French General Elections of March 1973." *Parliamentary Affairs* 26: 274-395.

Heath, Anthony, Roger Jowell, and John Curtice. 1985. *How Britain Votes*. Oxford: Pergamon Press.

Heath, Anthony, Roger Jowell, John Curtice, G. Evans, J. Field, and S. Witherspoon. 1991. *Understanding Political Change: The British Voter, 1964-1987*. Oxford: Pergamon Press.

Héran, F., and D. Roualt. 1995. "Le Tableau sociologique de la nonparticipation électorale." *Insée première* 414 (November): 1-4.

Hoffman-Martinot, V. 1992. "La Participation aux élections municipales dans les villes françaises." *Revue française de science politique* 42, no. 1: 3-35.

Hout, Michael, Clem Brooks, and Jeff Manza. 1995. "The Democratic Class Struggle in the United States, 1948-1992." *American Sociological Review* 60 (December): 805-28.

Inglehart, Ronald. 1997. *The Silent Revolution.* Princeton: Princeton University Press.

———. 1990. *Cultural Shift in Advanced Industrial Societies.* Princeton: Princeton University Press.

Jackson, R. 1995. "Clarifying the Relationship between Education and Turnout." *American Politics Quarterly* 23 (July): 279-99.

Jaffré, Jérôme. 1977. "M. Le Pen peut-il faire battre la majorité?" *Le Monde,* 18-19 May, 14.

———. 1980. "The French Electorate in March 1978." In *The French National Assembly Elections of 1978,* ed. H. Penniman. Washington, D.C.: American Enterprise Institute.

———. 1986. "Le Front National: La relève protestataire." In *Mars 1986: La drôle de défaite de la gauche,* ed. Elisabeth Dupoirier and Gérard Grunberg. Paris: PUF, 211-30.

———. 1997a. "La Décision électorale au second tour: Un scrutin très serré." *Revue française de science politique,* June-August, 426-37.

———. 1997b. "Les Élections législatives de 1997." *Revue pouvoirs* (June/August): 133-50.

———. 1998. "De 1995 à 1997, l'opinion publique, l'impopularité et le vote." In Perrineau and Ysmal, *Le Vote surprise.*

Jérôme, Bruno, Véronique Jérôme, and Michael S. Lewis-Beck. 1999. "Polls Fail in France: Forecasts of the 1997 Legislative Election." *International Journal of Forecasting,* 15: 163-74.

J.M.S. 1997. "Le Congrès de Tours à l'envers." *Le Point,* 29 November.

Jospin, L. 1976. *Les Socialistes et le tiers monde.* Paris: Flammarion.

———. 1995. *1995-2000: Propositions pour la France.* Paris: Stock.

Julliard, J. 1997. "Inventez, Jospin!" *Nouvel Observateur,* 18 June.

July, S. 1997. "L'Alternance de la dernière chance." *Libération,* 31 May.

Kaid, Lynda Lee, and Christina Holtz-Bacha. 1995. *Political Advertising in Western Democracies: Parties and Candidates on Television.* Thousand Oaks, Calif.: Sage.

Katz, Richard S., and Peter Mair. 1995. "Changing Models of Party Organization and Party Democracy: The Emergence of the Cartel Party." *Party Politics* 1, no. 1: 5-28.

Keeler, John, and Martin Schain, eds. 1996. *Chirac's Challenge: Liberalization, Europeanization and Malaise in France.* Basingstoke, England: Macmillan.

Kitschelt, Herbert, with Anthony Mac Gann. 1995. *The Radical Right in Western Europe: A Comparative Analysis.* Ann Arbor: University of Michigan Press.

Klitgaard, R. 1988. *Controlling Corruption.* Berkeley: University of California Press.

———. 1998. "La Coopération internationale contre la corruption." *Finances et développement* 35, no. 1: 3-6.

Kriesi, Hanspeter. 1989. "New Social Movements and the New Class in the Netherlands." *American Journal of Sociology* 94: 1078-1116.

Krueger, A.O. 1974. "The Political Economy of the Rent-Seeking Society." *American Economic Review* 64 (June): 291-303.

Krugman, Paul. 1997. "Is Capitalism Too Productive?" *Foreign Affairs* 76, no. 5 (September/October): 79-94.

Lafay, J.D., and J. Lecaillon. 1993. *The Political Dimension of Economic Adjustment.* Paris: OECD.

Lafay, J.D., and B. Jérôme. 1991. "Qualité de la gestion municipale et résultats électoraux des maires sortants: Analyse empirique des élections de mars 1989." In *Economie 1991.* Perpignan: Université de Perpignan, 35-50.

Lambert, Yves. 1995. "Vers Une Ère post-chrétienne?" *Futuribles: Analyses et perspectives* 200 (July-August): 85-111.

Lambert, Yves, and Guy Michelat. 1992. *Crépuscule des religions chez les jeunes Jeunes et religion en France.* Paris: L'Harmattan.

Lancelot, Alain, and Pierre Weill. 1971. "Les Transferts de voix du premier au second tour des élections de mars 1967." In *Les Élections législatives de mars 1967.* Paris: Armand Colin.

Lancelot, Marie-Thérese, and Alain Lancelot. 1971. "Géographie des élections des 5 et 12 mars 1967." In *Les Élections législatives de mars 1967.* Paris: Armand Colin.

Laurens, André. 1988. "De l'Ouverture ratée à l'obligation d'ouverture." *Les Élections législatives, 5 juin, 12 juin 1988.* Paris: *Le Monde: Dossiers et documents.*

Lavau, Georges. 1986. "L'Électeur français devient-il individualiste?" In *Sur l'Individualisme,* ed. Pierre Birnbaum and Jean Leca. Paris: Presses de la FNSP, 301-29.

Lavau, Georges, Gérard Grunberg, and Nonna Mayer, eds. 1983. *L'Univers politique des classes moyennes.* Paris: Presses de Sciences Po.

Lawson, Kay. 1980. "Political Parties and Linkage." In *Political Parties and Linkage: A Comparative Perspective,* ed. Kay Lawson. New Haven: Yale University Press.

Lawson, Kay, and Colette Ysmal. 1992. "France: The 1988 Presidential Campaign." In *Electoral Strategies and Political Marketing*, ed. Shaun Bowlder and David M. Farrell. New York: St. Martin's.

Lazarsfeld, Paul, B. Berelson, and H. Gaudet. 1944. *The People's Choice*. New York: Columbia University Press.

Lecaillon, Jacques. 1994. "Economie des 'affaires' politiques." *Analyses de la SEDEIS* 98: 23-29.

Leclerc, G., and F. Muracciole. 1997. *Lionel Jospin: Hériter rebelle*. Paris: Lattès.

Le Gall, Gérard. 1997. "Succès de la gauche quatre ans après sa déroute de 1993." *Revue politique et parlementaire*, September, 6-25.

Le Monde: Dossiers et documents. 1988. *Les Élections législatives, 5 juin, 12 juin 1988*. Paris.

———. 1994. *Le Second Tour des élections cantonales, 29 mars 1994*. Paris.

———. 1995a. *L'Élection présidentielle 23 avril-7 mai 1995*. Paris.

———. 1995b. *Le Second Tour des élections municipales, 20 juin 1995*. Paris.

———. 1997. *Les Élections législatives, 25 mai, 1er juin 1997*. Paris.

Lévy, J.-P., and J.-L. Validire. 1997. "Questions à MM. Chirac et Jospin." *Libération*, 27 August.

Levy, M. 1978. "Le Corps électoral." *Population et société* 110 (February).

Lewis-Beck, Michael S. 1984. "France: The Stalled Electorate." In *Electoral Change in Advanced Industrial Democracies*, ed. R.J. Dalton, S.C. Flanagan, and P.A. Beck. Princeton: Princeton University Press, 425-48.

———. 1985. "Un Modèle de prévision des élections législatives françaises (avec une application pour 1986)." *Revue française de science politique* 35, no. 6 (December): 1080-91.

———. 1988. *Economics and Elections: The Major Western Democracies*. Ann Arbor: University of Michigan Press.

———. 1993. "The French Voter: Steadfast or Changing?" In *The French Voter Decides*, ed. D. Boy and N. Mayer. Ann Arbor: University of Michigan Press, 1-13.

———. 1995. "Comparaison de prévision des élections présidentielles en France et aux Etats-Unis." *Journal de la société de statistique de Paris* 136: 29-45.

———. 1997. "Le Vote du 'Porte-Monnaie' en question." In Boy and Mayer, *L'Électeur a ses raisons*, 239-61.

———. 1998. "Class, Religion, and the French Voter: A 'Stalled' Electorate?" *French Politics and Society* 16, no. 2 (Spring): 43-51.

Lewis-Beck, Michael S., Anne Hildreth, and Alan Spitzer. 1988. "Was There a Girondist Faction in the French National Convention 1792-1793?" *French Historical Studies* 15, no. 3 (Spring): 519-48.

Lewis-Beck, Michael S., and Glenn Mitchell II. 1993. "French Electoral Theory: The National Front Test." *Electoral Studies* 12, no. 2 (June): 112-27.

Lewis-Beck, Michael S., and Tom W. Rice. 1992. *Forecasting Elections.* Washington, D.C.: CQ Press.

Libération. 1997. *Histoire secrète de la dissolution.* Paris: Plon.

Lipset, Seymour Martin, and Stein Rokkan. 1967. *Party Systems and Voter Alignments.* New York: Free Press.

Lodge, Juliet, ed. 1996. *The 1994 Elections to the European Parliament.* London: Pinter.

Macé-Scaron, J. 1997a. "PC: Les miettes d'un mythe." *Le Point*, 27 September, 66-69.

———. 1997b. "Parti Socialiste: Discipline dans les rangs." *Le Point*, 4 October.

Macridis, R.C. 1975. *French Politics in Transition: The Years after De Gaulle.* Cambridge, Mass.: Winthrop.

Malpot, Jean-Jacques, Véronique Paquel, and Daniel Verger. 1993. "Budgets et patrimoines." *Données sociales 1993.* INSEE, 385-94.

Manceron, C., and B. Pingaud. 1981. *François Mitterrand: L'homme, les idées, le programme.* Paris: Flammarion.

Mano, Jean-Luc, and Guy Birenbaum. 1997. *La Défaite impossible.* Paris: Éditions Ramsay.

Martin, Pierre. 1996. *Le Vote Le Pen.* Paris: Notes de la Fondation Saint-Simon, no. 84.

Martin, Virginie. 1993. *Les Comportements politiques des chômeurs.* Paris (mémoire de DEA, IEP de Paris: dir. Jean Charlot).

Mauduit, Laurent. 1995. "Le Programme economique de Lionel Jospin de plus en plus audacieux." In *L'Élection présidentielle, 23 avril-7 mai 1995* , ed. Michel Noblecourt. Paris: Le Monde.

———. 1997a. "Les Conseillers très spéciaux de Martine Aubry et de Dominique Strauss-Kahn." *Le Monde*, 7 June.

———. 1997b. "M. Jospin a changé d'Europe." *Le Monde*, 21 November, 1.

Mayer, Nonna. 1986. *La Boutique contre la gauche.* Paris: Presses de la FNSP.

———. 1995. "Les Choix politiques des agriculteurs." *Cahier du CEVIPOF.* 12 March.

———. 1996. "Du Communisme au Front National." *L'Histoire* 95 (January): 110-13.

———. 1997. "Du Vote lepéniste au vote frontiste." *Revue française de science politique* 47, no. 3-4 (June-August): 428-53.

———. 1998. "La Perception de l'Autre." In Perrineau and Ysmal, *Le Vote surprise.*

Mayer, Nonna, and A. Percheron. 1990. "Les Absents du jeu électoral." *Données sociales.* Paris: INSEE, 398-401.

Mayer, Nonna, and Pascal Perrineau. 1989. *Le Front National à découvert.* Paris: Presses de la FNSP.

Mayer, Nonna, and Etienne Schweisguth. 1985. "Classe, position sociale et vote." In *L'Explication du vote*, ed. Daniel Gaxie. Paris: Presses de Sciences Po, 263-85.

Mechet, Philippe. 1997. "Bonne tenue des sondages, mais difficile maitrise de la projection en sieges." *Revue politique et parlementaire*, July/August, 58-64.

Mercier, A.S., and B. Jérôme. 1997. *Les 700 Jours de Jospin.* Paris: Plon.

Michel, Patrick, and R. Luneau. 1995. *Tous Les Chemins ne mènent plus à Rome.* Paris: Albin Michel.

Michelat, Guy. 1993. "In Search of Left and Right." In *The French Voter Decides*, ed. D. Boy and N. Mayer. Ann Arbor: University of Michigan Press, 65-90.

Michelat, Guy, and Michel Simon. 1977. *Classe, religion et politique.* Paris: Presses de Sciences Po/Editions sociales.

Morin, J. 1983. "Un Français sur dix ne s'inscrit sur les listes électorales." *Economie et Statistique* 152, no. 2.

———. 1987. "La Participation électorale." *Données sociales* 152: 606-10.

———. 1989. "La Participation électorale d'avril 1988 à mars 1989." *Insée première* 32 (July): 1-4.

Morray, J.-P. 1997. *Grand Illusion: François Mitterrand and the French Left.* Westport, Conn.: Praeger.

Mossuz-Lavau, Janine. 1993. "Le Vote des femmes en France (1945-1993)." *Revue française de science politique* 43, no. 4 (August): 673-89.

———. 1997. "La Percée des femmes aux élections législatives de 1997." *Revue française de science politique* 47: 454-61.

Mueller, J.E. 1970. "Presidential Popularity from Truman to Johnson." *American Political Science Review* 64: 18-23.

Muet, Pierre-Alain. 1997. *Lack of Economic Growth and Unemployment: The Cost of Non-Cooperation.* Paris: Notre Europe, Research and Policy Paper, no 1.

Nannestad, N., and M. Paldam. 1994. "The VP-Function: A Survey of the Literature on Vote and Popularity Functions after 25 Years." *Public Choice* 79, no. 3-4: 213-46.

Paldam, M. 1986. "The Distribution of Election Results and the Two Explanations of the Cost of Ruling." *European Journal of Political Economy* 2: 5-24.

Parkin, Frank. 1968. *Middle Class Radicalism: The Social Bases of the British Campaign for Nuclear Disarmament.* Manchester, England: Manchester University Press.

Parodi, Jean-Luc. 1978. "L'Échec des gauches." *Revue politique et parlementaire* 80: 9-32.

Parti Socialiste. 1997. *Changeons D'Avenir.* Paris: PS.

Patrait, Claude. 1992. "Pouvoirs régionaux en chantier . . ." In Habert, Perrineau, and Ysmal, *Le Vote éclaté.*

Péan, P. 1994. *Une Jeunesse française: François Mitterrand, 1934-1947.* Paris: Fayard.

Pégard, C. 1996. "Histoire d'un mensonge d'État." *Le Point,* 27 January, 42-45.

———. 1997. "Le PC mal dans sa peau." *Le Point,* 1 November, 10.

Percheron, A. 1986. "Les Absents de la cène électorale." In *Mars 1986: La drôle de défaite de la gauche,* ed. E. Dupoirier and G. Grunberg. Paris: PUF.

Peron, René. 1993. *La Fin des vitrines. Des temples de la consommation aux usines à vendre.* Cachan: Les Editions de l'ENS de Cachan.

Perrineau, Pascal. 1993. "Le Front National la force solitaire." In *Le Vote sanction,* ed. Philippe Habert, Pascal Perrineau, and Colette Ysmal. Paris: Presses de la FNSP/Dept. d'Études Politiques du Figaro.

———. 1995a. "La Dynamique du vote Le Pen: le poids du gaucho-lepénisme." In *Le Vote de crise,* ed. Pascal Perrineau and Colette Ysmal. Paris: Presses de la FNSP.

———. 1995b. "L'Élection Européenne au miroir de l'Hexagone: Les résultats de l'élection européenne en France." In *Le Vote des douze: Les élections européennes de juin 1994,* ed. Pascal Perrineau and Colette Ysmal. Paris: Figaro/Études Politique & Presses de Sciences Po.

———. 1997a. "Le Premier Tour des élections legislatives de 1997." *Revue française de science politique* 47, nos. 3-4 (June-August): 405-15.

———. 1997b. *Le Symptome Le Pen.* Paris: Fayard.

Perrineau, Pascal, and Colette Ysmal. 1998. *Le Vote surprise: Les élections legislatives des 25 mai et 1er juin 1997.* Paris: Presses de Sciences Po.

Pierce, R. 1995. *Choosing the Chief: Presidential Elections in France and the United States.* Ann Arbor: University of Michigan Press.

Philippe, A., and D. Hubscher. 1991. *Enquête à l'intérieur du parti socialiste.* Paris: Albin Michel.

Platone, F. 1993. "The French and Their Political System: A Measured Support." In *The French Voter Decides,* ed. D. Boy and N. Mayer. Ann Arbor: University of Michigan Press.

Platone, François, and Henri Rey. 1996. "Le FN en terre communiste." In Mayer and Perrineau, *Le Front National à découvert,* 249-67.

Ponceyri, Robert. 1997. "L'Étrange Défaite de la droite." *Revue politique et parlementaire,* September, 26-49.

Portelli, H. 1997. *Le Parti Socialiste.* Paris: Montchrestien.

Poulat, Emile. 1994. *L'Ère post-chrétienne: Un monde sorti de Dieu.* Paris: Flammarion.

Ranger, J. 1993. "Are the French Interested in Politics?" In *The French Voter Decides,* ed. D. Boy and N. Mayer. Ann Arbor: University of Michigan Press.

Rey, Henri. 1996. *La Peur des banlieues.* Paris: Presses de Sciences Po.

Rose, Richard. 1974. *Electoral Behavior: A Comparative Handbook.* New York: Free Press.

Ross, George. 1995. *Jacques Delors and European Integration.* Cambridge, England: Polity/Oxford.

Rose-Ackerman, S. 1978. *Corruption: A Study in Political Economics.* New York: Academic Press.

Safran, W. 1988. "Rights and Liberties under the Mitterrand Presidency: Socialist Innovations and Post-Socialist Revisions." *Contemporary French Civilization* 12, no. 1 (Winter-Spring): 1-35.

Sawicki, F. 1997. *Les Reseaux du parti socialiste.* Paris: Editions Belin.

Schain, Martin A. 1987. "The National Front and the Construction of Political Legitimacy." *West European Politics* 10, no. 2 (April): 229-52.

———. 1996. "The Immigration Debate and the National Front." In Keeler and Schain, *Chirac's Challenge.*

Schickler, E., and D.P. Green. 1997. "The Stability of Party Identification in Western Democracies." *Comparative Political Studies* 30, no. 4 (August): 450-83.

Schlesinger, Joseph A., and Mildred S. Schlesinger. 1990. "The Reaffirmation of a Multiparty System in France." *American Political Science Review* 84: 1077-1101.

———. 1995. "French Parties and the Legislative Elections of 1993." *Party Politics* 1: 369-80.

———. 1998. "Dual Ballot Elections and Political Parties: The French Presidential Election of 1995." *Comparative Political Studies* 31: 72-97.

Schlesinger, Mildred S. 1978. "The Cartel des Gauches: Precursor of the Front Populaire." *European Studies Review* 8: 211-34.

Schneider, R., and D. Carton. 1997. "Cocos d'amour." *Nouvel Observateur*, 18 June.

Schweisguth, Etienne. 1995. "La Montée des valeurs individualistes." *Futuribles* 200 (July-August): 131-60.

Shields, James G. 1995. "Le Pen and the Progression of the Far Right in France." *French Politics and Society* 3, no. 2 (Spring): 34-35.

Singly, François de, and Claude Thelot. 1988. *Gens du public, gens du privé: La grande différence.* Paris: Dunod.

SOFRES. 1989. *L'État de l'Opinion 1989.* Paris: Seuil.

———. 1996. *L'État de l'Opinion 1996.* Paris: Seuil.

Strauss-Kahn, Dominique. 1997. *Intervention de Dominique Strauss-Kahn ministre de l'économie, des finances et de l'industrie: Présentation du projet de la loi des finances pour 1998.* Paris: Ministry of Finances.

Sublieau, F., and M.-F. Toinet. 1985. "L'Abstentionnisme en France et aux Etats-Unis." In *L'Explication du vote*, ed. D. Gaxie. Paris: Presses de la FNSP.

———. 1992. "La Participation aux régionales: Une divine surprise?" *Revue politique et parlementaire* 958, no. 2.

Teixeira, Ruy. 1992. *The Disappearing American Voter.* Washington, D.C.: Brookings Institution.

Toinet, M.-F. and F. Sublieau. 1993. *Les Chemins de l'abstention.* Paris: La Découverte.

Tullock, G. 1967. "The Welfare Costs of Tariffs, Monopolies, and Theft." *Western Economic Journal* 5 (June): 224-32.

Verba, Sidney, and Norman Nie. 1972. *Participation in America.* New York: Harper & Row.

Viannson-Ponte, Pierre. 1971. *Histoire de la République gaulienne 2.* Paris: Fayard.

Vichniac, Judith. 1991. "French Socialists and *Droit à la différence.*" *French Politics and Society* 9, no. 1 (Winter).

Weil, Patrick. 1997. *Mission d'étude des législations de la nationalité et de l'immigration.* Paris: La Documentation Française.

Wilson, Frank L. 1988. "When Parties Refuse to Fail: The Case of France." In *When Parties Fail: Emerging Alternative Organizations*, ed. Kay Lawson and Peter Merkl. Princeton: Princeton University Press.

Witkowski, D. 1996. "Les Jeunes en 1996: Le bonheur est dans le privé." In SOFRES, *L'État de l'opinion 1996*, 161-92.

Wolfinger, Raymond, and Steven Rosenstone. 1980. *Who Votes?* New Haven: Yale University Press.

Wyplosz, C. 1997. "Silence sur le chômage: Ne troublez pas la campagne électorale." *Libération*, 20 May.

Ysmal, Colette. 1986. "D'une Droite en sursis à une droite défaite, 1974-1981." In Boy and Dupoirier, *1981: Les élections de l'alternance.*

———. 1996. "France." *European Journal of Political Research* 30: 331-45.

———. 1999. "French Political Parties: A State within the State?" In *Political Parties and the Old Orders*, ed. Philip Davies and John White. Albany: SUNY Press.

Zorgbibe, Charles. 1993. *Histoire de la construction européenne.* Paris: PUF.

Index

Contributors

Andrew M. Appleton
Department of Political Science, Washington State University.

Daniel Boy
Research Director, Centre d'étude de la vie politique française (CEVIPOF—Center for the Study of French Political Life) and Fondation nationales des sciences politiques (FNSP—National Foundation of Political Science), Paris.

Bruno Cautrès
Director, Banque de données sociopolitiques (BDSP—Socio-Political Data Bank), University of Grenoble.

Gérard Grunberg
Research Director, Centre d'étude de la vie politique française (CEVIPOF—Center for the Study of French Political Life) and Centre national de la recherche scientifique (CNRS—National Center for Scientific Research), Paris.

Jean-Dominique Lafay
Director, Laboratoire d'économie publique (LAEP—Public Economy Laboratory) and Professor of Economics, University of Paris I.

Kay Lawson
Professor of Political Science, San Francisco State University, and Visiting Professor of Political Science, University of Paris (Sorbonne).

Michael S. Lewis-Beck
F. Wendell Miller Distinguished Professor of Political Science, University of Iowa.

Nonna Mayer
Research Director, Centre d'étude de la vie politique française (CEVIPOF—Center for the Study of French Political Life) and Centre national de la recherche scientifique (CNRS—National Center for Scientific Research), Paris.

George Ross
Morris Hillquit Professor in Labor and Social Thought, Brandeis University, and Minda de Gunzburg Center for European Studies, Harvard University.

William Safran
Professor of Political Science, University of Colorado at Boulder.

Martin A. Schain
Chair, Center for European Studies and Professor of Politics, New York University.

Joseph A. Schlesinger
Professor Emeritus of Political Science, Michigan State University.

Mildred S. Schlesinger
Adjunct Professor of Political Science, Michigan State University.

Etienne Schweisguth
Research Director, Centre d'étude de la vie politique française (CEVIPOF—Center for the Study of French Political Life) and Centre national de la recherche scientifique (CNRS—National Center for Scientific Research), Paris.

Marie Servais
Graduate Student in Economics, Laboratoire d'économie publique (LAEP—Public Economy Laboratory) and the University of Paris I.

Colette Ysmal
Research Director, Fondation nationale des sciences politiques (FNSP), Paris.